# THE RIGHTS OF CHILDREN

# THE RIGHTS OF CHILDREN

## Legal and Psychological Perspectives

*Edited by*

**JAMES S. HENNING, Ph.D.**

*Liaison Clinical Psychologist*
*Department of Psychiatry*
*Southern California Permanente Medical Group*
*Bellflower, California*

*Assistant Clinical Professor*
*University of California at Los Angeles Medical School*
*Los Angeles, California*

CHARLES C THOMAS • PUBLISHER
*Springfiel. • Illinois • U.S.A.*

*Published and Distributed Throughout the World by*
CHARLES C THOMAS • PUBLISHER
2600 South First Street
Springfield, Illinois 62717 U.S.A.


ISBN 0-398-04525-9
Library of Congress Catalog Card Number: 81-14409

*With THOMAS BOOKS careful attention is given to all details of manufacturing and design. It is the Publisher's desire to present books that are satisfactory as to their physical qualities and artistic possibilities and appropriate for their particular use. THOMAS BOOKS will be true to those laws of quality that assure a good name and good will.*

**Library of Congress Cataloging in Publication Data**
Main entry under title:

The Rights of children.

Bibliography: p.
1. Child mental health—Social aspects—United States. 2. Children's rights—United States. 3. Children—Legal status, laws, etc.—United States. 4. Social work with children—United States. I. Henning, James S.
RJ499.R53 362.7 81-14409
ISBN 0-398-04525-9 AACR2

*Printed in the United States of America*
PS-R-1

For
Jennifer and Johnny
two very special children

# CONTRIBUTORS

**Donald N. Bersoff** is associate professor of law at the University of Maryland and professor of psychology at the Johns Hopkins University. He serves as coordinator of the joint J. D.—Ph.D. program in law and psychology at those two institutions. In addition, he is a founding partner of the law firm of Ennis, Friedman, Bersoff, and Ewine, through which he represents the American Psychological Association. Dr. Bersoff received his Ph.D. from New York University and his J.D. from Yale Law School.

**Stephen Bittner** was graduated from the University of Chicago School of Medicine and trained in pediatrics at Yale University. As medical director of a neighborhood health center he helped organize a community child protection team and a parent aide program. While at Children's Hospital he pursued his interest in family violence and psychosocial origins of illness.

**Daniel D. Blaine** is a professor in the Department of Educational Psychology, University of Hawaii at Manoa. He received his Ph.D. from the University of Texas at Austin.

**Anne Chaleff** is a psychiatric nurse in the Child Outpatient Department of the Neuropsychiatric Institute, UCLA. She is presently engaged in the evaluation and treatment of sexually abused children and their families in the Family Support Program at the NPI/UCLA. She is the coordinator of the self-help component of the Family Support Program, Parents United.

**Richard A. Dubanoski** is a professor in the Department of Psychology, University of Hawaii at Manoa. He received his Ph.D. from the University of Minnesota.

**Thomas Grisso** is professor of psychology at St. Louis University. He received his Ph.D. in clinical psychology from the University of Arizona. His past research has focused on issues within law and juvenile justice. Currently he is engaged in a research project to study decision-making processes in juvenile courts.

**Michael S. Grodin** is presently a clinical fellow in pediatric cardiology at the Children's Hospital Medical Center, Boston. He completed his undergraduate training at the Massachusetts Institute of Technology where he studied molecular biology and philosophy. After receiving his M.D. degree from the Albert Einstein College of Medicine, Dr. Grodin completed postgraduate training at UCLA, Harvard, and Boston University.

**James S. Henning** received his Ph.D. in clinical psychology from the University of Wisconsin-Milwaukee. He was appointed clinical fellow in psychology at Harvard Medical School and postdoctoral fellow at Washington University School of Medicine. Currently he is liaison clinical psychologist in the Department of Psychiatry at Southern California Permanente Medical Group and assistant clinical professor at the University of California at Los Angeles Medical School.

**Sheldon G. Kirshner** received his Ph.D. in psychology from the University of Wisconsin-Milwaukee following which he served as a special fellow with the Center for Studies of Suicide Prevention, National Institute of Mental Health. Since 1971, he has been a member of psychology faculties including Northeastern Illinois and Roosevelt Universities. He received his J.D. degree from Lewis University College of Law and his LL.M. degree from Northwestern University School of Law. As an attorney he has served as assistant to the presiding judge of the Juvenile Court of Cook County, Illinois, and as guardian ad litem representing children. In private practice, he specializes in custody dispute resolution and litigation.

**Thomas Lovinguth** is a clinical psychologist in the St. Louis County Juvenile Court. He received his Ph.D. in clinical psychology at St. Louis University. His interests have focused on the application of psychological methods within the juvenile justice system and in the study of juveniles' rights. Currently he is researching questions in the area of the transfer of juveniles so that they can stand trial as adults in criminal courts.

**Margo McCaffery** received her B.S. degree from Baylor University, Waco, Texas, and her M.S. from Vanderbilt University, Nashville, Tennessee. She has authored numerous articles about pain as well as several chapters and books on pain. In 1980, she was voted a fellow in the American Academy of Nursing (F.A.A.N.). Currently she is self-employed in Santa Monica, California, as a consultant and workshop leader in nursing care of patients with pain.

**Gary B. Melton** is assistant professor of psychology at the University of Nebraska, Lincoln. He received his Ph.D. in clinical/community psychology from Boston University. His principal interests are in application of developmental research to the law and in psychology of rural communities.

**Teru L. Morton** is an assistant professor in the Department of Psychology, University of Hawaii at Manoa. She received her Ph.D. from the University of Utah.

**T. Kerby Neill** is a child psychologist. He received his Ph.D. in clinical psychology from Catholic University and postdoctoral training with children at the Menninger Foundation. He has directed children's services in an inner-city clinic, New Haven, Connecticut. Currently he directs the Graham B. Dimmick Child Guidance Service, Lexington, Kentucky.

**Eil H. Newberger** received an M.D. from Yale University and after an internship in internal medicine at Yale served for two years in the Peace Corps in Upper Volta, West Africa. During his pediatric residency at Boston Children's Hospital, he completed a master's degree in epidemiology at the Harvard School of Public Health and organized the Trauma X group at Children's, one of the first interdisciplinary child abuse consultant units in the United States. He has been director of the Family Development Study since 1972. He was given the Annual Award for Improving the Welfare of Children by the Massachusetts Society for the Prevention of Cruelty to Children for 1976. In 1977, he was elected president of the Massachusetts Committee on Children and Youth. He is assistant professor of pediatrics at the Harvard Medical School and lecturer on maternal and child health at the Harvard School of Public Health.

**Morris J. Paulson** is a professor of psychiatry and biobehavioral sciences in the Department of Psychiatry at UCLA School of Medicine. He graduated from the University of Alberta and was awarded the Ph.D. from the University of Kansas. He has been on the faculty of UCLA since 1956. In the last 15 years, he has focused his research efforts on intervention and treatment of physically and sexually abusing families.

**Sharon F. Schwartz** is presently a lecturer in ethics at the University of Massachusetts, Boston. Ms. Schwartz received her Bachelor of Arts and Master's Degree in philosophy from Boston University, where she is presently a Ph.D. candidate. She has worked extensively in the area of medical ethics and is actively involved in studies concerning ethics and decision making in the Neonatal Intensive Care Unit at Massachusetts General Hospital.

**Kay Blanton Stevens** is an instructor in special education at the University of Kentucky. She received her M.S. from U.K. in 1979. She taught regular classes in elementary schools for two years and special education for six years. She has also worked as a residential teaching parent at Learning House, Palo Alto, California.

**David Sachs Stern** is currently professor of law and faculty advisor to the International Law Society, Northern Illinois University College of Law. A graduate of the Harvard Law School, he also holds the degrees of LL.M. in comparative law and doctor of juridical sciences from New York University Law School as well as Doctor en Ciencias Sociales y Derecho Publico from Universidad de la Habana, Cuba.

**Louise Strouse** was trained in the biological sciences and obtained her graduate degree in cardiovascular physiology at the University of Chicago. She has been associated most recently with an international rural health and family planning program administered by the School of Public Health at the University of California at Los Angeles.

**I. David Todres** is the director of the Neonatal and Pediatric Intensive Care Units of the Massachusetts General Hospital, Boston and assistant professor of pediatric anesthesia at Harvard Medical School. He did his undergraduate training in physiology and medicine at the University of Cape Town, South Africa, with postgraduate training in Oxford and London, England.

**Judith S. Wallerstein,** Ph.D. received her master's degree in social work from Columbia University and a doctorate in clinical psychology from the University of Lund in Sweden. She was trained in child psychoanalysis at the Topeka Institute for Psychoanalysis. Dr. Wallerstein is currently director for the Center for the Family in Transition. She holds the position of senior lecturer at the School of Social Welfare at the University of California at Berkeley.

# FOREWORD

Recently, a New Jersey couple was charged with child abuse for allegedly trading their fourteen-month-old boy for a three-year-old sports car. The story of the baby and the Corvette appeared in the paper two days before another story in another city's newspaper about "throwaway" children: troublesome children expelled by parents from their own homes. There are approximately 64 million children under the age of eighteen in the United States today, about one-third of the entire population. The demographic data suggests that 53.5 million are white; 9.4 million are black; 4.8 million are Hispanic; and 1.3 million are Asian or American Indian. According to the United States National Commission for the International Year of the Child, one child out of six is poor and one-quarter of the children live on aid to families. It is estimated that over 500,000 children grow up outside of their natural homes in foster homes, group homes, or institutional care. It was further reported that one million children are child abuse or neglect victims, ten million have no source of regular health care, and mental health services are not available to an estimated 90 percent of the children who need such services.

Our society needs to question its basic molecular structure, the family unit, and to investigate the well-being of children when it perceives the measure of love owed to a child to be a function of parents' or society's convenience.

This book is addressed to all those people who are concerned about the welfare of children. Specific audiences in the health care sciences and the legal profession will discover articles that fit both particular and general needs. The aim and scope of this book is to help those adults who work with children understand basic needs and rights of those children.

The articles reflect the variety of professions that touch children's lives and make contributions to the well-being of children. The authors have advanced the frontiers of children's rights by delineating the knowledge of those rights, identifying problematic areas, consulting and implementing unique and advantageous programs, and describing direct service to children and their families. Leading professionals in their fields have written about their own views of child development and enhancement: experiential, theoretical, and investigative. The diversity of the articles may surprise some readers. However, there are few areas of human existence that do not impinge on the lives of children. It is the editor's hope that some readers will take up pen and will advance in their own writing and research the knowledge of children's needs.

The concept of the book arose out of a symposium held at the American Psychological Association Convention in 1978. At that time, a panel was selected to discuss the issues of children as they interfaced with the legal profession. The problems were already legion and the courts across the nation were beginning to face a new and voiceless minority—children. The symposium through its success clarified the deficiencies and discrepancies of care of children.

As more and more disciplines began to investigate their own policies toward this new minority, more inadequacies surfaced. The last years of the seventies brought a new struggle into the areas of public conscience—The Rights of Children. Mental health professionals and aligned medical specialties took a closer look at children's treatment, and what they saw frightened them. In 1979, the United Nations proclaimed an International Year of the Child, a prolegomenon to the study of children's needs. Since that time, academia and the legal-judicial profession have maintained an interest in the promotion of the rights and development of children. Frequently, however, the productivity was insular and unconnected to other disciplines. It is within the last years that multi-disciplinary contributions to children's problems have surfaced. Acceptance of such collaboration, without fear of loss or disciplinary identity, still needs to be forged on the anvil of progress. This book is one step.

There are several themes that resonate throughout the book, although each author was invited to write a particular statement on an important issue. First, *there is a historical context in which the field of child welfare has evolved.* Specifically, an understanding of the settings in which children live and function presumes an understanding of the position of children in world history. There is no such thing as a context-free problem; each issue carries the baggage of tradition on its shoulders. Children are no different. To analyze children's problems we need to look at previous processes and previous solutions.

The second theme, obvious to many and acted upon by few, is that *children are evolving emotionally, intellectually, and physically.* Children are learning, not learned. They need the opportunity to act and the freedom to grow. They need limits and support. It is a challenge to the adult world to provide them their inalienable rights to life, liberty, and the pursuit of happiness. Is there also not a mandate for adults to protect and ensure an enriching world in which children will find themselves ten to twenty years from now?

The final theme is the *interdigitation of knowledge and its direct application to the enhancement of children's lives.* The chapters in this book display the warp and woof of children's lives: birth, growth, family, sickness, education, and the law. When issues are investigated that directly affect one part of a child's life, it is discovered that it affects another part also. The emotions affect school performance; the family affects the recovery from an illness; the law affects who gets born and who is resuscitated. When theory is researched and the research is applied, then more is discovered, and much more still waits to be discovered and applied. The contributors in this book have taken on the responsibility of advancing discoveries. The authors have met the demand to be socially responsive. The baton is now passed to those others who will be responsible to further the cause of children's rights.

There are many people who contribute to a book. The authors, publisher, and editor are the visible contributors. Grateful and admiring credit also belongs to Daniel B. Gilreath for punctiliously correcting grammar and spelling, to Anne Bell for collaboration on format, and to Mrs. Ramona Kelly who typed part of the manuscript against many odds of meeting deadlines and other commitments. To all of you who are part of this book, children and contributors alike, thank you in grateful appreciation.

James Scott Henning

Los Angeles

# ACKNOWLEDGMENTS

The editor would like to express his gratitude to the *Judges' Journal*, a quarterly publication of the Judicial Administration, for permission to print an updated revision of the article, "The Child in the Divorcing Family," and also to the *Journal of Family Law* for permission to reprint materials from the article, "Child Custody Determination—A Better Way."

# CONTENTS

# THE RIGHTS OF CHILDREN

Chapter 1

# CONFLICT'S CHILDREN IN THE CONFLICT OF LAWS

DAVID S. STERN

THE CONFLICT OF LAWS is divided into three great parts: jurisdiction, choice of law, and judgments. This chapter deals with each of those parts even though most of the important problems that impact on the child arise in the field of jurisdiction and enforcement of judgments. Each of the three great parts will also be studied from the three major levels of authority in the United States legal system: the state, the national, and the international.[1]

A brief definition of each of the parts is necessary at the outset. Jurisdiction has two main subparts. The first, legislative jurisdiction, determines when a governmental unit has the authority to assert its power over persons, things, or activities within its territory. This territorial foundation has caused many of the complexities in conflict's law. The second main subpart, judicial jurisdiction, deals with the assertion of power by a court and the limits on that power.

Choice of law is the part that considers the various means whereby useful rules from units outside the territory in which the court sits might be employed to solve a legal problem before the forum. There are many different modes of describing this process. The fact that these concepts are embodied in legislation in the

[1]Throughout this chapter I have kept the citations to further authority to the most accessible references, although in a few places I have expanded beyond that minimum in in the interest of completeness. With few exceptions, they are current to June, 1980.

civil law system has created one of the really difficult problems for the international branch of this subject.

The final great part deals with the scope to be given to a judgment procured in another jurisdiction. Under our federal constitution, this is regulated by the full faith and credit clause. Other judgments outside the scope of that clause, both domestic and international, are enforceable, if at all, on the basis of comity, which leaves the matter of enforceability, as well as the extent of the validity of the prior judgment, up to the discretion of the court to which the foreign judgment has been brought.

Within just the United States there are fifty-one squared variables. If one were to include all of the other organized units on a world-wide basis, the possible arithmetic product goes beyond the ordinary power of imagination.

For each of these major parts, this chapter will treat the most important current difficulties with concrete cases. Some of these are models based on many actual cases. Some will be modern classic cases themselves. For each division of the conflicts law, the case will take a substantive area of law of the child. The case will be discussed first in the light of the most important prevailing solutions reached in the United States, and then it will be considered briefly from the transnational point of view. It is my position that the practitioner in this field can no longer view domestic problems in isolation.

Legislative and judicial jurisdiction will be considered through an adoption case; choice of law, through a case of legitimation; and effect of judgments, through a custody case. My conclusion will stress the importance of real cooperation between the law and all of the allied professions having an interest in the freedom and dignity of future generations.

The field of conflict of laws is needed to help the decision makers, especially the courts, to the best possible solutions for problems arising in complex societies, which necessarily have complex rules. If all humans and their products were to remain fixed in one set of rules, no conflict of laws would be needed. Only internal local differences would have to be solved. The distance we have moved from that situation makes clear the need for devices to bring in relevant data from outside sources. This need is increased when the use of that data can avoid the violation of the individual's sense of injustice, whether maker or consumer of justice.

The first typical case[2] involves the Brown family, which consists of George, the father, a widower, employed by Intercontinental Services Corp., and William, his eight-year-old adopted son. On a business trip to Amsterdam, George is negligently injured by a passing vehicle while on his way to a business meeting. His injuries result in total and permanent disability, but he is still able to function as a "parent." William had been adopted by the Browns when George was resident manager for Intercontinental in Belgium.

Considered solely from William's point of view, two immediate problems exist. He is a dependent minor whose father cannot maintain the previous level of support, even if that support were to be measured only in economic value terms. The first problem is simply stated: Does William have a cause of action against the party in Amsterdam? Does he have any rights? If the answer to the basic question is in the affirmative, the problem would be to ascertain where he can exercise those rights. The substantive question remaining would be whether the existence or scope of his right of action is controlled in any way by the fact that he is an adopted rather than a biological child.

As to the first problem, the law in the United States is clearly split. There seems now to be two dominant groups among our federated units. One group would deny all rights of the minor for negligent harm to one or both parents. The trend, however, seems to be one of favoring the right to recover for loss of support. The more progressive states have extended the notion of support to include loss of companionship, affection, and other incidental benefits of parenting.

If this were a purely domestic United States case, no difference would be noted among the adoption statutes of the several states. Although the English common law did not have any provision

---

[2]My typical case is based on cases collected in 69 A.L.R.3d 528 revealing the split already emerging within the federated states and comments made concerning similar cases in Europe by Rodolfo de Nova in ADOPTION IN THE PRIVATE INTERNATIONAL LAW 104, Receuil (Hague Lectures) 69 passim (1962).

for adoption, an adaptation of the civil law tradition produced far greater uniformity of law than any other legal part that came down with the common law tradition.[3] Thus, it is not strange that, within the civil law system itself, a similar length of time of descent from Roman law led to differences in adoption among the many countries where that Roman law was received.

One thus encounters a curious result. Both the Netherlands and Belgium would recognize the rights of the child to support, or at the least a monetary substitute for support, from the person who negligently injures the parent, but the laws of these two countries would make the right of recovery depend on the difference between biological and adopted children. Having no alternative source of support, the biological child would always recover, but the adopted child would recover damages only if he legally lost all rights in his natural family and became legally the same as a biological child for the adopting parent. A Belgian court deciding a domestic case would deny the right to the adoptee on the grounds that the natural family still had the alternative duty of support, while the Dutch court would allow the recovery against the negligent harmdoer.

Now William Brown is faced with the problem of finding a place where he can assert his right. Assuming that the Dutch wrongdoer has never had anything to do with the United States, William is limited to bringing his action in the Netherlands. A Dutch court would then have to face the question of the law governing the legal significance of William's adoption. The Dutch rule for choice looks to the law of nationality. As William was a United States national at the time of his adoption, the Dutch court would be faced with the challenge of the "pluri-legislative" law in place of the usual unitary one. For the Dutch court, the easiest way out of that difficulty is to find a law within the array of states with which George and William might be said to have had the most meaningful connection.

Suppose, however, that the car which struck George Brown was driven by an employee of Allproducts, the largest general

---

[3]Restatement 2d, Conflict of Laws, deals with adoption in §.78 and Comments; *see also* Note, *Doe v. Risher*, 20 How. L.J. 277-78 (1977).

manufacturing corporation in the Netherlands, and that its wholly owned subsidiary, Allproducts, USA, Inc., has its central management, assembly, and distribution center in the state of residence of George and William. In these circumstances, the case might be litigated in the Brown's home state. However, there would still be the possibility that the state court might decide that it would be more convenient for the matter to be litigated abroad. Since means now exist for gathering evidence abroad, and proof can always be made of any foreign law needed as data for decision, the convenience to William might overcome the reluctance of the court to litigate what is, in large measure, a foreign tort.

Since we have posited presence of the defendant corporation, William must still overcome the obstacle of lack of jurisdiction over the subject matter. This kind of a suit for support requires jurisdiction over the person of the defendant, and that by present constitutional norms calls for a meaningful connection between factors: the place of litigation, the defendant, and cause of action. The limits of these constitutional control norms would not be stretched beyond present bounds if an action in the Netherlands were held to cause an effect in the state of William's residence, provided that Allproducts' activities within that state were of such a volume and value to Allproducts that defense could not be deemed unfair in the constitutional sense.[4]

The next difficulty for William falls in the area of legislative jurisdiction. State legislatures rarely indicate territorial limits to their statutory generalization. The local adoption statute would not say whose law should govern an adoption outside of the state and the United States. Since all were United States nationals at the time of adoption, the court might apply its own law as most likely to meet the expectations of the parties to the adoption.

The court of William's home state is aware, however, that if it

---

[4]Exactly how the unsettling effects of the decisions of the Supreme Court in *Shaffer*, *Kulko*, and *Worldwide Volkswagen* will eventually be rationalized within the United States jurisdictional battleground is unclear. My position is that the two fields, enterprise risk distribution (the personal injury side of the case) and human dignity maintenance (the child support side), should be kept as separate as professional ingenuity can arrange. For the most recent doctrinal confrontation, *see* the Twerski-Mayer proposals in their article in 74 NW. U. L. REV. 781 (Dec. 1979) and the trilogue of commentaries thereon in the 7 HOFSTRA L. REV. 807-843.

artificially localizes this adoption, it may have to apply its substantive law, which denies the adoptee the right to recover for injuries to the parent. The court would like to move away from that rule and to adopt the "better rule," allowing recovery. It sees a way of doing this without directly overruling precedents by referring this kind of adoption to the law of the place of injury. It has thus decided that it will use the forum's law to create the relationship based on George and his deceased wife's connection with the forum but to measure the rights flowing from that relationship by the law of the place of injury.[5]

Jurisdictional concepts call for a number of generalizations. The single greatest source of confusion in this field stems from the fact that jurisdiction in child status cases is dominated by ideas flowing from commercial, industrial, and manufacturing activities—the creating and transmitting of wealth. This dominance is so great that the current revolution in jurisdictional ideas, and supposed demise of the jurisdiction *quasi in rem,* and the serious threat to the *in rem* jurisdiction, based on presence of a thing, took place in a series in which the human problem, modification of the amount owing for child support, was bracketed by two commercial cases.[6]

---

[5]On the "better rule" and the other choice-influencing considerations, *see* ROBERT A. LEFLAR, AMERICAN CONFLICTS LAW (3d ed. 1978). A more recent tribute to Leflar's general contribution, a most noteworthy one, can be found in a Symposium, 31 S.C.L. REV. 409 (Feb. 1980 #3). Using the realistic methodology, the composite approach, the forum could well look to the law of the place of adoption, one of many choices possible, and finding the right kind of adoption there, use its law rather than that of the place of injury (*lex loci delicti*). It can certainly be argued that there is less accidental quality to the act of adoption, which requires some official recognition of private intent, than a true accident.

[6]In date order, the cases are Shaffer v. Heitner, 429 U.S. 803 (1977); Kulko v. Superior Court (Calif.), 436 U.S. 84, rev. 564 P.2d 353 (1978); and Worldwide Volkswagen v. Woodson, 48 U.S.L. W. 4079 (1980). Most of the recent commentary, which is overwhelming in volume, is cited in the articles mentioned in note 4 *supra.* To that I would add two most recent comments on *Worldwide*: Woods, *Pennoyer's Demise: Personal Jursidiction After Shaffer and Kulko and a Modest Prediction on Worldwide Volkswagen v. Woodson,* 20 ARIZ. L. REV. (1978); and Sorg, *World-wide Volkswagen: Has the United States Supreme Court Taken Ill. CPA 17-1(b) out of the Gray Zone?* (1980), SO. ILL. L. J. 137. This latter comment is important because Illinois pioneered the constitutionally maximum long-arm statute both in text and judicial construction. While eventually segregation of the norms may occur, we are not yet at that point, so the happenings in the more clearly economic sphere will continue to impact on family-child status matters.

Reduced to simple terms, the rule now dominant is that there must be a real relationship between subject matter of the suit, the defendant, and the forum. However, a defendant-oriented subject matter jurisdiction overlooks the reality of children in the law. The only possible exception could be emancipated children, but they are no longer children for the purpose in question. Add to that basic rule the fact that subject matter can no longer serve to force a defendant to litigate in an inconvenient forum. If any obligation of a valuable type is to be effected, personal jurisdiction is needed, and that must be on reasonable notice, with a meaningful opportunity to defend.

If *in rem* jurisdiction is to be limited to interests in local land and unity of administration of estates, Professor G. Hazard's suggested interstate venue is destroyed.[7] The choice may be to return to a presence theory or neoterritorialism a la *Pennoyer*.[8] It is no wonder that the Supreme Court moves cautiously in the family-child law area. The Court is well aware that the traditional linkages of persons to territory, such as domicile or even residence, have turned to fiction and should seldom be relied upon as connecting links.

The normally impassioned debates in choice-of-law methodology have largely passed by the field of child status questions. Most of the more meaningful choices here tend to be derivative. This is a legacy from the era in which children were thought of as a special kind of property, whose rights would always be derivative of those of the parents or the family. Movement away from that older condition has been slow and often hesitant.

I have, therefore, chosen to consider choice of law to determine legitimacy. Again, my case is revelatory of the many difficulties in the path of a court that will not come right out and declare an independent right of the child to be legitimate, but that must achieve the result by indirection. More than any other single

---

[7]His article (contributed to a symposium entitled *The State Courts Role in the 80's & Beyond* in honor of Walter V. Schaefer) deals with his valuable suggestion that true multistate problems would have to be dealt with under a new interstate venue, based on the use of a new version of the *res:* 74 Nw. U.L. Rev. 711 (1979) especially at 713 (demise of diversity) and 719 (the obligation as *res*).

[8]Pennoyer v. Neff, 95 U.S. 714 (1878)—landmark foundation case on personal jurisdiction.

influence, one must admit the reality of the judges importing into decisions in child status matters their own moral standards.[9]

The following typical case best illustrates the strained quality of the devices used to solve matters of legitimacy: Fleeing from a conventional marriage to a more glamorous single's apartment in Manhattan, Mrs. Marblehed soon adds a male companion to the household. The relationship with Bill Brisk results in the birth of Samuel late in 1970. The companionship continues on the same informal basis, and early in 1972, another child, Sally, is born. Shortly thereafter, Mrs. Marblehed decides to become Mrs. Brisk. To do this she first procures a Haitian divorce from Marblehed. Two days later she and Bill appear on the Mexican side of the border, where they are duly married.

This happy "family" packs up the apartment in Manhattan, and all move to Massachusetts. Some few years later, Mrs. Brisk decides to terminate her marriage to Brisk. Out of this rather ordinary litigation dealing mainly with property questions arises the question of the status of the children. There is also a question about the name they should bear, as well as some doubt about the rights of Bill Brisk to maintain the role of "father."

The conventional rule on choice of law, which prevails in Massachusetts, is that the legitimacy of children domiciled in the Commonwealth will be settled by reference to the law of the jurisdiction that created the status. This means that both creation of the status and measurement of the effects of that status will be controlled, in this case, by the law of New York.

The conclusion of the trial judge was that if the children would be found to be legitimate under the law of New York, they would be legitimate under the law of Massachusetts. The result would be that Bill Brisk would continue to have the rights and duties of a father and that these children would bear his name.

---

[9]Typical of such a reaction is the recent decision of the Illinois Supreme Court in Jarrett v. Jarrett, 36 Ill. Dec. 1, 400 N.E.2d. 421 (1980) where the majority, over a stinging dissent by two conservative members of that court, prospectively construed the new Marriage Dissolution statute's custody provisions so as to bar a "fit" mother from retaining custody of minors because she had brought her "paramour" into the marital home. The main ground of the dissent was that importation of judges' moral biases in this area was inexcusable.

The process of reasoning, which the Supreme Judicial Court of the Commonwealth approved, was the following: New York had adopted a law which made it very clear that strong public policy of the state favored making all children legitimate if that could be done. The history of the statute indicated that even children of admittedly bigamous marriages should be legitimate if the fathers so wished.

The Massachusetts court had, therefore, only to tie these children to New York at the time of their births. This was easy to do since children automatically have the domicile of the mother. Records confirmed that Mrs. Marblehed was a resident there and the putative "marital" domicile was there as well.

The quality of the Mexican marriage could have been a serious problem for both of the children because the lawyers for Mrs. Brisk pointed out that an unauthorized marriage would not be sufficient. New York decisions had made it clear that this marriage would only be deemed void, thus bringing it within the statute favoring legitimacy of children "born out of wedlock."[10]

The extent to which a court faced with choice of law in child status matters will utilize the domicile connecting factor may very well be controlled by the result to be achieved. When dealing with the issue of polygamous or incestuous marriages, the result may be controlled by the particular issue before the court. If the matter is one of support or inheritance, and the forum has a strong policy of favoring legitimacy and the independent rights of children, the issue may be decided in favor of legitimacy. On the other hand, if the court can find any policy declarations favoring legitimacy within its own law, and the choice reference is to a system disfavoring legitimacy, the court may refuse the choice.

It is now clear that two real dangers for the practitioner exist in this subfield. The first danger is a result of the dissolution of the concept "status." Originally, "status" was tied to the total

---

[10]Based in very general terms on Fuss v. Fuss, 372 Mass. 64, 368 N.E.2d 271 (1977). *See also* Section 287-288, Rest. 2d, Conflict of Laws. Many states have statutes legitimating children of void and annulled marriages. The New York statute construed in *Fuss* is Dom. Rel. L. § 24(1) McKinney Supp. 1976. For the construction see *In re* Estate of Flemm, 85 Misc. 2d 855, 381 N.E.2d 573 (N.Y. Sur. Ct., 1975).

dependence of the child. It could then be thought of as a "res," a thing that could be tangibilized.[11]

The beginning of the process of making the child independent saw the splitting of single-choice methods into issue determination. Once the courts admitted that various references might be necessary to determine all of the child status issues, pragmatism forced them to view the results. It did not take the more realistic courts very long to see the unrealiability of domicile. No comfort was available in redefinition to residence, presence, or other words of that kind. In the struggle between the extreme need of unity of choice for some policy purposes and the equally extreme need of diversity for others, we are left with the fortunate compromise of favoring legitimacy. This touchstone will most frequently lead to the best interests of the child in real terms.

The last great part of the conflict of laws presupposes a prior proceeding. That proceeding may be formally judicial or substitutional, such as arbitration by agreement. Our legal system has always had a fundamental rule that there should be an end to litigation. The common law method of achieving this result led to the formulation of several principles. The most important was the notion that the cause of action merged in the judgment and that any subsequent proceeding would have to be on the judgment. This principle was accompanied by notions of preclusion, *res judicata,* to bind parties and their privies and to cover all matters that might have been litigated originally, and estoppel, to preclude issues where a common matter arises in litigation that is not between the original parties.[12]

Further reinforcement of the notion of putting disputes to rest came with the adoption of the full faith and credit clause of the United States constitution. That clause, as activated by Congressional legislation from time to time, established the rule that a judgment should be entitled to the same force and effect in the courts of all of the states that it had in the state where it was

[11]HAZARD, *see* note 7, *supra*, 716 and 719.

[12]The general background and the latest developments in preclusion can be found in an article contributed by Professor Scoles to the Symposium in note 7 *supra*, especially 74 NW.U.L. *REV*. 743 (1979).

rendered. The Supreme Court, in construing the clause over the almost two centuries of its existence, set forth certain basic limits on the second state's discretion in effecting or refusing enforcement of other states' judgments. These are keys to other basic clauses providing for the establishment of norms for the nation—mainly due process and equal protection. Full faith itself may be denied if the face of the judgment shows a lack of jurisdiction over person or subject matter; it may also be denied if the judgment is not final. Originally, the clause was thought to apply only to money judgments, but it was early extended to include decrees in equity that met the other requirements.

Today the clause is used in many settings. The recent Indian Child Welfare Act provides for full faith and credit to certain judgments of tribal courts, while the same result has been reached by the Supreme Court of Washington by judicial construction.[13] It may be even more significant, however, that the alternative voluntary granting of interstate effect to prior proceedings through comity has begun to blur the formal lines. Comity is also the principle used to grant extranational judgments force and effect within the United States.

The sum total of all of these policies has not been sufficient to settle the question of interstate enforceability of decrees in the custody field. The particular focus of the custody questions in the cases that led the Supreme Court finally to the holding in *May v. Anderson*[14] was lost in the historical process that went on in spite of, rather than because of, that holding. The chaos was not the result of that decision, however. The breakdown of the family and the increased ease of mobility in the United States would have happened anyway and would have produced the present interstate warfare for the control of minor children. The latter, not the decision, is what has created the reality of parental kidnapping.

---

[13]The Indian Child Welfare Act is codified to 25 U.S. Code § 1901-63. P.L. 95-608, 92 Stat. 3069 (1979). Very ably commented on in the *Indian Child Welfare Act—Tribal Self-Determination through Participation in Child Custody Provisions*, 2979 Wisc L. Rev. 1202; and Jones, *Indian Child Welfare, A Jurisdictional Approach*, 21 Ariz. L. Rev. 1123 (1979). The Washington case in *In re* Adoption of Buehl, 87 Wash. 2d 649, 555 P.2d 1334 (1976).

[14]345 U.S. 528 (1953), that personal jurisdiction over the parties is required for custody determination.

To remedy this problem by criminalizing the conduct might be a politically satisfactory response,[15] but it will not serve the interests of the children, even if those were to be defined in terms matching the legal and social reality of 1880, rather than 1980. It is impossible to define with exactitude, even with the help of the best allied professionals, those interests. One reason for this impossibility lies in our present inability to measure or evaluate parental concern for children. So long as the disputes remain to be settled in the law process rather than by some multi-disciplinary alternative resolution process, the children will continue to suffer. Their suffering derives largely from the attempt on the part of our society to maintain a fiction. That fiction is that the nuclear family is the norm and that the single parent family or the non-family affection unit is abnormal. When, additionally, the interests of the child are measured in economic terms, the dilemma for resolution is even greater. Given the present reality of multitudes of children of divorce, separation, or abandonment, and given the critical need to nurture the successive generations, finality or prior custody decrees may be the smallest concession to reality.

Progressive and talented courts can move in the direction of giving effect even to modifiable judgments not normally entitled to full faith effect. For the greater mass of overburdened trial courts, help was needed. When the problem of the snatched child reached serious proportions, courageous leadership in the Uniform Law Commission resulted in the adoption of the Uniform Child Custody Jurisdiction Act (hereinafter, The Uniform Act.)[16]

---

[15]Typical of the language used is the title of the reintroduced proposal of Sen. Wallop, Parental Kidnapping Prevention Act (S.105,95th, 1st Sess.) and by Bennett in the House, HR 1290. The Senator's comments may be found in 15 TRIAL (Amer. Trial Lawyers Assoc.) 34 (May 1979).

[16]The Uniform Child Custody Jurisdiction Act, 1968 Official Text, may be found in 9 ULA (Unif. Laws Anno.) (Matrimonial, Family & Health Laws) at 1 (1979). The Pocket Part at 8 gives the list of jurisdictions that have adopted the act (35), the modifications to the official text, and the statutory citations, for the adopting states. The principal advisor to the Commissioners for this act was the late Professor Brigitte Bodenheimer, and her articles on it are fundamental for those desiring more details, especially the foundation article on the Act in 22 VAND. L. REV. 1207 (1969) and the update, *Progress under the Act*, 65 CALIF. L. REV. 978 (1977). There is also a recent summary of cases construing the act in 96 A.L.R. 3d 968 (1980).

The act provides mechanisms that allow for nearly full faith and credit treatment to prior custody decrees.

Since thirty-five states have now adopted the Act, the run of decisions is beginning to show relief of the more acute cases. There remain weaknesses, and I would cite two. The first is the fact that the Act still relies on the concept of the "home state," to be established by presence for a fixed period of six months. It is dangerous to make such a delicate mechanism depend on a revised version of "domicile." Conservative courts may make an equation that could result in the reintroduction into this field of the old artificiality.

The second weakness is not of the Act's making. It stems from those commercially originated changes in constitutional control of jurisdiction discussed earlier. The major threat[17] is that the child-centered proceeding to determine custody may terminate parental rights without personal jurisdiction when the Supreme Court's decisions indicate that this type of proceeding is required. Even though the Act requires due process notice, limitation at the constitutional level of the "long-arm," successfully used until now for certain support matters through the continuing jurisdiction fiction, might defeat that portion of the Act. That, at this time, would be a really tragic regression. Hopefully, the enactment of the sound portion of the Wallop proposal, calling for full faith and credit to valid Uniform Act prior-custody awards, would indicate to the Court the intention of Congress to avoid such a regression.

There is no question that our social fabric has worn sufficiently thin and that some control over the "children of divorce" is required. I have two reasons for being concerned with the way in which this control has been exercised to date. My first concern is that litigation is not the best means for resolving disputes in child status matters. My second is that the techniques of conflicts law brought to bear in the field will prove to be a failure. These failures will cumulate the frustration, which must in turn lead inevitably to further federal statutory and common law control of

---

[17]*See* Lozoff, *The Due Process Dilemma of the Uniform Child Custody Jurisdiction Act*, 6 Ohio Nor. .. Rev. 586 (1979).

the field. Professor Leflar has stated it well: "New federal common law to govern a number of essentially national matters, eliminating state choice-of-law litigation accordingly, is both desirable and inevitable. That, however, is not a part of conflicts law, but rather an escape from conflicts law."[18]

The difficulties in this field are demonstrated by *Williams v. Zacher.*[19] This case presents a custody litigation in the hands of a most sensitive court. The Oregon Supreme Court would do all that it could to support the purposes of the Uniform Act. It is also a case in which neither of the custodial contestants had "clean hands." The facts are not unusual, nor are they as sensational as some custody battles that have been fought through two or three states and six or seven rounds.

Here Williams (H1) and Zacher (W) had married in early 1973, in Denver, Colorado, and the child (C) was born there later that same year. All lived in Denver until August, 1975, at which time they separated, and H1 and C arrived at the home of Williams' parents, taking up residence by December, 1975. That home was in Oregon, and the two had come by way of Utah and Wyoming.

On August 8, 1976, W obtained a decree dissolving the marriage. She alleged that H1 had taken the child from Denver by force, but because C was out of the state at the time of dissolution, the Colorado court reserved jurisdiction over the question of

---

[18]Leflar, *Choice of Law: A Well-Watered Plateau,* 41 LAW & CONTEMP. PROB. 10 at 26 (1977). Although the statement was often repeated throughout his writing, it was in his 1968 Hague Lectures that Ehrenzweig made his most direct attack on the general principles of private international law as the "superlaw." He said: "An attack on the validity of such principles...can show that, *even in the law of persons,* such principles are just another fragile and deleterious product of the continuing illusion of a non-existing superlaw." (Emphasis added.) 125 HAGUE LECTURES 167 at 242 (1968).

To appreciate the change in attitude and the need for real refinement in basic terminological definitions, contrast that statement with his earlier comment on "true rules" that are binding and beyond debate, such as the law of the domicile to provide for unity of administration of estates: "Most important...among those formulated precedential rules which...must be excluded from any discussion of *a priori*...status. These areas include such personal relationships as marriage and legitimacy by birth, to which international or national customary rules have given a modicum of super-law of 'public-law' content." *A Proper Law is a Proper Forum: A "Restatement" of the "Lex Fori Approach,"* 18 OKLA. L. REV. 340 at 342 (1965).

[19]35 Or. App. 129, 581 P. 2d 91 (1979).

custody of C. H1 was not given personal service of the Colorado action.

On January 12, 1977, Zacher and her second husband, accompanied by a private investigator, removed the child from his Oregon home by force and then flew directly to Denver. The next day the Colorado court awarded custody of C to W. In the later Oregon proceeding, that court noted that H1 had filed a motion to quash the custody award with the Colorado court, that the motion had been denied, and that an appeal therefrom was then pending. H1 had begun the Oregon proceeding in February, and W was served at her current residence in Idaho in March, 1977.

The Oregon trial court ruled that H1's petition was an initial petition and denied it under the "clean hands" rule. On appeal the Oregon Supreme Court refused to rule on the question of whether the adoption of the Uniform Act by Colorado would preclude any collateral attack on the Colorado decree. It simply held that this was not the right case for the determination of that question and found, instead, that the Colorado custody award failed on two grounds. The first ground was that Colorado was not the "home state," so that it had no custody jurisdiction under the Act. The second was that for all custody awards to be effective under the Act, whether interstate or international, notice and opportunity to defend, which would satisfy due process standards, must be given all indispensable or necessary parties. It needed no underlining to point out that H1, as father and then custodial parent, was such a party.

The Oregon Supreme Court considered the question of a "more appropriate forum," as well, and found that at the time of this appeal, there was none. Since only a month, at most, could have elapsed from the time of the Colorado decree and the commencement of the Oregon proceeding, and since W had appeared in Idaho during that time, Idaho could not have become a "home state," because that process takes six months.

On remand, the Supreme Court instructed the trial court to determine whether a change in fact might have made another jurisdiction a "home state" during the half year of appeal process. The remand also ordered the trial court to make certain that all of the Act's conditions protecting the custodial parent be complied with in the event that the court should order a transfer of the litigation to another jurisdiction. This kind of meticulous care should be lavished on the delicate determinations affecting the life of a child. There is, however, the danger, as with joint custody, that the remedy may be available only to those who have the patience and the financial ability to litigate.

Mobility is no longer limited to the federated United States. It is increasingly transnational. In accordance with Section 23 of the Uniform Act the same respect is given suitable foreign country custody awards as to those of the several states. *Miller v. Superior Court of Los Angeles County*[20] gave to an Australian custody award greater than full faith and credit under this section of the Act. The decision has been criticized on that ground alone. There was vigorous dissent at the intermediate appellate level, and the California Supreme Court upheld the decision 4-3, with another vigorous dissent. The major thrust of both dissents was that the enforcement of this particular award raised, in a most extreme setting, the weakness of a jurisdictional foundation that really lacked sufficient notice and a fair hearing to both custodial contestants. Had the decision involved countries other than Australia and the United States, the criticism would have been even more intense. There was also no meaningful confrontation with the currently difficult question of the impact of custody awards of this kind on the constitutionally protected right to travel.

The facts essential for the discussion of the *Miller* decision are easily summarized: H1 and W had entered into a complex custody arrangement involving two children, both of whom had dual Australian and United States nationality. W thereafter married another Australian and left California for Australia. There followed subsequent modifications of the original custody arrangement, but custody remained in W. She then took both children once again to California. In an Australian proceeding, in which H1 alleged that the children had been removed without his consent, custody was awarded to him. He then sought enforcement of that award in California. The decision of the Supreme Court's majority, that the Act made the award enforceable in California, raised the subsequent disputes.

---

[20] 22 Cal. 3d 923, 151 Cal. Rptr. 6, 587 P.2d 723 (1978).

Professor Brigitte Bodenheimer, as *amicus curiae*, had argued against that enforcement on the main ground that the Act does not favor giving any effect to punitive decrees and that this award was clearly punitive. The majority of the Court disagreed. The holding itself is significant as a dramatic extension of the Act into the international sphere, but it has an additional significance in that it reveals the extent to which language designed to create uniformity may be subject to extremely variant interpretations. There have been other instances, most notably the Uniform Reciprocal Enforcement of Support Act (URESA), where the very process of getting a Uniform Act adopted by all jurisdictions has destroyed the very uniformity sought. The judicial interpretational process adds to the risk of inconsistency. Notwithstanding, the Act represents a very important advance in custody litigation because it focuses on the child in a realistic recognition that the child is the party whose interests are to be adjudicated.

The United States has now participated officially in both The Hague Conference and Unidroit for almost twenty years. Both bodies are concerned with the development of international conventions in the family law field. Before that, our country took the simplistic position that such matters were within the area controlled, for lawmaking purposes, by the federated states.[21] While the international trend may be in the direction of the creation of what deNova has called plurilegislative nations,[22] the rapid evolution of transnational relationships will inevitably create more cases in which courts in the United States will have to consider the other major legal systems of the world.

Once again, a typical case is cited: the important decision of the European Court of Human Rights in *the Marckx case*.[23] There

---

[21]A leader in the struggle to bring about official participation, Kurt Nadelmann is still pioneering new ideas in this field. *See* especially his scholarly note on *Internationales Privatrecht* in 17 Harv. Int. L. J. 657 (1976) with its Postscript; *id.* at 675, calling for an Amer. Journal of Private International Law.

[22]*See* his Hague Lectures on Private Intn'l Law, 118 Receuil (1966) 443 at 554-6 (commenting on U.S. representatives to Hague Conference on Private Law difficulties with proposed conventions and his use of the term during his discussion of *In re* O'Keefe, id at 546 et seq.

[23]*Judgment in the Marckx case*, 19 INTN'L LEGAL MATERIALS (Amer. Soc. Int. L.) 109 (Jan. 1980).

are several reasons for its importance. First, the decision validates a trend in favor of abolition of the negative status of illegitimacy; second, it shows the importance of the emergence of a supranational norm in this sensitive field; and finally, it stands as a lesson to decison makers in this country in techniques that might be used to overcome the sociological differences frequently encountered in domestic litigation.

Simply stated, the action was brought on behalf of mother and daughter, by the mother, Paula, a Belgian national who was unmarried and a journalist by profession. The essence of the case was whether provisions of the Belgian civil code, which forced mothers of children born out of wedlock to choose between freedom of disposing of property and adoption of the child, violated "the right to respect for [her] private and family life," which is the key provision of the European Convention for the Protection of Human Rights and Fundamental Freedoms. The Court found that attitudes had changed in Belgium between 1950, when discrimination against illegitimate children was a norm, and 1978, when submission of a bill to bring Belgium into line with the earlier conventions that had contributed to reversing that discrimination.

While the Convention leaves the means of creating equality up to each member nation, the Court felt that to rest the power of making gifts, legacies, or invasion of "forced shares" depend on the distinction between "married" and "unmarried" mothers was indefensible under the Convention.

It is true that the United States government has not obtained the necessary Congressional action to make the several Hague conventions binding on the states under the supremacy clause. It is also true that where prestigious United States scholars have participated in the formulation of those conventions, and the conventions in turn are accepted as creating valid international norms, that process will inevitably influence developments here.

In his recent McCormick lecture at the University of Arizona College of Law, Judge Joseph Sneed commented: "...(T)he task of deciding which are the predominant values of a given social group is certainly not one that lawyers are trained for."[24]

---

[24] 21 ARIZ. L. REV. 926, n.33, at 934 (1979).

The universality that shines through that statement makes it as applicable to the needs of law in dealing with the child as it originally stood as part of his plea for coherence in the federal judiciary. Two other comments are brief but highly appropriate. The first is from a U.S. family law practitioner: "...(O)ne of the greatest deficiencies in law...has been the failure to undertake a thoroughgoing review...concerning the consequences of family breakup."[25] The second is that of a distinguished Danish scholar and practitioner: "...(I)t is worthy of respect that the study [of Private Int'l. L.] leaves no stone unturned.....(A)lthough it is useful to provide lawyers and judges with a good instrument, one should be careful not to refine it so much that only the instrument makers themselves are able to use it."[26]

---

[25]Fain, *Family Law—Whither Now?*, 1 J. OF DIVORCE 31, at 41-2 (1978).

[26]Phillip, *General Course on Private Intn'l Law*, 160 RECEUIL (Hague Lectures) (1978) 9.

Chapter 2

# MORAL DILEMMAS AND PROBLEMATIC DECISION MAKING IN NEONATAL INTENSIVE CARE

MICHAEL S. GRODIN, SHARON F. SCHWARTZ, AND I. DAVID TODRES

> "If we are to improve our human condition, we must act for ourselves; if we are to achieve full humanity, we must regard others as not less than ourselves; and that, life being short and art long, we cannot await final answers but must act upon the best of what we know; time lost is beyond recapture."
>
> Eisenberg, 1975

THE PRACTICE OF MEDICINE may be described as a teleological activity in the sense that it is a means to certain ends or goals. These ends or goals may be tacitly understood and may be described as the prevention and treatment of disease, the alleviation and minimizing of pain and suffering, the maintenance and care of the ill, and the preservation and enhancement of the "general well-being" of the patient (MacIntyre, 1979; Wartofsky, 1980). The meaning of "medicine" and the corresponding terms in other languages is, in short, the art of healing individually, as it is so defined by Aristotle (Pye-Smith, 1900). It is these ends or goals of medical practice that serve as value premises for decision making with regard to the administering of treatment and care.

With the rapid advances and successes of modern medical technology, decisions as to what is "appropriate" for the patient in terms of treatment and care have come under scrutiny. In particular, decision making has become problematic with respect to the critically ill patient, as life-support technology can now sustain and prolong life in some cases almost "indefinitely", (Duff, 1973, 1976; Eisenberg, 1975; Grodin, 1978; Jonsen, 1975; Waldman, 1976). For some critically ill patients life may be extended and prolonged, but pain and suffering may continue, disability may remain unchanged or even worsen, and the patient's "general well-being" may be seriously threatened. Thus, with the advances of sophisticated medical technology, it is not always clear how the critically ill patient *ought* to be treated, as the goals of medical practice are pursued. Choices may often involve morally relevant alternatives, in the sense that the ends or goals of medical practice seem to be in competition or conflict with one another as choices of treatment and care are made. Value premises seem to conflict as the patient, the physician, the family and others offer one goal to be more relevant than another, thus offering one choice of treatment or care to be of more value than another. Decision making becomes problematic as those involved attempt to reconcile what "ought" to be done in the face of what *can* be done.

In the case of the *competent* patient, decision making with regard to treatment choice is usually based upon how the individual patient assesses the explicit directives. Competency then is a pivotal and crucial criteria for ensuring the legitimacy of the "said wishes" of the patient. However, in the case of the *incompetent* patient, for example in the case of the critically ill newborn, *proxy* consent is then said to be taken as the "said wishes" of the patient. Incompetency then adds a new dimension to decision making as projected "wishes" or values of the incompetent patient are inferred.

The Newborn Intensive Care Unit could be said to represent the most sophisticated and advanced uses of life-support technology (Jonsen, 1978; McCormick, 1974; Moore, 1973). The corresponding obligations and responsibilities in the use of such technology are often problematic. Conflicts regarding treatment and care arise for the following reasons: (1) the newborn is seen as an *incompetent* patient with no "said wishes"; (2) the goals of treatment and care for the newborn may not be clear; (3) there may be conflicts with regard to the roles, the interests, and the responsibilities of those involved in the decision making. Strict criteria or "scie ıtific" data do not exist for evaluating all of neonatal intensive care, and each case will be unique with its multiple variables: medical, social, and economic factors. What would be fitting or proper for the newborn is never fixed, and decision making is inescapably contextual and contingent upon the particular surroundings and particular persons involved (Avery, 1973; Fletcher, 1975; Hauerwas, 1975; Shaw, 1973).

A discussion of problematic decision making and the critically ill newborn will make explicit the complexities and difficulties involved in treatment and care choices for the incompetent patient. The *low-birth weight* infant will be offered as a "model" for such decision making. Consider the following three cases.

CASE ONE—TRISOMY 13: Miss Smith is eighteen years old, unmarried, and in her third trimester of pregnancy. She has already made arrangements for the adoption of her expected child. In fact, Miss Smith states if it had been within the legal time period she would have aborted her current pregnancy. Miss Smith goes into spontaneous labor, is taken to her local hospital, and delivers a four pound male infant. At the time of delivery the infant is noted to be blue, unresponsive, and apparently asphyxiated. Through therapy, the infant is intubated, given cardiac massage, and placed on a respirator. The infant is then transferred to a newborn intensive care unit (NICU) in critical condition. Upon arrival at the NICU the infant is noted to have siezure activity and on careful physical examination dysmorphic features are noted. A genetics specialist is called to consult on the baby and a presumptive diagnosis of Trisomy 13 is made. The geneticist explains to the mother that chromosomal substantiation of the diagnosis is necessary and this may take several days. In the interim period, it is decided to support the infant with all means possible. The mother is also informed that 40 percent of babies with Trisomy 13 die in the first month of life and 95 percent are dead by one year. All these infants are retarded and developmentally vegetative. After chromosomal confirmation is obtained, the respirator is disconnected from the infant and all life-support measures discontinued. The baby is transferred to a chronic care institution, where he eventually dies at eleven months of age.

CASE TWO—MENINGOMYELOCELE: Baby Girl James, the first

born child to the James family, is found at delivery to have a high lumbar meningomyelocele (spinal defect), mild hydrocephalus (enlarged head), and lower extremity paralysis with urinary and bowel incontinence. The parents, both professors at a local college, have decided they do not wish to sign the surgical permit necessary to close the spinal defect. Through a court order the hospital physicians and staff take the infant to surgery where the defect is closed and a ventriculoperitoneal shunt placed to relieve the increased intracranial pressure associated with hydrocephalus. The baby is institutionalized and over the years requires a series of operations for the numerous complications that arise. The child, though unable to walk and confined to a wheelchair, is able to mobilize herself and travel about. Moderate retardation prevents self-sufficiency; however, the child is able to interact with peers and appears to achieve pleasure from such interactions. The possibility for adoption, though slight, is actively explored.

CASE THREE—LOW-BIRTH WEIGHT INFANT: Mrs. Jones, a thirty-six-year-old female, has been childless for the past eight years. She is seven and one-half months pregnant and both she and her husband consider this baby to be a "premium" one. Mrs. Jones suddenly goes into premature labor and is admitted to her local hospital. The local pediatrician is called and discusses what appears to be the forthcoming premature delivery. The parents stress their past failures at childbearing and their wishes for a baby "at all costs."

Mrs. Jones delivers an 870 gram (approximately two pounds) female infant that, because of severe distress, requires positive pressure ventilation with oxygen and suction. In the nursery the infant develops further distress and a chest x-ray reveals severe respiratory distress syndrome. The baby is intubated, intravenous lines placed, and mechanical ventilation instituted. The baby becomes hypoglycemic and acidotic, her blood pressure and blood count fall, and following a bloody lumbar puncture the presumptive diagnosis of intraventricular hemorrhage is made. A C.A.T. scan confirms a moderate to severe bleed, and mechanical ventilation must be totally initiated as the baby is without spontaneous respirations.

A meeting of the housestaff, nursing, clergy, and ancillary

personnel is held to discuss the prognosis with the parents. The parents want "everything possible" to be done for the baby as they state they can accept a "little" retardation. However, if the baby is to be severely retarded, they would prefer for the "baby's sake," as well as their own, that she be allowed to die. Institutionalization is suggested as an alternative, but the parents do not want to see the baby "suffer" in an institution. In the face of mixed emotions, medical uncertainties, and competing interests and values, medical orders must be written and a future course of action plotted.

The three above cases represent the kinds of decision making common to the NICU. Each case has its own history, characters, scenario, and outcome, and no two cases are alike. All such cases have degrees of confidence and areas of concern within the decision-making process.

In Case One the infant has Trisomy 13, a fixed, known genetically determined disease (Warkany, 1966). There is little uncertainty with respect to the degree of present and future disability, as in the case of Tay-Sachs disease. The prognosis is certain and inevitable (Smith, 1976). While "supportive" care is thought to be reasonable, "extraordinary" life-support therapy seems to be prolonging an inevitable death. Disability is fixed and known, while pain and suffering will ensue. Treatment and care is thus chosen on the basis of known and future outcome, where medical knowledge of the given genetic disorder is known with certainty.

In Case Two the infant is born with a meningomyelocele, a lesion of the spine visible at birth. Further complications associated with the meningomyelocele include hydrocephalus, bladder and bowel problems, and degrees of mental retardation (Brocklehurst, 1971; Freeman, 1974; Lorber, 1971, 1974, 1975). Unlike a fixed, known disorder as in Case One, this infant's projected "fixed" disorder is questionable and unknown. Though it is known that the infant will have some degree of functional and cognitive difficulty, the nature and extent of difficulty cannot be assessed with any degree of certainty. Prognosis in this case is limited by experience and observation. The future of these infants is often an open question. Statistics will allow for some prognostication, but with little specificity.

In Case Three, the low-birth weight infant presents added difficulties. Advanced technology has allowed more and more infants to survive at lower and lower birth weights. Less is known about ensuing difficulties or disabilities in these small infants. The *very* low-birth weight infant is a new phenomenon brought about with the help of complex life-support technology. Prognosis as a heuristic guide for decision making and treatment choice is not useful here in that the numbers of cases, histories, and outcome are even more limited (Hack, 1979; Steward, 1974).

A description of the workings of the Newborn Intensive Care Unit provides the contextual framework necessary for analyzing decision making and the critically ill newborn. The neonatal intensive care unit (NICU) is a spatially isolated area where all personnel are involved exclusively in the care of critically ill newborns. The unit, as such, is maximally equipped with all the equipment and supplies required for life-support and specialized care. The number of beds in the NICU is dictated not only by the level of the nursery (level III = advanced life support) but also by the size of the delivery service and numbers of high risk pregnancies managed at that hospital. Regionalization of perinatal care has come about as a direct extension of specialization and it is often necessary to transfer pregnant women at high risk prior to delivery and/or the infant following delivery to a level III center. Thus, occupancy is also a function of each unit's capability to accept the transfer of an infant. The allocation of limited bed resources is based on availability as well as factors of prognostication and the ability to manage and care for the complete needs of a critically ill newborn.

The goals of NICU care are the same as those for the general practice of medicine. The pursuit of these goals is contingent upon carefully constructed and implemented diagnostic and therapeutic plans. As multiple parties are involved in assessment of neonatal care there are frequent contraindications in the pathways toward goal attainment. The problematic nature of such controversy requires detailed analysis of each member of the NICU team. Understanding of the explicit and implicit roles, responsibilities, and considerations of each group is thus imperative.

The primary ir. lividual to consider with respect to decision making, in general, is the patient. The relationship between the patient and physician ought then to be one of shared goals and mutual understanding. Treatment and care is justified, given this relationship, where the physician's understanding of the disease will include the beliefs and intentions of the patient. (As Aristotle pointed out, the physician practices the art of healing, *individually.)*

As was mentioned earlier, the incompetent patient, i.e., the patient in the NICU, adds another dimension to that relationship. The parent or legal guardian must then contribute to such a relationship where it is his or her responsibility to act in accordance with the patient's wish if the patient were competent to express it. In addition to proxy consent, a consideration of new ideas and techniques may in some cases be implemented prior to a full understanding of their effect on ultimate patient outcome. Thus, "objective" treatment plans may not be available in the case of the critically ill newborn.

The parents and family of the newborn infant are its extrauterine full form of support, for it is the family, in the case of the healthy infant, who must feed, nurture, and financially support the child until he or she is old enough to care for itself. In the case of the sick neonate, many of these classic responsibilities and forms of care are carried out in the NICU itself. Although the parents, as legal guardians, hold the primary role in decision making for their sick child, they are for the most part uninvolved in much of the caring. Parents become not only concerned with their interpretation and protection of the newborn's "rights" but also are quite concerned with doing what is "right." The family quickly finds itself delving into issues of "quality of life." Because it is the parents who ultimately must care for the infant following discharge from the NICU, they understandably question what deficits or disabilities their child may eventually have. Such handicaps may have far-reaching effects on the integrity and form of their family unit. If the parents' concept of "quality of life" comes in conflict with what the "State" feels are the legal or moral rights of the infant, then the State may, in some cases, deem it necessary to accept legal guardianship to speak in "the best interests of the child."

It is the physician who all too often either is delegated or chooses to accept the responsibility for decisions in the NICU. The physician, however, is no better prepared to deal with some of the issues related to "quality of life" and the incompetent's "right" than any other party. The neonatologist is in the position of gathering and assessing objective medical and scientific data, and from this must make treatment plans for further decisions. In attempting to make "objective" medical decisions, the physician must have a clear understanding of what prognostic indicators of ultimate outcome are available. As the technology of neonatal care far surpasses both the experience and often the expertise of the practitioner, prognosis itself becomes problematic. Iatrogenicity generates an important question. Many of the "life-saving" therapies cause serious and long-lasting deficits and disabilities. The oxygen used to ventilate the baby who might otherwise die from immaturity of the lungs may ultimately cause chronic pulmonary insufficiency and blindness. The physician finds himself weighing risk factors and deciding which will have a graver consequence—the disease or therapy itself. The uncertainty of prognosis, along with the possible iatrogenic consequences of care, make the lack of objective data on which decisions are made all the more unsettling. The general practitioner who is involved in the referral to the ICU, and who will be the primary care provider on discharge, is often not equipped with the knowledge or expertise to participate in these decisions.

In addition to family and physicians, many personnel are actively involved in neonatal care such as nurses, social workers, psychologists, technicians, and clergy. These groups may independently or collectively take an active role in their involvement with decision making. The nursing staff serves not only as key administrators of treatment plans but also as the primary caretakers of the infant. Nurses feed, nurture, and initially supply the major component of the parenting role. When this role is carried to excess it occasionally interferes with the necessary transition from the caretaker role assumed by the professional to that of parent. Parents often feel disjointed and disconnected from their sick newborn (Bandman, 1978; Benfield, 1976). It is for these reasons that parents are encouraged to become actively involved in early caretaking in the NICU and, as the clinical condition warrants, to accept more and more of that primary responsibility.

The social workers and psychiatric support services concern themselves with the enormous social, physical, mental, and economic stresses the parents must endure. These staffs often base problematic decision making in the NICU on a "quality of life" principle. Finally, the clergy may play an important role in specific cases. This group has concerned itself with the "sanctity of life" as well as the "quality of life" principle on which to make treatment and care choices (Fletcher, 1974; McCormick, 1978; Reich, 1978).

Hospital administrators, governmental and legal bodies, and political and social advocates complete the personnel concerned with neonatal care. Though these groups may not be as directly involved in specific case decisions, their force in light of public policy and standards is far-reaching. The hospital administration must concern itself not only with the economics and utility of the NICU but also with the management and allocation of resources. Governmental bodies must look into broad social and economic plans for future medical care (Bunker, 1978). The judiciary has become increasingly outspoken with regard to nontreatment decisions and in the assessment of liabilities as they relate to rights and responsibilities (Dinnerstein, 1978; Quinlan, 1976; Saikewicz, 1977). Finally, political and social advocates apply utilitarian principles in analysis of problematic decision making where the greatest good for the greatest number is the operating principle.

At some point, some or all NICU personnel are involved in decision-making dilemmas relating to specific newborn cases. The roles and responsibilities of each group, whether communally or individually, are often implied yet not always defined. The inherent conflicts of roles, obligations, and principles that result may compound the difficult problems facing the sick newborn. Thus discussions involving all of those in the decision-making process will include particular moral or ethical principles as well as medical criteria and data on which decisions are to be based. Discussions concerning nontreatment or withdrawal of life-support technology for selected infants raise particular moral questions, as principles often are in conflict. In the absence of reliable clinical criteria for predicting outcome in severely ill newborns, the question of what *ought* to be done in particular cases has required much discussion, including those from within as well as those from without the medical context. Attempts to formulate guidelines for treatment and care choices by public policy have been under scrutiny, given this absence of exact physiologic measurement and predictability of disease outcome. Some have argued that *guidelines,* as such, would not be of any use, given the fact that in the NICU many cases are unique in presentation and outcome. Two such cases would be the following: (1) An infant with the "Short Bowel Syndrome," where it is unclear how much intestine is necessary to maintain continued independent life. Intravenous alimentation is given in the hopes that enough gut regeneration will occur to eventually replace such dependence. (2) An infant with a congenital heart defect where a paliative procedure may be performed in order to prolong life in the hopes that an eventual "corrective" procedure will be developed.

Thus, where prognosis as a heuristic guide to treatment and care choice is often absent, other principles are considered to be fundamental in guiding treatment choices. Discussions involving ethical or moral principles are introduced.

Questions are raised as to whether there are certain "inalienable" or "absolute" rights belonging to those who are involved in decision making, where such rights would supersede other considerations. A "right" might be defined as a relationship between persons where there is a right-holder and a right-ower. Similar to the case of a legal right, an "inalienable" or "absolute" right would have a logical structure. To say "X has a right" would mean that there ought to be a law or regulation or protection in upholding that right (Ladd, 1979). In the case of the critically ill newborn, there may be those who argue that the infant has an "inalienable" or absolute right to all available life-support technology; however, there may be others who would argue that parents (or legal guardians) have certain "inalienable" rights over those of the infant and those would take precedence. Treatment and care choices resulting from these two views might then be very different. It is important to n te that before invoking a "rights" claim in this context, the following considerations should be investigated: (1) Who is involved in the decision-making procedure and are there "rights" that would impose particular duties on particular persons? For example, the parent or legal guardian has the right to make treatment decisions for their infant but there may not be a correlative duty on the part of the physician to uphold that right if there is disagreement. Alternatively, if the infant is said to have a right to available life-support treatment, then the parents and/or physician would have a duty to uphold that right. (2) What kind of action would be required by the right-ower? For example, what kind of action would be required by a "right-to-life" argument? (3) What is the origin of the assumed right, i.e., is the right acquired by virtue of a contract, a certain role or relationship, or by certain circumstances? (4) Are there circumstances where this assumed right could be exercised and when it could be waived? For example, the parent or legal guardian has the right to choose whether or not to withdraw or withhold life-support treatment but such a right need not be exercised in light of other considerations (Ladd, 1979).

If one reflects on the three cases presented, it will be evident that decisions made in the NICU are not based on a proprietary rights model alone, as treatment choices cannot always be definite, uniform, or objective. There are likely to be competing or conflicting rights so that a rights model in decision making and the critically ill newborn that is understood as peremptory or proprietarial will not be helpful where the problem of adjudicating such rights becomes necessary. A rights model or rights principle for such decision making may then be subordinate to other more fundamental principles.

The principle that all life ought to be preserved and prolonged at any and all costs is a "sanctity-of-life" principle, where the choice of total life-support therapy would follow. In other words, the obligation to prolong and preserve life would be commensurately all-encompassing according to a "sanctity-of-life" principle. This principle would imply total life support in at least two of the above mentioned cases. A "right-to-life" principle may be a principle similar in its absoluteness. It would be argued that no life ought to be taken, implying, however, that total life-support intervention may not always be indicated, and that there may be cases where life-support intervention would be contra-indicated.

A "quality-of-life" principle is one where precedence is given to the "capacity" of a patient to have or attain a certain "level" or "standard" of life. This principle can be elusive and its meaning may be relative to the context and to the person making the judgment. Such a principle might be translated into the following: all life ought to be preserved, or all life is good, but emphasis is placed on the meaning of the "good life." Biological life would have a relative value, having meaning only when it would contribute to the betterment of a patient's condition (Reich, 1978). Nontreatment decisions in the critically ill newborn might be justified on this principle where the newborn's physical condition would not contribute to its "well-being," and where treatment might in some way diminish a certain quality of life. Thus, decision making based on a quality-of-life principle may omit some or all life-support intervention because of certain "justifying" circumstances. Such "justifying" circumstances have, for example, been formulated in terms of "personhood" or "humanness," whereby partial, total, or no life-support intervention would be indicated based on particular traits as representing the essence of "personhood" or "humanhood" such as neocortical function, self-consciousness, and the ability to have relationships with others and with God (Fletcher, 1974; McCormick, 1974, 1975).

In analyzing what it would mean to use such a principle in decision making, the following questions would have to be considered: (1) Which quality or qualities of human life are to be of value, and what do we mean by a quality? (2) How does a quality become a value, and what do we mean by value? (3) How is a "valued quality of life" principle used in a normative statement indicating what sort of action is permissible or impermissible? (4) How is the normative criterion (based on this "valued quality of life") applied to the actual situation, particularly when values are in conflict (Reich, 1978)?

Two further points could also be raised: (1) In listing what qualities could be valued, the list could be innumerable—those that are general and universal, particular and measurable, and those that are abstract and generally immeasurable. (2) Whatever one's normative criterion is, it would influence how "quality-of-life" principles are applied, making these judgments extremely relativistic.

Such a principle would indicate varying degrees of life-support treatment or intervention, depending on *who* is making the decision, and depending on what is considered to be of value. For example, an infant born with mental retardation might be viewed as "unacceptable" to parents who value a highly technical and competitive life-style. Mental retardation would then be sufficient grounds for moderation of treatment. The same child might be otherwise "acceptable" with a more physical deformity rather than cognitive impairment. On the other hand, a child with similar cognitive disability might be "acceptable" to the parents who value physical labor over intellectual capacity. Thus physical deformity rather than retardation would to them be sufficient grounds for moderation of treatment. Decision making based on this principle is easily seen to be problematic as there can be competing values, depending on who is making the decision and what is taken to be of value.

Using this quality-of-life principle, emphasis may be placed on the moral claims of a certain "value" of life that is based on predictable qualitative consequences for either the individual infant, or for others whose interests might be of concern (e.g. family or society) (Reich, 1978). Life-support treatment or intervention may or may not be indicated, depending on how the calculus is applied. If the principle is taken to be that of the greatest good for the greatest number, life-support intervention would be based on the maximization of some particular kind (or quality) of consequence of an action, depending on what is singled out for maximization. That is, the utility of an action would be defined in terms of the productiveness of what those affected by it *believe* to be intrinsically good (Narveson, 1967). Thus, treatment decisions would be made on the basis of whether or not the consequences of those decisions would produce a greater net amount of what is valued by those involved. Choice of treatment may or may not be indicated, depending on the resultant equation and the net value, either individual or social.

Utilitarianism may then result in social or societal based decision making where the value of individuals would be calculated against, for example, the "good" or value of society in general (Lyons, 1965). One might argue, however, that a utility-based decision may not close the gap between what might be termed "social morality" and individual or "personal morality" (Ladd, 1979). In addition, one might argue that a principle of utility is never just a consideration of utility, but requires a background of beliefs and evaluative commitments before the principle is applied, i.e., there are implicit decisions made about how the world ought to be viewed, how experience ought to be structured, and that "the world is one of discrete variables of a reasonably high degree of predictability" (MacIntyre, 1977).

In conclusion, each case is in itself complex and individual, and decisions with regard to these newborns may reflect various principles, roles, and responsibilities, unique to that newborn. Medical and moral considerations are case-specific or contextual and thus may not be applicable even when presented with what might appear on "medical grounds" to be a similar child. One must be wary at any attempt to draw up policies or guidelines for decision making. All the various aspects of patient care must be weighed and considered individually with respect to each individual child.

The process of decision making is never static. It is a dynamic process constantly being evolved and refined to better apply to rapidly changing possibilities. Decisions to initiate, continue, or withdraw life-support technology for the infant can be uniquely problematic for the medical staff and family. The uniqueness is manifested in a number of ways. The infant is an incompetent patient in the decision-making process and thus the medical-ethical judgments are in the hands of the parents or legal guardians. Decision making then poses questions to rights of others to make decisions for the incompetent. While parents appropriately assume this responsibility, the infant may need protection from parents whose concerns for their infant may be secondary to their own personal needs or beliefs. The physician's role in the decision making should be one of directing the medical management towards therapeutic goals and acting on behalf of the newborn and its parents towards these goals. Where life-support technology may not provide these therapeutic goals but only bring about the survival of a "severely compromised individual," the wisdom of using sophisticated medical technology will require the attention of all those involved in the care of the infant. This group should include, in addition to the caring physicians, those who have established personal ties with the parents and infant, namely nursing personnel, family pediatricians, and clergy.

One other aspect of newborn care is the uncertain potential for future well-being following the insult of a critical illness. The newborn is at the beginning of its life and there is no known life with which to make comparisons or determine how that particular life may be changed by the insult of the illness. The prognosis for the infant is uncertain. New developments in medical diagnosis, therapy, and technology are constantly changing the outlook for this infant. Data are only recently available and even then there are many gaps in medical knowledge. Basing future outcomes on treatment procedures carried out ten years ago may not be relevant to the infant we are treating *today*. The infant's "powers" of recovery are often staggering, making decisions based on future "quality of life" very difficult.

Although the "correctness" or "rightness" of any one decision may ultimately remain in doubt, the necessity for making decisions is absolute. The responsibility for such action must be accepted with thoughtfulness, reflection, and solemnity. With an understanding of the moral, as well as medical, dimensions of the care of the critically ill newborn, it should be possible to pursue the healing art in a humane, compassionate, and trusting manner that will ensure the future well-being of those who need our protection most—our children.

> "If I am not for myself, who is for me? And if I am for myself (alone) what am I? And if not now, when?"
>
> Hillel, Mishnah, Torah

## References

Bandman, B., & Bandman, E. (Eds.). *Bioethics and human rights.* Boston: Little Brown, 1978.

Benfield, D.G., Laeb, S.A., & Reuter, J. Grief response of parents after referral of critically ill newborn to a regional center. *New England Journal of Medicine*, 1976, *294*, 975.

Bleich, J. Theological consideration in the care of defective newborns. In C. Swinyard (Ed.), *Decision-making and the defective newborn.* Springfield, Illinois: Charles C Thomas, 1978.

Bunker, J.J., Barnes, B.A., & Mosteller, F. (Eds.). *Costs, risks and benefits of surgery.* New York: Oxford University Press, 1977.

*In re* Dinnerstein, Mass. 380 N.E. 2d 134 (1978).

Duff, R., & Campbell, A. On deciding the care of severely handicapped or dying persons with particular reference to infants. *Pediatrics*, 1976, *57*, 4.

Eisenberg, Leon. The ethics of intervention: acting amidst ambiguity. *Journal of Child Psychology and Psychiatry*, 1975, *16*, 93.

Fletcher, J. Indicator of humanhood: a tentative profile of man. *Hastings Center Report*, 1974, *2*, 1.

Fletcher J. Choices of life or death in the care of defective newborns. In *Social responsibility: Journalism, law, medicine.* Lexington, Virginia: Washington and Lee University Press, 1975.

Freeman, J.M. To treat or not to treat: Ethical dilemmas of treating the infant with myelomeningocele. *Clinical Neurosurgery*, 1973, *20*, 134.

Grodin, M. Ethical issues in perinatology—the rights of the fetus and newborn. *Journal of Clinical Child Psychology*, Fall, 1978, 184.

Hack, M., Fanaroff, A., & Merkatz, I. The low birthweight infant—Evaluation of a changing outlook. *New England Journal of Medicine*, 1979, *31*, 1162-1165.

Hauerwas, S. The demands and limits of care-ethical reflections on the moral dilemma of neonatal intensive care. *American Journal of Medical Sciences*, 1975, *269*, 222.

Jonsen, A., & Garland, M. (Eds.). *Ethics of newborn intensive care.* San Francisco and Berkeley: University of California School of Medicine and Institute of Government Studies, 1976.

Jonsen, A., & Lister, G. Newborn intensive care: the ethical problems. *The Hastings Center Report*, 1978, *8*, 15.

Ladd, J. Legalism and medical ethics. *Journal of Medicine and Philosophy*, 1979, *4*, 70.

Lorber, J. Results of treatment of myelomeningocele: an analysis of 524 unselected cases with special reference to possible selection for treatment. *Developmental Medicine and Child Neurology*, 1971, *13*, 279.

Lorber, J. Selective treatment of myelomeningocele: To treat or not to treat. *Pediatrics*, 1974, *53*, 307.

Lyons, D. *Forms and limits of utilitarianism.* London: Oxford University Press, 1965.

McCormick, R. A proposal for "quality of life" criteria for sustaining life. *Hospital Progress*, 1975, 76.

McCormick, R. The quality of life, the sanctity of life. *The Hastings Center Report*, 1978, *8*, 30.

MacIntyre, A. Utilitarianism and cost benefit analysis. In R. Sayre (Ed.), *Values and the electric power industry*. Indiana: Notre Dame Press, 1977.

MacIntyre, A. *What does ethics have to learn from medical ethics*. Unpublished manuscript, 1979.

Moore, T. *Ethical dilemmas in current obstetric and newborn care* (report of the 65th Ross Conference on Pediatric Research). Columbus, Ohio, 1973.

Narveson, J. *Morality and utility*. Maryland: Johns Hopkins University Press, 1967.

Pye-Smith, P. Medicine as a science and medicine as an art. *Lancet*, August, 1900.

*In re* Quinlan, N.J. 355 A.2d 669 (1976).

Reich, W. Quality of life and defective newborn children: an ethical analysis. In C. Swingard (Ed.), *Decision making and the defective newborn*. Springfield, Illinois: Charles C Thomas, 1978.

*In re* Saikewicz vs. Superintendent of Belchertown State School, Mass., 370 N.E.2d 417 (1977).

Shaw, A. Defining the quality of life. *The Hastings Center Report*, 1977, *7*, 11.

Smith, D. *Recognizable patterns of human malformation*. Philadelphia: W.B. Saunders Company, 1976.

Stewart, A., & Reynolds, E. Improved prognosis for infants of very low birth weight. *Pediatrics*, 1974, *54*, 724.

Warkany, J., Passarge, E., & Smith, L. Congenital malformation in autosomal trisomy syndromes. *American Journal of Diseases of Childhood*, 1966, *112*, 502.

Wartofsky, M. Rights, risks and responsibility. In S. Spicker & H. Engelhardt (Eds.), *Philosophy and medicine*. Boston: Reidel Publishing Company, 1980.

Chapter 3

# INTRAFAMILIAL INCEST AND SEXUAL MOLESTATION OF CHILDREN

MORRIS J. PAULSON, LOUISE STROUSE, AND ANNE CHALEFF

WITHIN THE LAST FEW years, there has been increased public awareness of physical and sexual abuse of minors. Although society deplores the appalling incidence of maltreatment of children, we can feel encouraged that medical-legal-social intervention into domestic violence and abuse of children is developing in a more humanitarian and rehabilitative direction, rather than solely as a stepping stone to punishment and incarceration. History has shown how society in the past has sanctioned the sexual use of children, for the entertainment of adults (Aries, 1965). We have only to remember Victorian England and the world of Dickens to recall the extent of physical abuse inflicted upon children by adults and parents.

The literature on sexual abuse of children is extensive. The following discussion presents an overview of some of the major studies pertinent to a clinical understanding and treatment of sexually abused children and their families. The Sexual Abuse Treatment Program, Neuropsychiatric Institute, University of California, Los Angeles, will be discussed as one prototype for evaluating a community-based, university-hospital-sponsored, outpatient treatment program for families involved in intra-familial incest.

This paper was supported in part by Grant No. MC-R-060339, awarded by Maternal and Child Health, DHEW, and Catholics of Motion Picture, T.V., Radio and Recording Industry.

## Definitions of Incest

Incest has been defined as "sexual intercourse between persons so closely related that they are forbidden by law to marry" (Webster, 1967). Levi-Strauss (1956) postulates an almost identical definition suggesting, however, that the primary purpose for early cultural and anthropological taboos of incest was to preserve the good quality and exchangeability of women as a commodity. "The incest taboo, although generally prohibiting marriage among nuclear family members, is not aimed at the family. Rather, the taboo guarantees the exchange of women and from this fundamental exchange come all other exchanges..... goods, services, etc." (Rist, 1979). The definition of intrafamilial incest becomes even more difficult as we examine carefully the allowable degrees of affectional intimacy within a family which are prescribed by law, by the church, by one's culture group, and by the values within an individual family. A law enforcement charge of sexual molestation thus may become highly debatable even in a court of law. Finkelhor (1979) in discussing "What's wrong with sex between adults and children" states that a major argument against adult-child sexual behavior revolves around the condition of consent, and that children by their very nature are incapable of truly consenting to sex with adults. This argument, while having some merit, misses the more important point that sexual intimacy involves both physiological and psychological consequences having multiple impact upon the child beyond those related to consent and willing participation.

## Origins of the Incest Taboo

Scientific and anthropological literature is replete with historical references and theories specific to origins of the incest taboo (Lustig, 1966; Henderson, 1972; Sarles, 1975). In early psychoanalysis the concept of unconscious wishes and sexual fantasies played a significant part in the development of theories of infantile sexuality and the role of the Oedipus complex in shaping later adult psycho-sexual development. Freud (1954) viewed the incest taboo as a means of protecting the nuclear family from ruinous disruption and parent-child rivalry. Others

(Adams & Neel, 1967; Lindzey, 1967) posited a biologic "knowledge" that, through the ages, has been unconsciously sensed: a knowledge that inbreeding would produce defective offspring (Lukianowicz, 1972). Such a conceptual basis for the taboo has, however, been disputed by Lester (1972) who referring to Hutterite colonies that have been inbreeding for generations noted no apparently negative consequences upon succeeding generations of children.

Today there is a remarkable freedom for sexual experimentation. Contemporary studies of sexual behavior reveal rapidly changing and liberalizing attitudes towards heterosexual and homosexual intimacy, attitudes that have created much confusion among parents with respect to values and standards by which they wish to rear and educate their children (Cohen, 1978). A startling example of this is illustrated by a "Penthouse" (Nobile, 1977) article advocating "positive incest" as a means by which young girls can be lovingly introduced into sexual activity. Needless to say, this philosophy, distorted as it may be, produces premature aging among those professionals and parents who are daily witnesses to family disintegration subsequent to the disclosure of single or repeated incest between family members.

## Epidemiology of Incest

Many studies have examined not only the socioeconomic correlates of incest (Guttmacher, 1951; Riemer, 1940) but also sociocultural factors within both rural and urban society (Sonden, 1936). In spite of methodological concerns regarding a number of such studies, it is assumed by social scientists that the incest taboo is cross-cultural, and unrelated to social class, ethnicity, and socioeconomic status. Lester (1972), however, cautions that in spite of such universality, there is a higher incidence of reported incest in families from lower social classes—primarily because it is the disadvantaged, disorganized, economically indigent, and unstable families who have a higher probability of being identified or reported by social welfare and/or law enforcement agencies. The affluent, cosmopolitan family, often with the collusion of the family physician and the resources of an attorney, is able to keep intrafamilial molestation of a child secret (Schechter, 1976).

Burgess (1978) has recently shown that approximately 78 percent of sexual abuse and molestation of children takes place within the home by members of either the nuclear or extended family. The perpetrators, most of whom are males, are diverse and heterogeneous in attitudes and behavior. McCreary (1975) found in a heterogeneous group of molesters a relationship between severity of personality disturbance and greater frequency of prior offenses. Bell and Hall (1971) state that child molesters have a basic character disorder shown by schizoid and passive traits, as well as a profound dread of adult sexuality. Cohen, Seghorn, and Calmas (1969) describe three types of child molesters: one having relatively normal psychosocial functioning, another having poor social-sexual functioning, and a third group is cruelly and viciously involved in sexual assault of children. It is thus apparent that in studying the epidemiology of sexual abuse of children, one must examine its origins from many points of view. No unidimensional pattern is etiologic; incest of children by parents is diverse and complex.

## Sequelae for the Child Victim

The emotional consequences of incest are as varied as are its determinants. Kaufman, Peck, and Tabuiri (1954), Sloan and Karpinski (1942), and Bender and Grugett (1952) all claim that incest and sexual molestation in early childhood are less traumatic and less emotionally damaging than when occurring in adolescence. On the other hand, Katan (1973), in a study of children raped at ages three and four years and untreated until later in life, confirmed permanent and acute pathology, which earlier had been identified also by Lewis and Sarrel (1968). Frequently, girls who feel abandoned by their mothers turn to an incestuous alliance with a father or stepfather, which for many then leads to a later life of prostitution. Benward and Densen-Gerber (1975) and Weiner (1964) found that some girls passively submitting to incest later appear surprisingly capable and mature; yet as Rist (1979) states, "The primary defenses (of such girls) are denial, repression, and, sometimes, projection. Often, guilt feelings are avoided by denying enjoyment from the sexual activity and behaving in an outwardly passive manner." Mother-son incest, although only rarely reported, invariably results in significantly greater emotional trauma and adult psychosexual maladjustment for the male victim, engendering "in the child a fear of both parents—the castrating father and the all-encompassing mother" (Rist, 1979). In addition to disorders in personality development, victims frequently feel to blame for incarceration of the father, for break up of the family, and for the stigma the community frequently directs to the victimized family. Somatic symptoms, depression, shame, and promiscuity then become additional, commonly recognized sequelae to the act of incest (Kaufman, 1954).

## The "At-risk" Child

Just as in the case of physical abuse, attempts have been made to identify the high risk, incest-prone family, in order to intervene with primary prevention procedures (Browning and Boatman, 1977; Paulson, 1974, 1975, 1978). In many families the identified risk factors are strikingly similar to those in physical abuse: (1) many mothers and fathers of incest victims have themselves been molested in their own early childhoods, (2) the child, feeling unloved, uses seductive-like behavior in order to receive emotional fulfillment, (3) children of depressed mothers and alcoholic fathers live within a family environment that, lacking in emotional affection, allows only the expression of a physical-sexual type of release of affect, (4) inadequate, passive-dependent fathers unable to experience personal esteem within the marriage, frequently turn to a child for gratification, knowing that there is now no pressure to satisfy the sexual partner in a mature, adult manner, and (5) unhappy remarriages have brought fathers, stepfathers, and stepchildren into relationships of potential intimacy. The rare mother-son and father-son incest are symptomatic of acute family pathology, in which the perpetrator may have a borderline or psychotic disorder (Schechter, 1976).

## The Dysfunctional Family

Many investigators have emphasized that intrafamilial sexual abuse is a symptom of a disorganized and nonfunctioning family (Giarreto, 1976; Lustig, 1966; Machotka, Pittman, & Flamenhaft, 1967; Summit, 1978). But, what is meant by this term? According to Lustig (1966), such a family is "unable to work together in an effective manner to pursue socially approved goals, within the limits of values defined by society. The members feel themselves threatened by incipient disintegration." Mothers faced with their own sexual inadequacies can become colluding partners, accepting or welcoming sexual overtures between husband and child as a means of avoiding intimacy in the husband-wife relationship.

For fathers in a dysfunctional family, there is often a need to maintain a strong patriarchial role as a compensation for deep-lying feelings of personal-social-sexual inadequacy. The family is often socially isolated from its neighbors, with the father's role marked by anxiousness, fear of outsiders, and inability to express normal feelings of intimacy, affection, anger, irritation, and conflict. However, there is one relationship within which the incompetent parent can experience a degree of fulfillment, and that is through an incestuous relationship with the child. On a deep and unconscious level the husband may be expressing intense feelings of anger and retaliation against his wife and women in general. The dynamics behind such rage is often rooted in early childhood relationships with a seductive, insecure, overly smothering, hysterical mother. In those rare cases of father-son incest, underlying homosexual tendencies have been identified (Awad, 1976; Raybin, 1969).

Mothers in the incestuous family frequently report a history of emotional deprivation, physical and sexual abuse, desertion by their own fathers, and multiple unhappy marriages in which each new spouse recreates aspects of her own early pathological childhood. The role-reversal phenomenon of physically abusive families is replayed with the daughter assuming the mother's role in the marital relationship and the mother regressing into a dependent, infantile status, unable to assert an adult role within the family. Lustig (1966) has suggested that such role-reversal and father-daughter incest may sometimes be an expression of the mother's unconscious homosexual love for her daughter, expressed and fulfilled through the incestuous relationship of father and daughter.

Many latency-age and adolescent-age girls, victims of intra-family incest, describe their mothers as demanding, depriving, jealous, and competitive for the affections of the father in the family. The angry, sexually precocious girl at times consciously seeks out a sexual encounter with the father or stepfather as the ultimate revenge against the affection-depriving mother. Outwardly, as previously mentioned, many of these girls appear socially and physically mature; on closer examination, they reveal anxiety, depression, and low self-esteem. The incest act is a means of reassuring themselves of at least momentary affection, and thus a way of temporarily denying inner affectlessness. Peters (1976) and Schultz (1973) have pointed out that the degree of experienced distress in daughters is proportional to the degree of emotional and behavioral responses of the parents. These authors make a special plea to parents that, in spite of the personal sense of loss and embarrassment that immediately follow disclosure of incest, parents try to be reasoned, supportive of the victim, and not hysterical. The dire consequences of incest can be even more compounded by the understandable but irrational behavior of the victimized parent (Ferracuti, 1972).

## Motivational Factors in the Treatment of Sexually Abusing Parents

Much has been written on success or failure of mandated treatment for criminal offenders. Imprisonment as a rehabilitative technique has had little positive outcome. Even when combined with institutional programs of psychotherapy, imprisonment has failed in deterring all age groups from a return to crime. But why? It is important to examine closely the role of the family in rehabilitating such offenders. If there is minimal identification with a nuclear group of caring persons, if the bonds of attachment with others are nonexistent, then the perpetrator finds his identity with another peer group, usually other criminal offenders. It is here that he/she finds acceptance, experiencing a sense of belonging with a social unit having like goals, values, and aspirations.

What can be done for the sexual offender who, subsequent to court disposition, is referred for outpatient psychotherapy? For the pedophile, unattached to a family unit, whose criminal offenses have involved commercial sex, vice, and "chicken-hawk" activities with young runaway children on the streets, psychotherapy appears to have little value. For such offenders there is an absence of guilt, and a minimum of conscience with regard to the consequences of sexual assault upon children. The primary goal of such persons is a return to a similar life-style of commercial sex but, "this time not get caught."

What can be done for the pedophile living within the context of intrafamily incest? Here there are usually existing interpersonal relationships, bonds of affection and attachment between family members, a cohesive family unit, and an economic commitment to others. Within such a context the pedophile has greater motivation for accepting a program of rehabilitation. Hopefully, his own personal needs and values will also be better gratified within the milieu of a caring family.

When first apprehended, most molesters feel they are unique in engaging in such kinds of abuse towards children. Their self-esteem is lowered, especially in terms of their position within the family. Immediate estrangement may occur from the marital partner who feels emotionally violated, sexually demeaned, and betrayed in a relationship of supposed trust. For a significant number of parents, suicide is felt as the only escape. This, therefore, is a moment of crisis that must be carefully evaluated by the professional, and if need be, temporary hospitalization must be provided to prevent a self-destructive acting out of overwhelming feelings of guilt and hopelessness. The experiencing of such anxiety, guilt, and depression can be, however, an initial step towards therapeutic intervention, and a mobilization of emotional resources oriented to a resolution of those dysfunctional family dynamics that initially led to incest.

Many times identification of a one-and-only incident of incest makes for greater motivation on the part of perpetrator and family. Disclosure and apprehension may provide the necessary external impetus whereby immediate intervention can have its greatest potential for success. If, however, the incest has been occurring over a period of time, and especially involving more than one member of the family, then the perpetrator may have already incorporated or developed many rationalizations about the incest. Not having been identified at the first incident, the now chronically incesting parent becomes blasé, anxiety-free, feeling that he will never be caught. When apprehended, the initial concern is often related to being discovered, rather than related to any awareness of the psychological and physical trauma devastatingly inflicted upon the child and family.

Almost always in repeated incest of a child, the perpetrator has induced the victim to be a passive or willing participant. This may be by threat of violence, by granting of favors, by giving of gifts, or by convincing the child that "daddy loves you very much and this is alright." If he remains undiscovered, the abuser may over a period of time minimize the consequences of his actions. With minimum guilt, he incorporates a self-acceptance of the ongoing incest and denies the significance of the taboo act(s) itself. Feelings of self-alienation that occur subsequent to incestuous acts may become suppressed. Remorse and shame decrease as the perpetrator continues those sexual acts, which have escaped attention and condemnation. The conscious ego and the primitive, archaic primary drives have "made peace" with conscience, super-ego, and culture values. For many it is the ultimate discovery of incest with its manifest legal and family involvements that acts as the stimulus and motivation for terminating the incestuous acts.

The sexually assaulting parent may only grudgingly accept professional intervention in order to preserve the nuclear family, to prevent divorce, or to keep himself from prison. What is needed manifestly is a deep and meaningful commitment to therapy, based on a desire to respect the right of the child to grow physically, emotionally, and sexually in a family milieu that provides freedom from assault by parents. For a small number of fathers and mothers actively and passively involved in family incest, motivation for treatment is insufficient to either keep them in therapy or to contribute meaningfully towards successful rehabilitation. It is at such times and with such parents that long-term foster home placement may have to be considered. For other families with even poorer prognoses, there may be a need for permanent relinquishment of parental rights. Adoption becomes for some children the only way of assuring them of a home that will provide at least minimal bonds of affection, care, love, and protection.

### Interviewing the Incested Child

For the verbal-age child, being interviewed can be a source of great anxiety, fear, embarrassment, and anger. Tact, understanding, and a nonthreatening environment in which to conduct the interview are necessary. Most often such a session comes after a law enforcement investigation, in which the victim has already been confronted with questions specific to the physical act of incest. In the meantime, there frequently has been family pressure on the child, direct and indirect, to change statements in order to avoid the consequences of incriminating testimony. Recognizing fear of disclosure within the child, the interviewer must be patient, supportive, and objective in conducting a fair and impartial inquiry into those events associated with the alleged incest. A hostile confrontation of the child, when apparent changes in testimony are given, must be avoided. Denial and fabrication are for many children the only defenses for coping with the trauma of sexual abuse, the attendant consequences of family disintegration, and probable incarceration of the guilty parent.

It must be remembered that in spite of the nature and severity of sexual assaults, parents are, in the eyes of the victim, still the parents, the ones who have provided support, security, and varying degrees of emotional fulfillment. Therefore, direct testimony, confession, and disclosure can be experienced as betrayal. For some victims, the potential removal of the guilty parent induces acute separation fears. For other children, fear of retaliation by the abuser and fear of being blamed by siblings and other family members are emotionally devastating concerns.

It is important not to create in the interview an adversary type of family relationship based upon given testimony from the victim and earlier testimony given by one or both parents. For many victims, the nonintervention of a mother, knowledgeable about earlier incest, is seen as betrayal and lack of concern for the child's best welfare. Yet, unknown to the child, this lack of assertive intervention may well be a function of mother being emotionally paralyzed by this partial awareness of incestuous relationships between her child and her "significant other." Fear of physical intimidation or abuse by the sexual perpetrator keeps many dependent mothers in bondage and secrecy. Anxiety over loss of income, anticipating probable break up of the family, dreading rejection from both the extended family and the community of neighbors, not quite believing that incest could actually have occurred—all these areas keep many parents from disclosing suspected or observed incest.

There is increasing evidence that many parents directly or indirectly participating in the incest were themselves victims of similar incest in their own early childhoods. This "secret" has invariably been kept from all family members. The reappearance of molestation in the present family now exacerbates many long-repressed fears and feelings of shame associated with the earlier incest. Facing full awareness of a failing marriage, with increased doubts about her own sexuality and womanhood, jealous of the daughter who now becomes a rival for her husband's affections, many mothers must, in order to preserve any degree of emotional balance, either massively deny the incest or attribute partial or full blame to the seductive behavior of a maturing young child.

For many of the victimized children, the supportive milieu of a well-conducted interview allows for a therapeutic catharsis in which the victim is able to verbalize the trauma of molestation, without fear of rejection or intimidation. Once the secret is known, the victim may experience a positive, abreactive-like response. However, it is important to follow through on such an interview, for often there is a post-cathartic reaction of guilt, shame, fear, and regret at testifying against the parent. These are feelings that must be recognized by the interviewer and that the victim must also accept. Full and complete disclosure may be professionally gratifying for the interviewer, but, for the child, too early and complete "purging" can have delayed consequences that must be anticipated, monitored, and dealt with in an appropriate and professional manner.

It is also important for the interviewer to remember that sometimes children fabricate incest stories in order to intimidate and blackmail a parent. This is especially so when resolution of an earlier incest has allowed the perpetrator to return home. The young child, aware of the consequences of a further allegation of incest against the perpetrator, can use this knowledge to threaten, coerce, and defy conformity and discipline demands within the family. The socially precocious, seductive young girl can make normal hugging and kissing between parent and child grounds for further allegations of molestation. The stepparent may be jealously seen by the child as depriving him/her of rightful attention and affection from the biologic parent. For such a child, the potential power of fabrication can be used in a devastatingly harmful and manipulating manner. For mothers there is constant anxiety and distrust, wanting to trust both child and parent, yet constantly suspicious and torn between the child and the mate.

When the history given by a known jealous child is in marked contrast to history provided by a "suspected" perpetrator, and if the child's stated information appears dubious, then the interviewer must be particularly alert and skillful in order to obtain a valid history. In such situations, several shorter interviews over a period of time allow for validation of earlier given information, allowing the interviewer an opportunity to relate less as an interrogator and more as a concerned person trying to understand the events presented. Children show a variety of responses to both single and multiple interviews. They may be angry, defiant, sullen, nonverbal, accusatory, and suspicious. Others are repentant, tearful, depressed, and often grateful for having an opportunity to finally tell their secret. Whatever the feelings, they must be accepted in an understanding, nonjudgmental, nonhostile manner. If the gross and carnal details cannot be verbalized, the child should not be coerced into disclosure. The use of dolls becomes an appropriate way in which the victim can demonstrate in a nonverbal manner the physical nature of the sexual assault. Whatever the degree of abreaction shown by the victim, the short-term and long-term consequences of disclosure are profound, both for the child and for family members. The initial interview can hopefully be that moment when the first positive step is taken towards therapeutic intervention. It is the interviewer's responsibility to maximize this rehabilitative opportunity.

## Interviewing the Parents

The initial interview is frequently shaped by the time lapse between the first disclosure of incest and initial referral for help. Where the incest is very recent and the family is faced with multiple problems such as arrest of the accused, posting of bail, seeking medical attention for the victim, and overwhelming anger and depression on the part of the family members, the intake worker will be faced with many problems that interfere with the parent(s) giving a coherent, logical, and complete history of the sexual assault. As noted elsewhere, the personal degradation and humiliation felt by many mothers is so overwhelming that they cannot share a joint interview with the accused spouse. Under these conditions sensitive listening, gentle fact finding, and emotional support are the important ingredients of such an interview. Emotional blocking and silence must not be viewed as collusion or indifference, but as the single and most important ego-preserving defense for the shattered parent. Tears and words of anger are to be accepted; judgmental statements about the accused should be avoided; the goal of that first session should be to sustain the family member(s) through this moment of crisis.

Where the incest has been identified earlier, where legal procedures have now been established and the family is referred for rehabilitation, then the emotional impact of the earlier incest may not be as devastatingly reexperienced in the interview. At such times documents from cooperating community agencies can provide much needed information. It is important to ask the parent(s) what at that moment they want from therapy, and through careful listening try to determine the degree of motivation for help. Confronting the parents together is often antitherapeutic, for many times the couple is not yet ready to share with each other the details of the incest and the events leading to such sexual assault. The joint interview at such time does allow, however, an appraisal of the strengths and weaknesses within the marriage relationship that can help or hinder therapeutic intervention.

Where disclosure is impossible in an initial joint interview, it is then recommended that each of the parents be seen separately by different intake workers. This allows a more unbiased milieu, wherein the individual parent will hopefully feel a degree of trust, and an ability to be open about the incest. Separate interviews also aid in assessing the authenticity of the history given by each parent. Suspicions of earlier incest can be more effectively explored with the nonaccused spouse having an opportunity to ventilate feelings of shame and anger at herself for knowing earlier that incestuous behavior was occurring within the family, yet taking no steps to actively intercede. For many mothers the guilt associated with not interceding earlier is so acute that they will initially deny previous knowledge or suspicion of incest. Later in the security and support of the mothers' group therapy meetings many are then able to admit for the first time their extended collusion with the perpetrator. Even though Freud correctly stated that one of the goals of analysis (psychotherapy) is to make the unconscious conscious, this tenet cannot be directly applied in the early therapy of sexual abusers and their families.

It is most important that in the first, initial interview parents be clearly and fully informed about mandatory reporting requirements for professionals. Parents must know that suspected abuse and molestation of a child will be reported to either a social welfare or law enforcement agency. They should be informed of all the probable events that will then automatically be forthcoming. They must know that in some states, depending upon the severity of the incest, that the first agency involvement may be with the law enforcement. If at that time there is evidence of a felony having been committed, this can mean immediate arrest, incarceration in jail, and possibly removal of the child and siblings, if the home is deemed unsafe. While such information to the family may arouse intense feelings of anger, betrayal, and even paranoid-like threats of intimidation to the interviewer, such disclosure is nonetheless needed.

Professionals working in the area of abuse of children should also know that in most states, the confidential therapist-patient relationship does not hold in cases involving physical and sexual abuse of children. Further, there are liabilities that can be imposed upon those who by law are mandated to report suspected abuse of a minor and do not. Over and beyond these criminal and civil liabilities existing for nonreporting are recent legal opinions suggesting that physicians convicted of criminal failure to practice those standards of medical practice that require compliance with mandated reporting of child abuse may in fact not be covered by their existing malpractice insurance (Paulson, in press). Knowing the ethical and legal issues involved in mandatory reporting, the interviewer is in a more informed position to undertake an interview with openness, honesty, and professional responsibility.

### Perpetrator Response to Reported Incest

For most court-referred or agency-referred sexual abusers, the initial response at intake is denial. Like parents of physically abused children, they have many fears about the consequences of disclosure and confession. There is a need within themselves to verbally deny in order to preserve some semblance of self-esteem. Physically abusive parents can often justify their severe punishment of a child as righteous, seeing it as an attempt to teach the child respect for parents and adult authority. Many also feel that physical punishment is a socially accepted right of parents for effectively controlling behavior of children. For the incestuous parent, however, such rationalizations and beliefs are rare, even though there are occasional cultist-type statements about "positive incest" and "sex before eight, or else it's too late."

Identification of the suspected perpetrator in almost all cases results in either placement of the child (if the accused stays within the home), or court-ordered separation of the father from the family in order to protect the future welfare of the child and siblings. For the abusing parent there is an immediate fear of even short-term incarceration, for it is well known that in the prison hierarchy child abuse, both physical and sexual, has the lowest order of acceptability. This code of the prison places the perpetrator in high risk of sexual mutilation or death at the hands of fellow prisoners. Thus from the moment of identification and arrest there is a life-saving need to deny the incest. This need to deny becomes strongly reinforced when the accused is suddenly confronted with added personal, marital, family, social, and economic consequences of the molestation. At times the spouse is blamed for not sexually and emotionally gratifying the perpetrator; at times the incestuous behavior is attributed to drugs or alcohol intoxication; at other times, lesser acts of molestation such as fondling or exhibitionism are explained as accidental or "I was only teasing and tickling."

Subsequent to arrest and court disposition, perpetrators starting therapy are almost always initially guarded and defensive. There seems to be little overt anxiety. Whatever guilt is expressed does not appear to stem from pangs of conscience but rather from shame, disgrace, and the socioeconomic consequences now facing the family. For many of these fathers, it is impossible to say "I'm sorry.... I made a mistake.... please forgive me." Yet, in later stages of group therapy, depending upon support felt from group members, there is an increased openness and sharing of genuine emotions. The bonds of fraternal acceptance within a well-functioning group are esteem-producing agents of change. The shared guilt, the sense of not being alone, and the awareness that others are noncondemning and nonjudgmental are all outgrowths of group therapy that can produce increased self-acceptance and a more positive hope for the future. For a good number of parents they achieve significant emotional understanding and insight into the multiple family conflicts that earlier led to incest.

## Spouse Responses to Reported Incest

The spouse in almost all cases of family incest is the wife, who is now angry, shamed, full of disbelief, and deep in emotional shock. Where the incest is completely unsuspected, there are feelings of betrayal combined with retaliatory homicidal feelings towards the husband. For those wives who in some way collude to keep earlier incest a secret, there is guilt and remorse. Many of the more independent and self-sufficient mothers want the perpetrator out of the home immediately, not only to prevent a possible recurrence of incest, but also in order to separate themselves from the immediate proximity of the earlier trusted mate who they now feel has so devastatingly degraded the family.

Where the child is very young, mothers often feel especially guilty for not having been more observant and careful in monitoring the home situation. This is especially so when in a recent marriage there is a stepfather sharing a new and intimate family environment with children whose sleeping arrangements are lacking in privacy. With heightened rage about the violation of her child and the state of the marriage, the mother in a separate interview has for the first time an opportunity to verbalize her shame, anger, and desire for retaliation. These feelings must be gently explored and support provided for whatever emotions are precipitated by this intense reappraisal of all traumatic events within the family.

When the incest has been ongoing and mothers then acknowledge previous undisclosed suspicions of earlier molestation, they are then especially guilt-ridden and unable to forgive themselves. Some are so demeaned that they cannot even share the details of the incest, especially when oral sex is involved. They are able to talk more about rage and anger but have difficulty in sharing their feelings about the incest, or sharing details of their own sexual intimacy within the marriage. Guilt feelings surrounding collusion and nondisclosure must be explored, with the mothers many times justifying their own behavior in terms of socioeconomic needs, fears of assault and intimidation, anxiety over being left alone, and feeling that "it won't happen anymore." Surprisingly, after the shock of disclosure, many mothers will even in spite of repeated incest of one or more children in the family say, "But I still love the guy." Other mothers will affirm that "he has an illness, and I can't blame him when it isn't his fault."

It is surprising that so many families of incest have strong religious convictions, avowing that "if it is God's will, I'm going to stick by my husband." Religion is for many mothers and some fathers an ego-integrating strength, a source from which, in times of despair and hopelessness, they can find support and comfort. While many mental health professionals "play down" the value of religion within the personal life of an individual or family, we have found that for our mothers especially, religious beliefs are valuable and realistic adjuncts to psychotherapy, making unhappy marriages and lives at least more bearable and meaningful.

## A University Sponsored Sexual Abuse Treatment Program: A Prototype

The University of California, Los Angeles (UCLA), Neuropsychiatric Institute has since 1967 been involved in clinical research and treatment of self-referred and court-referred abusive parents. Previous UCLA publications (Paulson, Savino, Chaleff, Sanders, Frisch, & Dunn, 1974; Paulson, Affifi, Thomason, & Chaleff, 1974; Paulson & Affifi, 1975) have described varied kinds of interdisciplinary, outpatient programs used in the treatment of over 300 physically and sexually abusing parents and their children. More recently a specialty clinic for the treatment of intrafamily incest has been developed, using a bilingual, multicultural, interdisciplinary staff and faculty for the diagnosis and treatment of all members of the primary family unit (Paulson, 1978). Referrals are accepted from the courts, from social service departments, from community health delivery agencies, and from help-seeking families. Recognizing the acute psychological conflicts for all family members, especially at the time of initial identification of incest, a flexible and immediately available program of intake and early evaluation is implemented. It is at this time that the perpetrator is most anxious and fearful, not knowing whether he will be immediately incarcerated but knowing that the future of his family is at stake. It is also at this time that a careful inquiry must be made into the possibility of other children within the family being victims of incest by the same assaulting adult. This applies especially when the identified victim is the oldest of several children. Many case histories have indicated that incest has frequently involved the younger children as well, with all too frequently the siblings being aware of this multiple incest, but each afraid to tell the parent.

Although rehabilitation methods can be tailored to the needs of the family, our primary treatment combines a self-help component with traditional, insight-oriented group psychotherapy using a male-female, cotherapist model (Summit, 1978). The self-help component called "Parents United" is in part modelled after the successful Santa Clara County Sexual Abuse Program (Giarretto, 1976) presently being funded by the State of California, Office of Child Abuse Prevention. Fathers and mothers within Parents United meet weekly, working together to help resolve the tragedy of incest within the family. Electing their own officers, carrying on the business of an incorporated body of individuals, and serving as a support resource for each other, such a program becomes for each member and for each family a continuing, constantly available source of strength.

Following the first hour of business-social activities of Parents United comes a formal program of group psychotherapy. In contrast to the group treatment of our physically abusing parents, which included mothers and fathers together (Paulson, 1974), the present UCLA prototype for sexually abusing parents is organized so that initially mothers and fathers begin therapy in their own sex-specific group. This allows the mothers an opportunity to emotionally and therapeutically "work through" many painful stress areas, areas of conflict that often could not be explored and worked through if the fathers and mothers were within the same group. Separate groups for fathers similarly allow them to share feelings and phantasies, which, if expressed in front of their wives, could be too humiliating and catastrophic for an already precarious marriage. After at least one year in separate groups, and following resolution of many acute feelings of shame, betrayal and at times homicidal-like rage towards the perpetrator, the parents can then be brought together either for marital therapy, or in the more traditional group therapy model that provides for a mix of husbands and wives.

While the parents are in group therapy, the victimized children, and if need be, the siblings, are provided with a treatment program that is best suited to their idiosyncratic needs. For the more severely disturbed child, this may be individual therapy; for better functioning children it may be a group program with children having been similarly traumatized by family incest. Whether individual or group, the one-to-one identification with peers and therapist provides a sense of trust, acceptance, and reassurance, and opportunity to share the emotional and physical pains of earlier incest.

Recognizing the impact of differences in social-sexual maturity between latency-age and adolescent-age girls, the UCLA program has initiated separate age-specific groups. Experience has shown this to be a wise and therapeutic approach. A number of the older girls who participated somewhat willingly in the incest discuss significantly different problems and conflict areas than do younger girls. At the time of this writing, a group for sexually assaulted boys is being formed, boys who are presently being treated in an individual therapy format. In the same way that the group format for parents provides an opportunity for ventilation, sharing, support, and understanding, so does the group treatment of latency-age and adolescent-age children provide peer support, group identity, and an opportunity for catharsis, ventilation, and insight. Where, occasionally, internal conflicts are later overwhelming and therapeutic support from the group is not sufficient, then more intensive individual treatment for the child and/or parents is provided. In those more acute situations involving incapacitating depression, suicidal danger, or borderline or psychotic decompensation, the psychiatric inpatient service can provide immediate and acute-care treatment.

## Case History

Mary, age twelve, one of two female siblings, forced into oral copulation and vaginal intercourse with her stepfather, was referred to the UCLA Parents United program for psychotherapy by the legal system. The stepfather had admitted to sexual molestation and was placed on probation subject to his participation in a program of rehabilitation. Mary's mother was a passive-aggressive, depressed woman who herself had been molested in her own childhood by her biological father. The mother's early incest was a poorly kept secret from all the extended family. With Mary's recent incest becoming known, there was a revival of suppressed feelings of rage and shame in the mother.

One year of family therapy prior to joining Parents United provided only minimal understanding, and no significant family communication. Following the starting of a Parents United program, which the parents readily joined, the mother and father were each placed in their own sex-specific groups. Mary was initially seen for individual therapy, then later joined a group for young adolescent girls, all of whom were themselves victims of intrafamilial incest. Mary's subsequent psychotic decompensation led to psychiatric inpatient hospitalization, where intensive individual and group therapy within a structured ward milieu allowed Mary to return home after approximately two months hospitalization. The older, sexually acting-out sibling had initially been in family therapy and brief individual therapy, but due to minimal motivation soon withdrew from treatment.

After one year of group treatment in Parents United, considerable therapeutic progress has been shown by Mary and her parents. Mary is now nonpsychotic, functioning better in school, and more open with her parents. The mother is increasingly able to set appropriate limits upon her daughter's behavior, although still identifying closely with the daughter with respect to shame, guilt, and anger at the two generations of incest from which all have suffered. The perpetrator stepfather is himself much less depressed, less socially withdrawn, and more able to share feelings with his wife and his two stepdaughters. Yet, he realizes that within himself there are still conflictual aggressive-sexual feelings related to his own early childhood physical abuse, and the daily stimulation of two attractive, sexually mature adolescent stepdaughters within the home.

Identification, reporting, and legal intervention in all cases of incest can be traumatic for the family and may temporarily compound even more the many personal-financial-family pressures within the family. For Mary and her parents, the long-term effects of identification are positive and therapeutic. The chronic sexual exploitation of a child has been ended; a guilt-ridden, sexually obsessed stepfather has accepted a program of rehabilitation; a long-depressed mother whose own incest continued to fester with great emotional conflict was now able to talk about her own childhood trauma, and for the first time admit the tragedy of incest in her early life. Legal intervention provided the initial stimulus for treatment. A personal motivation to preserve the marriage and an acknowledged wish to resolve his incestuous sexual feelings are making for reasonably good emotional growth for the perpetrator stepfather. While the chronic family conflict is significantly decreased due to greater sharing, openness and insight, the tragedy of two generations of family incest has left an acute and permanent emotional scarring on each and every member of the family. Intensive, long-term treatment continues as a therapeutic necessity for all the family members.

Interdisciplinary liaison is essential in treating family incest. Liaison between the child's therapist and the team members of Parents United maximized treatment effectiveness for the entire family. The ward psychiatrist, the clinical social worker as primary-care therapist, and the nurse-psychologist teams working with the mother and father within the Parents United model, together were able to coordinate a treatment program effective for all the family members. Hopefully such a team approach, providing both inpatient and outpatient coordination, will maximize the treatment potential for each of the victims within the molested family.

In order to coordinate multiple treatment modalities and therapist interactions, it is necessary that all involved professionals meet regularly to share such goals and outcomes, to offer new insights and intervention plans, and to coordinate rehabilitation with the network of outside agencies that are always involved in the supervision and management of sexually abusing families. The team must have an opportunity to regularly share the content and conflicts of ongoing therapy, as well as conflictual counter-transference feelings. At times, therapists can become defensive, jealous, and protective of their particular group of parents, especially when the therapists' feelings are openly shared in the consultation supervision hour. If, in such supervision, recurring feelings of irritation or conflict are noticed, then it is important to look carefully at the process of interaction between therapists in order to identify elements of professional burnout. This is a potential danger for devoted and conscientious health professionals. It is a risk that is especially acute and impairing for professionals specializing in the areas of physical and sexual abuse of children. It is the wise supervisor-consultant who, observing these indices of internal stress, provides remedial resources and alternative professional responsibilities before burnout becomes emotionally disabling or, at the worst, even life-threatening to a therapist.

## References

Adams, M., & Neel, J. Children of incest. *Pediatrics,* 1967, *40,* 55-62.

Aries, P. *Centuries of childhood. A social history of family life.* New York: Vintage Books, 1965.

Awad, G. Father son incest: a case report. *Journal of Nervous and Mental Disease,* 1976, *162,* 135-139.

Bell, A., & Hall, C. *The personality of a child molester: An analysis of dreams.* Chicago: Aldine and Atherton, 1971.

Bender, L., & Grugett, A.E. Follow-up report on children who had atypical sexual experience. *American Journal of Orthopsychiatry,* 1952, *22,* 825-836.

Benward, J., & Densen-Gerber, J. Incest as a causative factor in antisocial behavior: an exploratory study. *Contemporary Drug Problems,* 1975,*4,* 323-340.

Browning, D., & Boatman, B. Incest: Children at risk. *American Journal of Psychiatry,* 1977, *134,* 69-72.

Burgess, A., Groth, A., Holmstrom, L., & Sgroi, S. *Sexual assault of children and adolescents.* Lexington: Lexington Books, 1978.

Cohen, Y. The disappearance of the incest taboo. *Human Nature,* July 1978, 72-78.

Cohen, M., Seghorn, T., & Calmas, W. Sociometric study of the sex offender. *Journal of Abnormal Psychology,* 1969, *74,* 249-255.

Eist, H., & Mandel, A. Family treatment of ongoing incest behavior. *Family Process,* 1966, *7,* 216-232.

Ferracuti, F. Incest between fathers and daughters. In H.L. Resnik & M.E. Wolfgang (Eds.), *Sexual behavior: Social, clinical and legal aspects.* Boston: Little Brown and Co., 1972.

Finkelhor, D. What's wrong with sex between adults and childen? Paper given as part of family violence research program. University of New Hampshire, February, 1979.

Freud, S. *The origin of psychoanalysis: Letters to William Fliess. Drafts and Notes.* London: Hogarth Press, 1954.

Giarretto, H. Humanistic treatment of father-daughter incest. In R. Helfer & C. Kempe (Eds.), *Child abuse and neglect. The family and the community.* Cambridge: Ballinger Publishing Company, 1976.

Guttmacher, M. *Sex offenses. The problem, causes and prevention.* New York: Norton and Co., 1951.

Harbert, T., Hersen, M., Barlow, D., & Austin, J. Measurement and modification of incestuous behavior: A case study. *Psychological Reports,* 1974, *34,* 79-86.

Henderson, J. Incest: A synthesis of data. *Canadian Psychiatric Association Journal,* 1972, *17,* 299-313.

Katan, A. Children who were raped. *Psychoanalytic Study of the Child,* 1973, *28,* 204-244.

Kaufman, I., Peck, A., & Taguiri, C. The family constellation and overt incestuous relations between father and daughter. *American Journal of Orthopsychiatry*, 1954, *24*, 266-277.

Lester, D. Incest II. *British Journal of Psychiatry*, 1972, *120*, 301-313.

Lustig, N. Dresser, J., Spellman, S., & Murray, T. Incest: a family group survival pattern. *Archives of General Psychiatry*, 1966, *14*, 31-40.

MacDonald, G., & de Furia, G. A guided self-help approach to the treatment of the habitual sex offender. *Hospital and Community Psychiatry*, 1971, *22*, 310-313.

Machotka, P., Pittman, F., & Flamenhaft, K. Incest as a family affair. *Family Process*, 1967, *6*, 98-116.

McCaghy, C. Child molesting. *Sexual Behavior*, 1971, *1*, 16-24.

McCreary, C. Personality differences among child molesters. *Journal of Personality Assessment*, 1975, *39*, 591-593.

Miller, H., & Haney, J. Behavior and traditional therapy applied to pedophilic exhibitionism, a case study. *Psychological Reports*, 1976, *39*, 1119-1124.

Nobile, P. Incest: The last taboo. *Penthouse*, 1977, 117-158.

Paulson, M. Incest and sexual molestation: Clinical and legal issues. *Journal of Clinical Child Psychology*, 1978, *VII*, 178-180.

Paulson, M., Savino, A., Chaleff, A., Sanders, R., Frisch, F., & Dunn, R. Parents of the battered child: a multidisciplinary group therapy approach to life-threatening behavior. *Life Threatening Behavior*, 1974, *4*, 18-31.

Paulson, M., Afifi, A., Thomason, M., & Chaleff, A. The MMPI: A descriptive measure of psychopathology in abusing parents. *Journal of Clinical Psychology*, 1974, *30*, 387-390.

Paulson, M., Afifi, A., Chaleff, A., Liu, V., & Thomason, M. A discriminant function procedure for identifying abusing parents. *Suicide*, 1975, *5*, 104-114.

Paulson, M. Early intervention and treatment of child abuse: our nation's mandate. *Psychiatric Opinion*, 1978, *15*, 34-38.

Paulson, M. J. *Identifying and helping the child abusing family*. In press.

Peters, J. Children who are victims of sexual assault and the psychology of offenders. *American Journal of Psychotherapy*, 1976, *30*, 398-421.

Raybin, J. Homosexual incest: three generations. *Journal of Nervous and Mental Diseases*, 1969, *148*, 105-110.

Riemer, S. A research note on incest. *American Journal of Sociology*, 1940, *45*, 554-565.

Rist, K. Incest: Theoretical and clinical views. *American Journal of Orthopsychiatry*, 1979, *49*, 680-691.

Rosenfeld, A., Nadelson, C., & Krieger, M. Fantasy and reality in patients' reports of incest. *Journal of Clinical Psychiatry*, 1979, *40*, 159-164.

Rosenfeld, A. *Incest: The victim perpetrator model*. In press.

Sarles, P. Symposium on behavioral pediatrics. *Pediatric Clinics of North America*, 1975, *22*, 633-642.

Schechter, M., & Roberge, L. Sexual exploitation in child abuse and neglect. In R. Helfer & C. Kempe (Eds.). *Child abuse and neglect. The family and the community*. Cambridge: Ballinger Press, 1976.

Schultz, L. The child sex victim: social, psychological and legal perspectives. *Child Welfare*, 1973, *52*, 147-157.

Sloane, P., & Karpinski, E. Effects of incest on the participants. *American Journal of Orthopsychiatry*, 1942, *12*, 666-673.

Sondon, T. Die Inzetverbrechen in Schweden und ihre Ursachen. *Acta Psychiatrica et Neurology*, 1936, *11*, 379-401.

Summit, R. Sexual abuse of children. A clinical spectrum. *American Journal of Orthopsychiatry*, 1978, *48*, 237-250.

Summit, R. Typical characteristics of father-daughter incest. A guide for investigation. Reprint from Harbor General Hospital, Los Angeles, CA, 1979.

Summit, R. Sexual child abuse, the psychotherapist and the team concept. In H. Donovan (Ed.), *Dealing with sexual child abuse*, Vol. 2. Chicago: National Committee for the Prevention of Child Abuse, 1978.

*Webster's Seventh New Collegiate Dictionary*. Springfield: Merriam, 1967.

Weiner, I. On incest: a survey. *Excerpta Criminologica*, 1964, *4*, 137-155.

Weitzel, W., Powell, B., & Penick, E. Clinical management of father-daughter incest. *American Journal of Disabled Children*, 1978, *132*, 127-130.

Chapter 4

# CHILD ABUSE: CURRENT ISSUES OF ETIOLOGY, DIAGNOSIS, AND TREATMENT

STEPHEN BITTNER AND ELI H. NEWBERGER

WHEN KEMPE AND HIS colleagues drew attention to the "battered child syndrome" in 1961, the attention of the American medical community was drawn to one of the most dramatic manifestations of family violence. Since, family violence has emerged as a major social problem in the United States, and the eyes of the pediatric community have been opened to familial causes of morbidity and mortality. The task of this chapter is to frame the knowledge base accumulated since the publication of the first Kempe (1962) report in a fashion accessible to pediatricians and members of the colleague disciplines, psychology and social work, with attention to present understanding of the family and social contexts in which child abuse is seen to occur and the major issues of differential diagnosis, intervention, and prevention. Kempe (1978) has noted that, notwithstanding a long period of concern with child welfare problems, injured and neglected children were ignored by the pediatric community because of "the process of denial that was unequal to anything I had previously seen in pediatrics." As medical literature has burgeoned in the interval since the report

Partial support for this work came from grants from the Administration for Children, Youth and Families, Department of H.E.W. (Project Number OCD-CB-141), and from the National Institute of Mental Health (Grant Number 1 T01 MH155 / Q1A2 CD).

of the "battered child syndrome," a number of diagnostic tags have been proposed to embrace the many manifestations and causes of child abuse. These include such family-oriented formulations as "the sexual misuse of children" (Brant, 1977), "the world of abnormal rearing" (Helfer, 1976), and "lack of empathic mothering" (Helfer, 1976), which do not, for the pediatrician, lend themselves easily to diagnosis. Management guidelines such as the need to choose "the least detrimental alternative" for the child (Goldstein, 1973) have been proposed but are often equally unclear. We propose in this paper to use the term "child abuse" to encompass the entire range of symptoms indicative of maltreatment of children, including physical injury, physical neglect, sexual abuse, and ingestion of harmful substances. We believe that this area of pediatric practice, so cluttered with jargon and so focused on symptoms, is analogous to the situation in the eighteenth century, when "fever" was proposed as a single disease with many manifestations (King, 1971).

## HISTORY, DEFINITION, AND PREVALENCE

Violence toward children has been condoned and endorsed through history, and it is deeply embedded in the social institutions and legal structures of industrialized societies. DeMause (1974) has suggested that "if today in America there are less than a million abused children, there would have been a point back in history where most children were what we would now consider abused." All but one of seventy children who lived prior to the eighteenth century whose biographies were studied were beaten by their parents (DeMause, 1974).

It has been proposed that the relatively recent concern with child abuse indicates an historical evolution in the position and worth of children in society. Fraser (1976) has noted that infanticide was approved as a legitimate practice at the time of the Code of Hammurabi, 2150 B.C. Under Greek Law, however, children could own property and the children of citizens could not be legally killed by their parents. Orphans could sue their guardians for improper care (Fraser, 1976). Yet infanticide was so widely practiced that it has been cited as a principal cause of the population decrease of Greece in the second century B.C.

(DeMause 1974). A general preference for males and an excessive exposure and lack of protection of female babies may have been responsible for a "large imbalance of males over females that was typical of the West until well into the Middle Ages" (DeMause, 1974). Late in the Roman era, possibly due to the influence of Christianity, infanticide was outlawed. This proscription, in 374 A.D., marked an early turning point in the care of children in Western civilization. In subsequent centuries in Europe it was more acceptable to abandon unwanted infants than to kill them, and in 787 A.D., the first foundling home was established in Milan. Infanticide continued, however, and there are reports of infants having been put to death in the nineteenth century in England in order to collect insurance premiums in what was called a "burial club" (Fraser, 1976).

Through the Renaissance and Enlightenment periods, there came an increased role of the state in the family life of poor people. Both the Elizabethan Poor Laws (circa 1601) and the Factories Act (circa 1800) provided for the intervention by religious and secular officials if parents were seen to be unproductive or inappropriately exploitative in raising their children. The English Court case *In re Spence*, in 1847, established the doctrine of *parens patriae*, in which the parent-child relationship was conceived as a trust for which the state would act as guarantor. This concept coincided with a dramatic increase in concern for the welfare of the children of the poor. Societies for the prevention of cruelty to children proliferated in the late nineteenth century. The first White House Conference on Child Welfare convened in 1909, and the United States Children's Bureau was established in 1912. Child guidance clinics proliferated in the 1920s to help "problem children," and child development research became a recognized scientific discipline (Parke, 1975).

Although concern for the adequate treatment of children had been voiced for fully a century prior to Kempe and colleagues' report of the "battered child syndrome," the awakening of the medical community to the more severe manifestations of child abuse was associated with an editorial outcry in professional and lay media and with the promulgation by the Children's Bureau of a model Child Abuse Reporting Law (Newberger, 1978). The conception of child abuse as a discrete set of symptoms that could be diagnosed and reported to child welfare agencies, which could provide rehabilitative treatment for the victims and their families, derives naturally from the late discovery of child abuse by the medical community.

These historic trends are not of incidental significance when contemplating the ineffectiveness and confusion associated with much current practice in regard to child abuse where the knowledge base is weak, and the promise of help in the Child Abuse Reporting Laws may largely be empty. Whether, indeed, child abuse can be defined with precision remains a question full of conflict even for experts. A recent paper by one of the more prominent scholars of family violence in the United States identifies the term *child abuse* as "'a political concept' that is the single greatest obstacle which stands in the way of gaining an insight into the problem of child abuse" (Gelles, 1978). Another scholar questions the individual focus of most clinical definitions and suggests that it is well to think of child abuse as "any act or condition...that wastes a child's developmental potential" (Gil, 1975).

## Prevalence

There are useful estimates but no good data on the frequency and extent of child abuse. Reporting practices vary; definitions differ from state to state and from researcher to researcher; and many of the studies that claim general validity are biased heavily toward the poor and socially marginal families who are most susceptible to study. When, in 1969, the Children's Bureau undertook to study the cases that were reported nationwide subsequent to the promulgation of its Model Law and the passage by every state of a Child Abuse Reporting Act, approximately 6,000 cases of child abuse were reported each year (Gil, 1970). In the decade after the first laws were passed, however, the concept of child abuse expanded, and most state laws were broadened to include child neglect, sexual abuse, emotional abuse, and deprivation of necessary physical and moral supports for a child's development. Similarly, the list of personnel mandated to report cases to departments of public welfare or police was expanded from physicians and other medical workers to virtually every person with responsibility for care of children. Case report statistics thus provide a diffuse and poorly differentiated estimate of the prevalence of child abuse.

When a nationally representative sample of American families were asked about their methods of childrearing in a recent survey, they gave responses that suggest a far greater prevalence of physical violence toward children than that suggested in the case report data (Straus, 1980). This survey, which asked respondents in intact families specifically whether children had been kicked, punched, bitten, beated up, or threatened with a knife or gun, suggested that 3.6% of children between the ages of three and seventeen are at risk for serious physical injury every year. In 1978, there were over 600,000 reports of the many problems now considered to be child abuse; 37% of the reports involved children under five years of age (American Humane Association, 1979). The finding in this survey of a high prevalence of violent acts toward children in middle and upper class homes suggests that the official case report statistics compiled from state agencies are heavily biased toward poor and minority children. The children of the affluent may receive different diagnostic labels for their problems ("accidents" rather than "abuse"), and practitioners may feel an obligation to protect more affluent families from the stigma of reports to public agencies (Gelles, 1978; Newberger, 1978).

## A MODEL FOR UNDERSTANDING CHILD ABUSE

The initial efforts to understand child abuse in the 1960s focused on the psychological problems of the parents of the victims. An influential study by Steele and Pollock pointed to abusing parents' distorted expectations of their children, frustrated dependency needs, personal isolation, and histories of having themselves been abused as children (Steele, 1974). Helfer (1976) suggested that the propensity for abuse has three elements: a child with qualities that are provocative; a parent with the psychological predisposition; and a stressful event that triggers a violent reaction. Social and cultural, in addition to psychological and familial, factors have been described in the recent child abuse literature, and it is useful to think of child abuse as culminating from a series of stresses that impinge on parents and children and culminate in harmful actions (Garbarino, 1975; Gelles, 1973; Light, 1973; Parke, 1975).

Table 4-I offers a framework for understanding the causes of child abuse in a social context. The "causes" presented in the table have been identified as risk factors by studying abused children and their families. They should not be construed as causal in any direct or linear sense nor should they be understood as *predictive*.

## Sociocultural Factors

At the top of Table 4-I are summarized the social and cultural factors that guide individual behavior. David Gil (1975), the author of the first national study of child abuse, notes that "the most fundamental causal level of child abuse consists of a cluster of interacting elements, to wit, a society's basic social philosophy, its dominant value premises, its concept of humans." Gil observed that in our culture, where competition is more valued than cooperation, physical force may be a normal way to resolve conflicts. Where the basic social structure is hierarchical and inegalitarian, the weak and dependent are necessarily near the bottom of the social ladder. Further, corporal punishment may be encouraged to prepare children for adult roles in a competitive social system.

The rights of children and the legitimacy of violence toward them by their caretakers are matters of great legal and social confusion. In 1967, the Court ruled *In re Gault* (1967) that children were entitled to due process before incarceration as delinquents. In the *Parham* (1979) decision, the right of parents to commit their children to institutions without professional review was affirmed. The Supreme Court has also ruled in favor of corporal punishment in the schools, and this may sanction violent practice in American homes. In *Ingraham vs. Wright* the *parens patriae* doctrine was cited in support of the right of teachers to inflict severe corporal punishment on children in the Miami public schools; were the victims, with their extensive

**TABLE 4-I**
MODEL FOR UNDERSTANDING CHILD ABUSE

***Social-Cultural Factors***

1. Values and norms concerning violence and force; acceptability of corporal punishment
2. Inegalitarian, hierarchical social structure; imbalanced interpersonal relationships
3. Values concerning competition vs. cooperation
4. Exploitative, alienating economic system; acceptance and encouragement of permanent poor class
5. Devaluation of children and other dependents
6. Institutional manifestations of all of the above: law, health care, education, welfare system, sports, entertainment, etc.

plus ***Family Stresses***

| Child-Produced Stresses | Social-Situational Stresses | Parent-Produced Stresses |
|---|---|---|
| 1. physically different (*e.g.*, handicapped)<br>2. mentally different (*e.g.*, retarded)<br>3. temperamentally different (*e.g.*, difficult)<br>4. behaviorally different (*e.g.*, hyperactive)<br>5. foster child | 1. structural factors: poverty, unemployment, mobility, isolation, poor housing<br>2. parental relationship: discord-assault, dominant-submissive patterns<br>3. parent-child relationship: attachment problems, perinatal stress, punitive childrearing style, scapegoating, role-reversal, excess or unwanted children | 1. low self-esteem<br>2. abused as child<br>3. depression<br>4. substance abuse<br>5. character disorder<br>6. ignorance of childrearing; unrealistic expectations |

with a ***Triggering Situation***
discipline
argument/family conflict
substance abuse
acute environmental problem

may lead to ***Maltreatment***
injury
inability to provide care
poisoning
psychological maltreatment

back and buttock bruises, to have been seen by a physician, a mandated report would have been required by Florida Law (Bourne, 1979).

Keniston (1975), among others, has noted that the low levels of support in public welfare programs also assure "perpetuation of exclusion" of children in families from the mainstream of American life. Also, the system mandated by statute to offer protection to abused children is generally perceived to be failing. It has been cited by Gil (1975) as an example of "socially structured and sanctioned abuse of children." Poverty, not parental failure, is cited by Gil (1975) as the principal abuse of children. Many poor children, reported as victims of child abuse and neglect, are placed in foster home care, not because of injury or severe deprivation, but because of serious economic and familial problems and a shortage of home-based services that might enable parents more adequately to care for their offspring. For nearly half a million children in the United States, foster home care and institutions, although in theory temporary, become the permanent settings for their growth (Gruber, 1973; Fanshel, 1978). Many of these foster homes and institutions offer inadequate care. Some, as was pointed out in Kempe's seminal paper in 1962, are outright abusive.

Violent entertainment in the cinema and on television may also affect how adults and children approach issues of conflict. Whether media violence is associated with aggressive behavior in childhood remains a subject for lively debate, but there is a developing consensus that a milieu of violence fosters actions of violence (Stein, 1975).

## Family Stresses

Social and cultural factors affect individual behavior and the quality of relationships within the family. It is helpful to think of "stresses" within the family as a way of organizing the complex data that accompanies a child with the symptoms of child abuse. It is well to bear in mind that the family stresses listed on Table 4-I prevail for many families in which there is no child abuse. Although available prevalence data suggest that family violence and child abuse are widespread, we do not yet know enough to be able to predict child abuse in a given family with certain levels and qualities of stress. In fact, it is the capacity to protect one's children from these stresses that seems to enable most of us to protect our children most of the time.

### *Social-Situational Stresses*

STRUCTURAL FACTORS: Case report data suggest that the great number of children reported as victims of child abuse are poor (American Humane Association, 1979). Although these data must be considered critically, several studies suggest that the situational realities of life in poverty may importantly increase the risk of child abuse. These include unemployment, greater geographic mobility, lower levels of parental education, and inadequate, crowded living quarters (Straus, 1980; Steinmetz, 1974).

In a recent contribution to the growing literature on the relationship between child abuse and social class, Pelton (1978) noted that "to the degree of severity, child abuse correlates with the degree of poverty, that the lower one goes in the socioeconomic scale, the greater the incidence of abuse, and that after years of mandated reporting, there has been no change in the distribution of socioeconomic status of abused children." Pelton decries a "myth of classlessness" for which insufficient support is found in the literature. In the Straus, Gelles, and Steinmetz (1980) survey, certain types of violence against children occurred twice as frequently in low income families as in high income families. They also found that the most poor and the most well-to-do appeared to abuse their children least often. Members of the middle class suffered stresses including conflict between adult members around roles, money, and sex, and these were associated with high rates of violence. No differences were found between whites and nonwhites.

Social isolation has been suggested as a principal concomitant of child abuse. If parents are without friends (Young, 1964), have no telephone contact with the outside world (Elmer, 1967), or are detached from contact with other adults (Merril, 1962), they will have no access to support in times of trouble. Many families feel rejected by their communities (Gil, 1970), and variabilities of the employment market keep many families on the move (Straus, 1980). Yet, "isolation" can be both a characteristic of an individual parent's personality or the given family's style; it may also be imposed by the exigencies of the economic and social setting.

PARENTAL RELATIONSHIPS: Although most psychological studies of child abuse have focused on the adult adaptation of individual parents, recent studies suggest that the relationship between a child's parents may have as much to do with the occurrence of child abuse as any psychological qualities of individual adults. In homes where husbands and wives had used violence on each other in the past year, there was a 129% greater incidence of severe violence towards children (Straus, 1974). The intergenerational nature of child abuse was supported in this study, which found that "respondents who reported that they had observed their parents hit one another had a much higher rate of violence towards their own children than respondents who said they had never see their parents hit each other" (Straus, 1974). A high level of "verbal violence" has been identified as a risk factor for physical violence (Steinmetz, 1974). How decisions are allocated in a family may also be associated with a risk of child abuse; a power domination by either parent, characterized as a dominant-submissive interpersonal pattern, was identified as a family concomitant in cases of child abuse (Straus, 1980).

PARENT-CHILD RELATIONSHIP: The parent-child relationship may be stressed by difficulties with the pregnancy and delivery, separations between child and parent during the first six months of life, and illness in the mother or child during the first year (Lynch, 1979; Goldson, 1978). Low birth weight infants are more likely to be abused than normal babies. Some studies have suggested that this increased vulnerability results from a failure to establish a normal bond attachment in the prenatal period (Klaus, 1976; Hunter, 1978).

There is increasing consensus on the association between the acceptance of violent means of socializing children and the occurrence of child abuse. Indeed, defining what is "abusive" as opposed to normal socializing of children in American homes has been noted to be a difficult conceptual impediment to research in this area (Straus, 1980). Corporal punishment is, of course, widespread. Among the few students of child abuse who have been willing to venture boldly with a recommendation for changing the current acceptance and promotion of violence toward children is Edward Zigler, former Chief of the United States Children's Bureau and now Sterling professor of Psychology at Yale University, who asserted that "undoubtedly the single-most important determinant of child abuse is willingness of adults to inflict corporal punishment upon children in the name of discipline" (Zigler, 1976).

Although corporal punishment appears to be accepted in all social classes, it is most frequent among the least affluent, who may also have less access to help outside the home in dealing with conflicts with their children; aggressive behavior outside the home appears to be fostered by violence within it (Erlinger, 1974). Families in which child abuse has occurred have been noted to administer corporal punishment inconsistently, in response to the child's failure to accomplish tasks, for behavioral expectations that may be unrealistic at the child's chronological age, and when the child is insufficiently responsive and nurturing to the parent, (Young, 1964) the so-called "role reversal" phenomenon.

When violence is the major mode of communication between parent and child, the relationship may take on a quality that maintains the violence (Parke, 1975). The child may behave provocatively in order to attract attention, even violent attention, from a parent who in turn may express remorse for "having" to beat the child. There may also be a passive acceptance or an active encouragement by the other parent, which may affect both the intensity and quality of the violence.

The number of children in a family may promote stress in ways that are not clearly understood. Straus, Gelles, and Steinmetz (1980) found the highest risk for violence occurred in families where there were five children. Families with two or three *or* more than six children had much *lower* overall levels of violence.

### *Child-Produced Stresses*

A child's own qualities may stimulate violence in his family.

These may include physical deformities, acute or chronic illness, slow intellectual development, psychiatric problems, and a temperament that is inadequately understood or tolerated by his parents (Friedrick, 1976). Historical circumstances may be associated with child-produced stresses, even in the absence of physical or behavioral idiosyncracies; a child may be born at a time of crisis and be identified as the bearer of trouble, or he or she may have been unwanted. Being a stepchild or foster child status may affect a family's behavior and increase the child's risk (Parke, 1975). It has been suggested that children who are at risk for abuse may remind their parents of their own traumatized past through behavior, physical characteristics, or developmental qualities (Green, 1976). Self-destructive behavior has also been observed in victims of child abuse (Green, 1978). This may be an expression of the child's acceptance of the "bad" self-image projected by the family.

### *Parent-Produced Stresses*

An abundant literature gives support to the notion that child abuse is accompanied by serious psychological problems in parents (Spinetta, 1972; Steele, 1974; Green, 1976), but there is no consensus that child abuse can be adequately explained by a psychologic profile of parent. Current research has necessitated more embracing causal models (Gelles, 1974; Green, 1976).

Most adults who abuse children are not crazy. In comparison to other adults, they may be lonely, feel helpless, seem depressed, express unfulfilled dependency needs, and may have little control over their angry impulses. Alcoholism may play a role in the violent interaction of some families. Other attributes that have been observed among parents are inadequate understanding of child care and child development, a misinterpretation of the meaning of such childhood behavior as crying or slow feeding or awakening at night, and a low tolerance for frustration.

The research base for understanding the parental attributes associated with child abuse is inadequate, although the literature is voluminous (Parke, 1975). Given the broad panoply of symptoms that are brought into focus as cases of child abuse, and the need to come to terms with the meaning of a child's symptoms in a particular family setting, it is well to approach each new clinical situation with an open mind and with few preconceptions about what one may find. Simply because a parent may have psychological difficulties does not confirm the diagnosis of child abuse in a situation where there is doubt; equally important, cases should not be dismissed because the parents do not seem crazy. Experienced clinicians in the field can all recount situations where victims of child abuse escaped detection for long periods because their parents appeared so "normal."

### Triggering Situation

There has been no systematic study of what happens to precipitate abusive events, and while some instances are acute and self-limited, others are of long duration. It is helpful nonetheless to consider the circumstances of the family's life in the period immediately prior to the injury that brings a child for care. Examples of triggering situations from clinical experience include a baby who, on a particular evening, would not stop crying; an alcoholic who was fired from his job; a mother who, after being beaten by her husband, could not make contact with her own mother; and the service of an eviction notice. Any of the stresses originating in a family stress can become the triggering event for an incident of abuse. It is helpful to think of the situation of the family who presents an abused child for care as a "crisis." A sensitive exploration of its origins and considerate attention to the recent family history by physician, nurse, and social worker can lead to clinical understanding of a given child's risk and can point the way to what will be necessary to diminish that risk in the future.

## DIAGNOSIS

### History

The pediatrician's first step must be to take a good history. The initial interview of a family in which child abuse or neglect is suspected has five objectives: (1) to understand the historical and especially medical antecedents of the child's injury, and to assess the plausibility of the history; (2) to determine the dimensions of the ongoing risk to the child, so as to inform the choice of protective or family supportive interventions; (3) to gather the past medical history of the child and the family members; (4) to form a relationship with the family that will foster and support their participation in subsequent diagnostic and therapeutic work with other professionals; and (5) to explain the case report and other aspects of the protective service process that the pediatrician and others will be doing to protect the child and to help the parents. This includes an honest reckoning with the parents about the concerns of the professional involved.

The first interview is never easy, but may be the first step in a long process, culminating in the child's return to a safe and nurturant home. The helping context of the hospital or pediatric office should be emphasized from the outset, and the pediatrician should convey a nonjudgmental stance of gentleness, sympathy, and a willingness to listen. Good interview technique allows parent and child to maintain the integrity of ego and family, such as it is, in each case. In the initial interview and in subsequent contacts, no direct or indirect attempt should be made to draw out a confession from the parent.

Denial is a prominent ego defense in virtually all abusing parents, and the bizarre stories often heard from them about how their children got their injuries ought not to be taken as intentional falsifications, but as repression in the face of threatening reality. These odd accounts often tell how profoundly distressing it is to a parent to acknowledge having an abused child. The third degree or its gentlemanly equivalent serves often to harden the defense or to promote more primitive defenses—resistance to talking about the problem at all, angry outbursts directed at the interviewer or at the hospital, or threats to take the child home immediately. Such defenses limit both the process of information gathering and the prospects for continuing helpful professional relationships; they may possibly endanger the child. Although skepticism about the proferred explanation also operates deleteriously, it is appropriate to emphasize the child's need for care—which may include his admission to a hospital—and the need to ensure that he is protected from harm.

The abused child arouses our sadness and outrage, and these feelings may be difficult to contain, especially if it is the pediatrician who feels obliged to remain calm and supportive, yet has to absorb some of the parent's anger and guilt in the interview situation. The channeling of feelings into effective action to relieve the family's distress is an important part of the case management from the beginning.

## Physical and Laboratory Diagnosis

Table 4-II summarizes the differential diagnosis of child abuse. A full physical examination with developmental screening and behavioral observations should be performed on any child who may be a victim of child abuse. As in assessing the familial origins of the problem, it is well to keep an open mind about the causes of a child's symptoms. The physical findings may be confusing and one should not rush to conclude that a given symptom is or is not diagnostic. Rather, the findings of the history and physical examination should guide the formation of hypotheses and a problem list, which will be better delineated in subsequent laboratory studies and social work and psychiatric consultations.

The cutaneous manifestations of child abuse may be ambiguous. Wilson has given a summary of the relationship between the color and the age of contusions. In the first twenty-four hours a bruise may be reddish, blue, or purple; from the first to the third day, the color becomes blue or blue-brown; with further metabolism of heme, the bruise acquires a greenish cast in the fifth to seventh day; and by the tenth day the bruise may appear to be yellow. Before disappearing completely in two to four weeks, the bruise may take on a brownish hue. These findings may vary or be difficult to interpret depending on skin color.

Manifestations of inflicted injury include bruises in the shape of a handprint, linear bruises or abrasions from whipping with a cord or rope, looped-shaped marks from cords which have been folded over, crescentic bite marks, alopecia or subgaleal hematoma from pulling of the hair, burn marks from cigarettes, and areas of abraded skin from where a child may have been bound or restrained.

Wilson (1977) notes that in addition to recording the distribution, shape, color, location, and approximate measurements of the bruises, it may be helpful to have photographs for purposes of

**TABLE 4-II**
THE DIFFERENTIAL DIAGNOSIS OF CHILD ABUSE

| Clinical Findings | Differential Diagnosis | Differentiating Tests |
|---|---|---|
| Cutaneous Lesions | | |
| 1. Bruising | a. trauma | |
| | b. hemophilia | PT, PTT |
| | c. Von Willebrand's | bleeding time |
| | d. anaphylactoid purpura | R/O sepsis |
| | e. purpura fulminans | R/O sepsis |
| | f. Ehlers-Danlos | hyperextensibility |
| 2. Local erythema or bullae | a. burn | |
| | b. staph impetigo | culture, gram stain |
| | c. bacterial cellulitis | culture, gram stain |
| | d. pyoderma gangrenosum | culture, gram stain |
| | e. photosensitivity and phototoxicity reactions | history of sensitizing agent, orally or topically |
| | f. frostbite | clinical history and characteristics |
| | g. herpes zoster/herpes simplex | scraping |
| | h. epidermolysis bullosa | skin Bx |
| | i. contact dermatitis, allergic or irritant | clinical characteristics |
| Occular Findings | | |
| 1. Retinal hemorrhage | a. shaking or other trauma | |
| | b. bleeding disorder | coagulation studies |
| | c. neoplasm | |
| | d. resuscitation | history |
| 2. Conjunctival hemorrhage | a. trauma | |
| | b. bacterial or viral conjunctivitis | culture, gram stain |
| | c. severe coughing | history |
| 3. Orbital swelling | a. trauma | |
| | b. orbital or periorbital cellulitis | CBC, culture, sinus x-rays |
| | c. metastatic disease | x-ray, CT scan; CNS exam |
| | d. epidural hematoma | x-ray, CT scan; CNS exam |
| Hematuria | a. trauma | R/O other disease |
| | b. urinary tract infection | culture |
| | c. acute or chronic forms of glomelular injury (e.g., glomerulonephritis) | renal function tests; biopsy |
| | d. hereditary or familial renal disorders (e.g., | |

Table 4-II continued

| Clinical Findings | Differential Diagnosis | Differentiating Tests |
|---|---|---|
| | familial benign recurrent hematuria) | history |
| | e. other: vasculitis, thrombosis, neoplasm, anomalies, stones, bacteremia, exercise, etc. | history, cultures, IVP |
| Acute Abdomen | a. trauma | R/O other disease |
| | b. intrinsic gastrointestinal disease (e.g., peritonitis, obstruction, inflammatory bowel disease, etc.) | x-ray studies, stool tests, etc. |
| | c. intrinsic urinary tract disease (infection, stone) | culture, IVP |
| | d. genital problem (torsion of spermatic cord, ovarian cyst, etc.) | history, physical exam x-ray, laparoscopy |
| | e. vascular accident as in sickle cell crisis | angiography, sickle prep |
| | f. other: mesenteric adenitis, strangulated hernia, anaphylactoid purpura, pulmonary dissease, pancreatitis, lead poisoning, DKA, etc. | as appropriate |
| Osseous Lesions | | |
| 1. Fractures (multiple or in various stages of healing) | a. trauma | |
| | b. osteogenesis imperfecta | x-ray and blue sclerae |
| | c. rickets | nutrition history |
| | d. birth trauma | birth history |
| | e. hypophosphatasia | decreased alkaline phosphatase |
| | f. leukemia | CBC, bone marrow |
| | g. neuroblastoma | bone marrow, biopsy |
| | h. S/P osteomyelitis or septic arthritis | history |
| | i. neurogenic sensory deficit | physical exam |
| 2. Metaphyseal and/or epiphyseal lesions | a. trauma | |
| | b. scurvy | x-ray and nutrition history |
| | c. Menkes Syndrome | decreased Cu, decreased ceruloplasmin |
| | d. syphilis | serology |
| | e. Little League Elbow | history |

| Clinical Findings | Differential Diagnosis | Differentiating Tests |
|---|---|---|
| | f. birth trauma | history |
| 3. Subperiosteal ossification | a. trauma | |
| | b. osteogenic malignancy | x-ray and biopsy |
| | c. syphilis | serology |
| | d. infantile cortical hyperostosis | no metaphyseal irregularity |
| | e. osteoid osteoma | response to aspirin |
| | f. scurvy | nutritional history |
| Sudden Infant Death | a. unexplained | |
| | b. trauma | autopsy |
| | c. asphyxia (aspiration, nasal obstruction, laryngospasm, sleep apnea) | autopsy<br>"near-miss" history |
| | d. infection botulism? | cultures, bacterial and viral |
| | e. immunodeficiency? | immunoglobulins |
| | f. cardiac arrhythmia? | autopsy |
| | g. hypoadrenalism? | electrolytes |
| | h. metabolic abnormality calcium? magnesium? | $Ca^{++}$, $Mg^{++}$ |
| | i. hypersensitivity to cow's milk protein? | |

documentation. The significance of obtaining informed consent for such procedures cannot be overemphasized. Parents will quickly sense any inquisitorial intentions on the part of the professional, and the utility of photographs needs to be explained openly and honestly; often, it may be well to omit the pictures in the interest of building and sustaining a helping relationship.

Four distinct patterns of inflicted burns have been described by Lenoski and Hunter (1977). Forced immersion yields a doughnut-shaped distribution of the burn with a spared area, frequently the buttocks or back, where the body may have been in contact with a container, and thus may have been protected from the heat of the water. A splash burn may produce nonuniform multiple burn areas, sometimes with an "arrowhead pattern" where the water has spread laterally as it rolls off the skin. If the child's body is immersed in a maximally flexed position, the skin folds of the thorax will be spared. This may give a striped pattern. When a burn is caused by contact with a hot object, such as an iron or radiator, the object may leave a distinctive mark on the skin.

Physical findings of child abuse may reflect internal injuries. A ruptured tympanic membrane may result from a blow to the side of the head or from a basilar skull fracture. Multiple Class I fractures of the teeth may result from repeated blows to the chin. A lacerated frenulum or other intraoral trauma may result from forced feeding with a spoon. Ocular injuries may include hyphema, corneal abrasion, subconjunctival hemorrhage, dislocation of the lens, detached retina, or retinal hemorrhages. The syndrome of the severely shaken infant (Caffey, 1972, 1974) is virtually always accompanied by retinal hemorrhages and may include no obvious cutaneous signs. Sudden thoracic compression and consequent increased intravascular pressure may also lead to retinal hemorrhages, the so-called Purtscher retinopathy (Tomasi, 1979). Occult internal injuries, as summarized by Touloukian (1968), include rupture of the pancreas and pseudocyst formation, lacerated liver or spleen, intramural hematoma of the bowel, retroperitoneal hemorrhage, renal laceration or contusion, intestinal perforation, rupture of the ureter or bladder, and chylous ascites.

The concomitant presentation of unusual chronic illness and child abuse has been noted in several recent reports. The term "Munchausen Syndrome by Proxy" has been applied to clinical situations where parents make their children sick in order to attract attention to their own problems (Meadow, 1977). A child with mysterious relapsing coma was found to have received sublethal doses of chloral hydrate by his mother (Lansky, 1974). Other reports include fever, bacteremia, recurrent idiopathic lesions of the skin, and sclerosed lesions of the cornea.

Laboratory studies are helpful in delineating the nature and extent of current trauma and in defining the presence of previous trauma. The radiologic findings of child abuse have been reviewed by Silverman (1974) and include multiple long bone fractures in various stages of healing, spiral fractures, epiphyseal fractures, and exaggerated periosteal reaction. A coagulation profile will exclude endogenous disorders of bleeding: prothrombin time, partial thromboplastin, platelet count, and bleeding time. Hemoglobinuria and hematuria are known to occur with major trauma (Rimer, 1977).

## Other Symptom Entities and Child Abuse

### *Ingestions and Child Abuse*

Childhood ingestions are seldom random, isolated events. Although their prevalence and morbidity have been reduced by the use of secure containers, recent studies suggest that family crisis is frequently present when a child is poisoned (Newberger, 1977).

Sobel's (1970) controlled studies of ingestions in 400 families noted that the variables correlating most closely with childhood poisoning were marital and sexual dissatisfaction, power struggles between parents and between parents and children, punitive disciplinary techniques, and psychological disturbances in the children. In McIntire's (1973) study of fifty subjects between the ages of six and eighteen who had ingested drugs, more than half were considered after careful interview to have been suicidal gestures. Many of these children, McIntire noted, displayed in their behavior the combination of a "cycle of rejection" in which rejection of their families was associated with the development of anger in the child. This anger, expressed outwardly, led to more rejection, and, expressed inwardly, was associated with the ingestion.

### *Failure to Thrive*

The diagnosis "failure to thrive" describes symptoms of growth failure for which no organic source can readily be found. The differential diagnosis of failure to thrive can be elaborate, time-consuming, expensive, and hurtful, both for the child and his family. Sills (1978) has suggested that the yield of laboratory studies not directly indicated from the history and physical examination is small.

When parents hear the diagnosis "failure to thrive" they immediately get the message that the "failure" is theirs. Moreover, in many states, the physician is obliged to report failure to thrive as a symptom of child abuse, notwithstanding the ambiguity of diagnosis. A diagnostic assessment of the family is as essential to the differential diagnosis as the laboratory data.

Although it has been estimated that up to 10% of victims of failure to thrive are also victims of physical abuse (Haton, 1977; Koel, 1969), a recent survey of the status of knowledge by Kotelchuck (1979) concludes that the understanding of the pathogenesis of failure to thrive is "primitive." Little support is found for the commonly held formulation that failure to thrive is caused by simple neglect. Among the familial concomitants of failure to thrive that have been cited in the pediatric literature are found failures of attachment, difficulties in feeding and infantile rumination, developmental immaturity, temperamental idiosyncrasy, and maternal depression (Fitch, 1976; Kotelchuck, 1979; Pollitt, 1976). Victims of failure to thrive are perceived by their parents to be sickly (Pollitt, 1976), and their patterns of feeding and crying suggest that they may have some innate disorder in the organization of their behavior that may interact with family factors to yield a strained relationship and an inadequate capacity to nurture the particular child (Kotelchuck, 1979; Lester, 1978; Pollitt, 1976).

### *Child Abuse and the Sudden Infant Death Syndrome (SIDS)*

Approximately 10,000 infants die in the United States each year without apparent cause. Sudden Infant Death Syndrome (SIDS) is the most common cause of death for infants between the ages of one week and twelve months and the second most common cause of death (after accidents) for all children between one week and fifteen years of age (Bergman, 1976). The relationship between SIDS and infanticide has been explored epidemiologically, although detailed comparative family studies are absent in the literature. SIDS is reported 100 times more frequently than infanticide, and there has been no change in the relative frequency since 1963, notwithstanding the increased awareness of both causes of death (Bergman, 1976; Kukull, 1977). Despite the importance of autopsy in understanding the cause of infant death, only a fraction of SIDS cases are examined pathologically. The low autopsy rate reflects both the inadequacies of the medical examiner system in many states and the reluctance of physicians to encourage the procedure to shocked and grieving parents. When autopsies are conducted, it is frequently difficult for a physician and family to find the results. Because most coroner medical examiner systems are established to detect crime, there is less emphasis than there might be on supporting families and improving the knowledge base (Cleveland, 1975).

The autopsy in SIDS may never delineate the precise cause of death, yet the information from the pathologic study is important in allaying the guilt and anguish of the family. Helpern has noted several dilemmas of interpretation that may arise from the autopsy findings: it may be difficult to determine if an autopsy finding, such as blood in the abdomen, occurred before or after the time of death; resuscitation attempts may result in injuries (such as fractures and hemorrhages) that are difficult to distinguish from inflicted trauma (Helpern, 1976).

A full history and review of any written records that may be available will help the pediatrician in the perplexing differential diagnosis of SIDS (Table 4-II). If there is a suspicion that the victim may have been abused, it is well to immediately obtain legal counsel. Law in all states requires that homicides be promptly reported, but where the possibility of SIDS is considered, an autopsy should be obtained to guide the choice of action. The pediatrician can protect the parents and siblings of the victim from certain hurtful legal processes. As SIDS occurs more frequently in families of lower socioeconomic status who may be more likely to attract the label of "child abuse" to their children's problems, it is well to avoid premature judgments and to provide support for the parents in their distress. Just as in the management of child abuse, a compassionate, reasonable demeanor will foster communication and promote the effective delivery of care by physician, nurse, social worker, and others.

### *Sexual Abuse*

Kempe (1978) has recently pointed out that sexual abuse remains a "hidden pediatric problem and a neglected area." Although increasing numbers of victims of sexual abuse are reported to county and state protective service programs, the case reports suggest that diagnosis is sporadic and action inconsistent (American Humane Association, 1979).

As with inflicted injuries, there is some conflict and ambiguity with regard to the definition, familial and parental concomitants, and role of the victim. Brant and Tisza (1977) suggest that the concept "sexual misuse" might be more appropriate to describe those situations where there is "exposure of a child to sexual stimulation inappropriate for the child's role in the family" as distinct from sexual abuse where there is forced sexual contact between a "victim" and a "perpetrator," which might cause great physical and psychological harm to a child.

Incest is defined as sexual abuse by a parent, sibling, or other close relative, including sexual intercourse. Molestation is defined as sexual abuse by a stranger with or without penetration. Modes of sexual contact include rape, which is defined as forced genital contact, usually introduction of the penis into the vagina of the female victim but occasionally including the forced penetration of an adult female by a boy's penis; sexual assault, defined as violent or nonviolent manual, oral, or genital contact with the genitalia of the victim; "immature gratification," defined as fondling, looking at, or kissing the genitalia of the victim; and confrontation by an exibitionist (Brant, 1978).

An adult who seeks sexual contact with children, in whatever mode, is labeled *pedophilic*. The sexual encounter may be coerced by the adult, or the child may be an active participant, seeking out or encouraging the adult because of needs for nurturance, mastery, or acting out aggressive feelings (Brant, 1978).

The line between loving caresses and sexual misuses may not be clear, and the pediatrician may be asked to draw the line. Clinical and survey data suggest that sexual interaction between children and adults is not infrequent, and it may be the personal reactions of the victim and the person to whom the victim goes for help that defines which cases receive diagnosis as cases of sexual abuse and are followed by intervention (Lardis, 1956; Asnes, 1972; Rosenfeld, 1977).

Finkelhor (1979) suggests that the current approach to sexual abuse is complicated by the historical context of sexual behavior between children and adults, and he notes that the process of discovery of sexual abuse has political dimensions. The women's movement has stimulated a consideration of the problem of sexual abuse as a variant of rape, and the proponents of protective services for child abuse have focused on the relationship with other forms of maltreatment. Neither approach fully considers the unique circumstances of most clinical situations that present as sexual abuse, and as a consequence the mobilization of the criminal process (as for rape of adult women) or the initiation of protective service intervention (as with cases of physical child abuse) can be unhelpful and insufficiently protective of the victim. Unlike rape, sexual abuse is usually perpetrated by a friend or an adult known to the child and may have importantly to do with the human relations within a particular family. It is more frequently chronic, does not necessarily involve physical force, and most frequently appears not to involve sexual intercourse. Unlike in physical child abuse, the "injury" is usually psychological rather than physical, and the motivation is usually for sexual gratification rather than as an expression of anger. The social stigma attached to abnormal sexual activity is much greater than for child abuse. These differences create confusion when one tries to comprehend the nature of the risk to a child, the needs of the family, and the therapeutic resources that can be brought to bear to prevent continued harm.

The social circumstances of victims of sexual abuse has only recently been systematically studied (1979). Finklehor's study of 795 undergraduate women revealed eight "vulnerability factors" in the women who were sexually victimized as children. These included 19% of the females in the sample. The factors included parental divorce and remarriage to a stepfather, a distant relationship with the mother, the experience of having lived away from the mother as a child, a quality of "sexual punitiveness" by the mother toward her spouse, the low educational status of the mother, few friends in childhood, and a gross family income under $10,000 (Landis, 1956; Asnes, 1972; Rosenfeld, 1977).

Among the presenting symptoms of victims of sexual abuse are enuresis and encopresis, hyperactivity, fears and phobias, sleep disorders, learning problems, compulsive masturbation, sexual

**TABLE 4-III**

SEXUAL ABUSE: DIAGNOSIS AND MEDICAL MANAGEMENT

*Signs and Symptoms*

1. Strong Evidence
   a. Gonococcal infection: Urethritis, pharyngitis, arthritis, conjunctivitis
   b. Trichomonas infection
   c. Venereal warts
   d. Syphilis
   e. Sperm or acid phosphatase present on body or clothes of victim
   f. Pregnancy
2. Probable Evidence:
   a. Vaginal or anal laceration
   b. Perineal bruises or abrasions
3. Possible Evidence:
   a. Monilial vaginitis
   b. Hemophilus vaginitis
   c. Hematuria (secondary to trauma)
   d. Behavioral symptoms: phobias, sexualized play, etc.

*Laboratory Evaluation of Sexually Abused Child*

1. Cultures: gonorrhea, monilia
2. Microscopic exam: sperm, trichomonas, monilia, hemophilus
3. Blood: syphilis serology and HCG beta-subunit assay for pregnancy
4. Urine: routine urinalysis for blood, sperm; culture for gonorrhea; pregnancy test
5. Miscellaneous: fingernail scrapings if there was a struggle, careful search for blood, pubic hairs, or semen on clothing

*Treatment*

1. Penicillin prophylaxis for several sexually transmitted diseases
2. Diethylstilbesterol to prevent pregnancy
3. Appropriate treatment if monilia, trichomonas, or hemophilus vaginitis found.

plague, perineal irritation, other genital injury and distorted, pseudo-mature personality development (Brant, 1978). Incest presents frequently when the child or mother reports the problem to someone outside the family. Often the child has been an active participant in a relationship over a long period of time. Incest may occur as mother-child, sibling-sibling, or father-child relationships, although the most common situation is father-daughter incest. The latter is described frequently as a triadic family system that includes a lonely dependent father, a depressed, withdrawn, but subconsciously encouraging mother, and a needy daughter who may believe that her secret relationship with her father is the only thing that holds her family together (Rosenfeld, 1977). It is well to think of incest as a symptom of a family's distorted emotional relationships, sadness, and inability to protect its children.

When sexual misuse or abuse is suspected, the clinical evaluation should include a calm, careful, sensitive interview of the child alone, allowing the child to communicate with pictures, toys, and play. The parents, other close relatives, and other caretakers can be interviewed to assess risk factors in the home and to establish relationships that will carry beyond the crisis to support the family, even in the event of ambiguous medical findings and uncertain diagnostic conclusions. The very suspicion of sexual abuse can be profoundly troubling to children and adults, and the force of the intrusions of the criminal justice and welfare systems when case reports are made can sometimes be more harmful than helpful to the psychological status of the victim and his or her family.

The physical examination of suspected victims of sexual abuse should first be carefully explained. The physical examination should be complete. When appropriate, there should be gentle aspiration with an eye dropper of vaginal contents for microscopic examinations and culture. Foreign bodies should be sought, and clothing examined for signs of semen or blood. The throat, rectum, and vagina should be cultured for gonococcus, and a serologic examination for syphilis should be performed. If vaginal discharge is present, microscopic examination for trichomonas and monilia, as well as culture and gram stain will be helpful in enabling prompt treatment of infection. Venereal warts may also be found on careful examination. It is well to keep in mind that the data one gathers may subsequently be reviewed in the criminal or civil court (Sgroi, 1978). For girls who are past menarche, the pregnancy test is done as a matter of routine where introduction of semen into the vagina is believed to have been possible. Treatment plans may include prophylactic antibiotic therapy and diethylstilbestrol to prevent pregnancy.

## THE INTERDISCIPLINARY MANAGEMENT OF CHILD ABUSE

Table 4-IV summarizes the management of child abuse and divides the pediatric role into two phases: diagnostic assessment and rehabilitation program. Principal questions are outlined, and interventions to protect the child and to help the family are summarized.

Since current understanding of child abuse regards the problem as a symptom of family distress, and because of an increasing acknowledgement that parental psychological problems are not the sole causation of child abuse, the evaluation of the meaning of the child's presenting physical and psychological data necessitates the coordinated diagnostic efforts of several personnel. A social worker should always be included in the initial diagnostic phase, and often a diagnostic interdisciplinary team will include a social worker, a pediatrician, a nurse, a psychiatrist, and an attorney. When such a diagnostic unit is not available, it will be necessary for the physician to work with his professional counterparts in other community agencies. It is helpful to develop guidelines for case management suitable for the resources of a particular institutional or community setting (Newberger, 1973; Schmitt, 1976, 1978). Child abuse case reports alone may not be sufficient to protect an abused or neglected child or to help the family.

Several ethical dilemmas confront the pediatrician in the diagnosis and management of child abuse (Green, 1975). The diagnosis itself is often made with difficulty, and the physician, concerned to give the parents the benefit of any doubt, may feel that the easiest, fairest, and most ethical approach when in doubt is to send the child home without reporting. Much uncompensated time is spent on these clinical problems and may create a disincentive to reporting.

There is conflict between the traditional doctrine of doctor-patient confidentiality and the laws that oblige reporting of privileged information when a child is suspected to be at risk. Fines and other civil liabilities have been imposed when physicians have been reluctant to reveal their knowledge of the family (Pfohl, 1977). The Hippocratic precept *"Primum non nocere"* is challenged when the reporting itself carries with it the risk of an incompetent intrusion into the lif of the family by a poorly

**TABLE 4-IV**
PHASES IN MANAGEMENT OF CHILD ABUSE

| Phases in Management | Primary Considerations | Interventions to Protect the Child and Help the Family |
|---|---|---|
| *Diagnostic Assessment:* | | |
| medical history<br>physical examination<br>skeletal survey<br>laboratory tests | Are the physical findings at variance with the history? | Provide more comprehensive medical workup. |
| | Is child abuse or neglect suspected? | Inform the parents of the suspicions and the physician's responsibility to protect the child. |
| photographs | What is the legal responsibility regarding suspected child abuse? | Make a report to the mandated agency. |
| | Is the home safe for the child? | Continue the evaluation on an outpatient basis. |
| | Is the child "at risk?" | Hospitalize the child for protection and further evaluation. |
| consultations for evaluation of family dynamics and child development | What is needed to make the home safe for the child's return? | Arrange for multidisciplinary conferencing for disposition planning. |
| *Rehabilitation Program:* | | |
| health needs | What resources will meet the needs of the child and the family? | Arrange for primary health care and appropriate treatment for the child and family. |
| physical, social, and environmental needs | | Mobilize community resources such as child care, homemaker service, foster home placement. |
| follow-up planning | Who will monitor the health and community services to the child and the family? | |
| medical care<br>social work services<br>nursing services<br>other services | | Provide coordination and integration of the helping resources. |

trained, inadequately supervised social worker from an overburdened and underfunded public child protection agency. The child may reflexly be separated from his home, or no help may follow. It is often difficult to choose "the least detrimental alternative," a concept suggested in the book *Beyond the Best Interest of the Child* (Goldstein, 1973) to guide a choice of management options when both may clearly carry the possibility of harm.

A consensus on seven axioms of interdisciplinary child abuse management appears in the literature on child abuse:

1. An abused child is at great risk for reinjury or continued neglect if nothing is done.
2. Protection of the child must be a principle goal of initial intervention, but protection of the child must go hand in hand with the development of a program to help the family through its crisis.
3. Traditional social casework alone may not adequately protect an abused child in the environment in which he received his injuries. Medical follow-up, too, is necessary, and daily contact with a child care center may help to encourage his healthy development.
4. In the event the child is reinjured, it is likely that the parents will seek care at a different medical facility from the one at which the diagnosis was originally established or suspected.
5. The problems of public social service agencies in both urban and rural areas—specifically in numbers of adequately trained personnel and in quality of administrative and supervisory functions—militate against their effective operation in isolation from other care-providing agencies. Simply reporting a case to the public agency mandated to receive child abuse case reports may not be sufficient to protect an abused or neglected child or to help the family.
6. There is rarely any need to establish precisely who it was who abused a child and how "intentional" the violence was. However strategic the "facts" may be to confirmation of diagnosis and treatment planning, clinical experience attaches the greater importance to the establishment of trust in the intervening professionals.

7. If there is evidence that the child is at major risk, hospitalization is appropriate to allow time for comprehensive assessment. Infants under a year of age with fractures, burns, or bruises of any kind are especially at risk for reinjury or for serious consequences of neglect.

The opportunity to observe parent-child interaction and the child's physical and psychological milestones (which might yield insight into the familial causes of a child's injury) may not be available to a physician in his office. Nurses in clinical and public health settings can and do, however, make such observations, which are fundamental in case-finding and evaluation. Their competence contributes uniquely to diagnosis, and their perceptions should be shared appropriately with the physician and social worker seeing the family. A home visit by a physician, public health nurse, or social worker is an important part of all initial assessments and is made to gather data for the discussion of the child's disposition. A psychiatric consultation is frequently a valuable diagnostic adjunct in the initial assessment. Often this consultant's perceptions lead to better understanding of what interventions can be most effective. Only rarely, however, can a psychiatrist work magic; his consultation should not substitute for careful diagnostic work and energetic advocacy by the social worker, physician, and nurse.

The development of programs that attend to these principles will require careful thought and planning. In the last analysis, the professional ability to convince patients or clients that they mean to help them depends on the ability to mobilize effective services for them.

When case management and interdisciplinary cooperation improves, health practitioners and other professionals who work with children will find it easier and more rewarding to make case reports and to participate in comprehensive service plans.

## References

*American Humane Association Annual Statistical Report,* National Analysis of Child Neglect and Abuse Reporting, 1977. National Study on Child Abuse and Neglect Report. The Association, Englewood, Colorado, February, 1979.

Asnes, R.S., et al. Gonococcal infections in children. *Journal of Pediatrics*, 1972, *81*, 192-193.

Bergman, A.B. Sudden infant death syndrome: an approach to management. *Primary Care*, 1976, *3*, 1-8.

Bourne, R. Child abuse and neglect: an overview. In R. Bourne and E.H. Newberger (Eds.), *Critical perspectives on child abuse*. Lexington: Lexington Books, 1979.

Brant, R. *Manual on sexual abuse and misuse of children*. Reprinted by The New England Resource Center for Protective Services. Judge Baker Guidance Center, Boston, Mass. 02115.

Brant, R., & Tisza, V. The sexually misused child. *American Journal of Orthopsychiatry*, 1977, *47(1)*, 80-90.

Bremner, R.H. *Children and youth in America: A documentary history*. Cambridge: Harvard University Press, 1971.

Caffey, J. On the theory and practice of shaking infants. *American Journal of Diseases of Children*, 1972, *124*, 161-169.

Caffey, J. Whiplash shaken infant syndrome. *Pediatrics*, 1974, *54*, 396-403.

Cleveland, A.P. Sudden infant death syndrome (SIDS): a burgeoning medicolegal problem. *American Journal of Law and Medicine*, 1975, *1*, 55-69.

DeMause, L. (Ed.). *The history of childhood*. New York: The Psychohistory Press, 1974.

Elmer, E. *Children in jeopardy: A study of abused minors and their families*. Pittsburgh: University of Pittsburgh Press, 1967.

Erlanger, R.S. Social class differences in parents' use of physical punishment. In S.K. Steinmetz & M.A. Straus (Eds.), *Violence in the family*. New York: Dodd, Mead, 1974.

Fanshel, D., & Skinn, E.G. *Children in foster care: A longitudinal investigation*. New York: Columbia University Press, 1974.

Finkelhor, D. *Sexually victimized children*. New York: Free Press, 1979.

Fitch, M.F., Cadol, R.V., Goldson, E., et al. Cognitive development of abused and failure to thrive children. *Pediatric Psychology*, 1976, *1*, 32-37.

Fraser, B.G. The child and his parents: a delicate balance of rights. In R.E. Helfer, & C.H. Kempe, (Eds.), *Child abuse and neglect: The family and the community*. Cambridge, MA: Ballinger, 1976.

Friedrich, W.N., & Boriskin, J.A. The role of the child in child abuse. *American Journal of Orthopsychiatry*, 1976, *46*, 500-590.

Gabarino, J. A preliminary study of some ecological correlates of child abuse: the impact of socioeconomic stress on the mother. *Child Development*, 1975, *47*, 178-185.

Gelles, R. A profile of violence towards children in the United States. Paper presented to the Annenberg School of Communications Conference on Child Abuse: Cultural Roots and Policy Options. Philadelphia, November 20, 1978.

Gelles, R. Child abuse as psychopathology: a sociological critique and reformulation. *American Journal of Orthopsychiatry*, 1973, *43(4)*, 611-624.

Gil, D.G. Unraveling child abuse. *American Journal of Orthopsychiatry*, 1975, *45*, 346-356.

Gil, D.G. *Violence against children. Physical child abuse in the United States.* Cambridge, MA: Harvard University Press, 1970.

Goldson, E., Ritch, M.G., Wendell, T.A., & Knapp, G. Child abuse: its relationship to birth weight, Apgar score, and developmental testing. *American Journal of Diseases of Children*, 1978, *132*, 790-793.

Goldstein, J., Freud, A., & Solnit, A.J. *Beyond the best interests of the child.* New York: Free Press, 1973.

Green, A.H. A psychodynamic approach to the study and treatment of child-abusing parents. *Journal of the American Academy of Child Psychiatry*, 1976, *15*, 414-429.

Green, A.H. Self-destructive behavior in abused children. *American Journal of Psychiatry*, 1978, *135*, 579-589.

Green, F.C. Child abuse and neglect: a priority problem for the private pediatrician. *Pediatric Clinics of North America*, 1975, *22*, 329-339.

Gruber, A.R. *Foster home care in Massachusetts: A study of foster children, their biological and foster parents.* Massachusetts Governor's Commission on Adoption and Foster Care, 1978.

Helfer, R.E., & Kempe, C.H. (Eds.). *Child abuse and neglect: The family and the community*. Cambridge, MA: Ballinger, 1976.

Helpern, M. Fatalities from child abuse and neglect: responsibility of the medical examiner and coroner. *Pediatric Annals*, 1976, *5*, 42-57.

Hufton, I.W., & Oates, R.K. Nonorganic failure to thrive: a long-term follow-up. *Pediatrics*, 1977, *59*, 73-77.

Hunter, R.S., Kilstron, N., Kraybill, E.N., & Loda, F. Antecedents of child abuse and neglect in premature infants: a prospective study in a newborn intensive care unit. *Pediatrics*, 1978, *61*, 629-635.

Ingraham vs. Wright, 45 L.W. 4364.

*In re* Gault, 387 U.S. 1 (1967).

Kempe, C.H. New vistas in the prevention of child abuse. In E.H. Newberger (Ed.), *Child advocacy and pediatrics. Report of the Eighth Ross Roundtable*, Columbus, OH: Ross Laboratories, 1978.

Kempe, C.H. Sexual abuse: the 1977 C. Anderson Aldrich lecture. *Pediatrics*, 1978, *62*, 382-398.

Kempe, C.H., Silverman, F.N., Steele, B.F., Droegemueller, W., & Silver, H.K. The battered child syndrome. *Journal of the American Medical Association*, 1962, *181(1)*, 17-24.

Keniston, K. Do Americans really like children? *Today's Education*, 1975, *64*, 11-12.

King, L.S. (Ed.) *A history of medicine, selected readings*. Baltimore: Penguin Books Ltd., 1971. Excerpts from William Cullen's *First Lines of the Practice of Physic*, 1786, p. 147.

Klaus, M.H., & Kennell, J.H. *Maternal infant bonding*. St. Louis: C.V. Mosby Company, 1976.

Koel, B.S. Failure to thrive and fatal injury as a continuum. *American Journal of Diseases of Children*, 1969, *118*, 565-567.

Kotelchuck, M. Non-organic failure to thrive: the status of interactional and environmental etiologic theories. In B. Camp (Ed.), *Advances in behavioral pediatrics, Vol. I.* Greenwich, CT: Jai Press, 1979.

Kotelchuck, M., Gordon, A., Jameson, J., & Newberger, E.H. Behavioral observations of non-organic failure to thrive children: a pilot study of attachment. In E.H. Newberger & M. Kotelchuck (Eds.), *The symptoms of child abuse.* Boston: Harvard University Press, 1979.

Kukull, W.A., & Peterson, D.R. Sudden infant death and infanticide. *American Journal of Epidemiology*, 1977, *106*, 485-448.

Landis, J.T. Experiences of 500 children with adult sexual deviation. *Psychological Quarterly Supplement*, Part I, 1956, *301*, 91-109.

Lanoski, E.F., & Hunter, K.A. Patterns of inflicted burns. *Journal of Trauma*, 1977, *17*, 842-846.

Lansky, L.L. An unusual case of childhood chloral hydrate poisoning. *American Journal of Diseases of Children*, 1974, *127*, 275-276.

Lester, F.M., & Zeskind, P. The organization of crying in the infant at risk. In T. Fried (Ed.), *The high risk infant.* Jamaica, NY: Spectrum Publications, 1978.

Light, R. Abused and neglected children in America: a study of alternative policies. *Harvard Educational Review*, 1978, *43*, 556-598.

Lynch, M. Ill-health and child abuse. *Lancet*, 1975, *2*, 317-319.

McIntire, M.S., & Angle, C.R. Psychological "biopsy" in self-poisoning of children and adolescents. *American Journal of Diseases of Children*, 1973, *126*, 42-46.

Meadow, R. Munchausen syndrome by proxy: the hinterland of child abuse. *Lancet*, 1977, *2*, 343-345.

Merril, E.J. *Protecting the battered child.* Denver: Children's Division, American Humane Association, 1962.

Newberger, E.H., & Bourne, R. The medicalization and legalization of child abuse. *American Journal of Orthopsychiatry*, 1978, *48(4)*, 593-607.

Newberger, E.H., Hagenbuch, J.J., Ebeling, N.B., Colligan, E.P., Sheehan, J.S., & McVeigh, S.H. Reducing the literal and human cost of child abuse: impact of a new hospital management system. *Pediatrics*, 1973, *51*, 840-848.

Newberger, E.H., Reed, R.B., Daniel, J.H., Hyde, J.N., & Kotelchuck, M. Pediatric social illness: toward an etiologic classification. *Pediatrics*, 1977, *60*, 178-185.

Parham, James, Individually and as Commissioner of the Department of Human Resources *et al.* vs. J.L. and J.R. Minors, *etc.* 47 L.W. 4740.

Park, R.D., & Collmer, C.W. Child abuse: an interdisciplinary analysis. In E.M. Hetherington (Ed.), *Review of child development research, Vol. V.* Chicago: University of Chicago Press, 1975.

Pelton, L.H. Child abuse and neglect: the myth of classlessness. *American Journal of Orthopsychiatry*, 1978, *48*, 608-617.

Pfohl, S.J. The "discovery" of child abuse. *Social Problems*, 1977, *24*, 310-323.

Pollitt, E., & Eichler, A. Behavioral disturbances among failure to thrive children. *American Journal of Diseases of Children*, 1976, *130*, 24-30.

Radbill, S.X. A history of child abuse and infanticide. In R.E. Helfer & C.H. Kempè (Eds.), *The Battered child* (2nd ed.). Chicago: University of Chicago Press, 1974.

Rimer, R.L., & Shane, R. Child abuse and hemoglobinuria. *Journal of the American Medical Association*, 1977, *238*, 2034.

Rosenfeld, A.A., Nadelson, C.C., Krieger, M., & Backman, J.H. Incest and sexual abuse of children. *Journal of the American Academy of Child Psychiatry*, 1972, *16*, 327-339.

Rosenn, D.W., Loeb, L.S. , & Jura, M.B. Differentiation of organic from non-organic failure to thrive syndrome in infancy. *Pediatrics*, 1980, *66*,698-704.

Sears, R.R. Your ancients revisited: a history of child development. In E.M. Hetherington (Ed.), *Review of Child Development Research, Vol. V*. Chicago: University of Chicago Press, 1975.

Schmitt, B.D., Bross, D.C., et al. *Guideline for the hospital and clinic: Management of child abuse and neglect*. U.S. Department of Health, Education and Welfare, User Manual Series, August 1978.

Schmitt, B.D., Grosz, C.A., & Carroll, C.A. The child protection team: a problem-oriented approach. In R.E. Helfer & C.H. Kempe (Eds.), *Child abuse and neglect, The family and the community*. Cambridge, MA: Ballinger, 1976.

Sgroi, S.M. Comprehensive examination for child sexual assault: diagnostic, therapeutic and child protection issues. In A.W. Burgess et al. (Eds.), *Sexual assault of children and adolescents*. Lexington, MA: Lexington Books, 1978.

Sills, R.H. Failure to thrive: the role of clinical and laboratory investigation. *American Journal of Diseases of Children*, 1978, *132*, 967-969.

Silverman, F.N. Radiologic aspects of the battered child syndrome. In R.E. Helfer & C.H. Kempe (Eds.), *The battered child* (2nd ed.). Chicago: University of Chicago Press, 1974.

Sobel, R. Psychological implications of accidental poisonings in childhood. *Pediatric Clinics of North America*, 1970, *17*, 653-685.

Spinetta, J.J., & Rigler, D. The child abusing parent: a psychological review. *Psychological Bulletin*, 1972, *77*, 296-304.

Steele, B.F., & Pollock, C.B. A psychiatric study of parents who abuse infants and small children. In R.E. Helfer & C.H. Kempe (Eds.), *The battered child* (2nd ed.). Chicago: University of Chicago Press, 1974.

Stein, A.H., & Friedrich, L. Impact of television on children and youth. In E.M. Hetherington (Ed.), *Review of child development research, Vol. V*. Chicago: University of Chicago Press, 1975.

Steinmetz, S.K., & Straus, M.A. (Eds.) *Violence in the family*. New York: Dodd, Mead, 1974.

Straus, M.A., Gelles, R., & Steinmetz, S.K. *Behind closed doors: Violence in the American family.* New York: Anchor/Doubleday, 1980.

Straus, M.A. Leveling, civility and violence in the family. *Journal of Marriage and the Family*, 1974, *36*, 13-19.

Tomasi, L.G., & Rosman, N.P. Purtscher retinopathy in the battered child syndrome. *American Journal of Diseases of Children*, 1979, *129*, 1335-1337.

Touloukian, R.J. Abdominal visceral injuries in battered children. *Pediatrics*, 1968, *42*, 642-646.

Wilson, E.F. Estimation of the age of cutaneous contusions in child abuse. *Pediatrics*, 1977, *60*, 750-752.

Young, L. *Wednesday's children: A study of child neglect and abuse.* New York: McGraw-Hill, 1964.

Zigler, E. Controlling child abuse in America. In *Proceedings of the First National Conference on Child Abuse and Neglect*, Department of Health, Education, and Welfare, 1976. Reprinted in R. Bourne & E.H. Newberger (Eds.), *Critical prespectives on child abuse.* Lexington, MA: Lexington Books, 1979.

Chapter 5

# THE CHILD IN THE DIVORCING FAMILY

JUDITH S. WALLERSTEIN

THE ROLE OF JUDGE on the Domestic Relations bench is surely one of the most difficult within the judicial system. Confronted daily with complex human problems that often appear insoluble and that evoke a combination of exasperation and moral anguish in most onlookers, the judge finds his or her task very much at odds with the model of judicious calm and carefully measured decisions to which the court aspires. It is, in fact, entirely comprehensible how competent and dedicated people of conscience would be fatigued and psychically depleted by this experience, and that only the judge with particular interest and commitment to this aspect of the law can spend several years dealing with family issues with equanimity and a sense of accomplishment.

Contributing to the judge's dilemma is the fact that the behavioral sciences have dragged their feet in researching the changes within the American family. We have, indeed, as a society been reluctant to recognize the phenomenon of divorce, particularly those aspects that pertain to children. We have been quick to believe that children are unhappy in a marriage that is unhappy for one or both of their parents. We have been remiss in providing the court-attached services and the community-based

The research reported in this paper has been supported since 1971 by the Zellerbach Family Fund, San Francisco. Dr. Wallerstein has been principal investigator; Joan B. Kelly, Ph.D., co-principal investigator.

Updated, with permission of the *Judges' Journal*, a quarterly publication of the Judicial Administration Division. Copyright 1980, American Bar ssociation.

services that divorcing families with children sorely need. Additionally, mental health professionals who have been involved in courtroom procedures often offer conflicting advice. This lack of unanimity among the members of the mental health profession reflects not only different orientations and schools of thought, but also the paucity of research. Essentially, the mental health practitioner who stands before the court has relied on his or her own clinical practice. While this practice may be extensive and illuminating, it is not the equivalent of the systematic study of many children. One cannot be even reasonably sure that the clinical experiences of any one practitioner, however extensive, can be appropriately applied to children from many walks of life who have not been identified as patients and have not come to treatment out of an identified need for help.

Only in recent years have the behavioral sciences begun to accumulate some systematic knowledge about the experiences of divorcing families with children. Findings from investigative projects, although too few in number, have been strikingly in accord with each other despite being conducted in different regions of the country (Hetherington, 1972; Hetherington, et al., 1976, 1978; Jacobson, 1978; Kelly & Wallerstein, 1976, 1977; McDermott, 1968, 1970; Wallerstein, 1977; Wallerstein & Kelly, 1974, 1975, 1976, 1980). It is these findings that may be of benefit to the judge, both by providing the information he or she may find specifically useful and in providing the sense that each decision does not derive entirely from individual experience. There is an emerging common body of knowledge that provides a social and psychological context within which complex issues can be understood and decisions facilitated.

The personal attitudes of the judge and the opinions of the court exercise a profound influence on American family life. Although the court sees only a minority of divorcing families, a percentage that has been variously estimated, but never counted, at approximately 10 to 12% of the divorcing families with children, the informal attitudes as well as the formal decisions of the court cast a long shadow. They influence the advice attorneys provide to the litigating and nonlitigating clients. They affect the values and expectations of the general community in regard to relationships between parent and children. Given the current rate of divorce, which shows no sign of diminishing, we can estimate conservatively that one-third of American children born within this decade will experience the disruption of their family. Thus, by virtue of its very magnitude, the divorce issue has moved to center stage in this society. It therefore becomes of great importance, both for the society as a whole and for the litigating families before the court, that the judge on the Domestic Relations bench speak with the available knowledge in addressing the issues that affect children within the divorcing family.

The findings we present here derive primarily from a five-year longitudinal study of 131 children from sixty divorcing families in a general northern California divorcing population.

Begun in 1971, the Children of Divorce Project had as its overarching goals the systematic exploration of the responses of children at various ages to divorce-related family change, as well as to those changes that occur consequent to the divorce within the parent-child relationship. Before the family disruption, all of these children had been considered by their parents and teachers to have reached appropriate developmental milestones. The children and their families were seen on an average of 14.2 interviews per family, extending over a six-week span, set within the context of a preventive planning service that was established at the county community mental health center. Families were referred by attorneys, schools, physicians, and other community agencies within no more than a year after the parental separation and preferably as close as possible to that separation. Initial data obtained in these four to six interviews with each family member over a six-week period were supplemented by independent information obtained from the children's schools. All family members were interviewed again individually by the same member of the clinical team within a year following this initial extended contact. For most of the families, the first follow-up occurred at about eighteen months after the parental separation.

In consideration of the finding of high incidence of continuing or increased distress among the children, it was decided to follow the original group further, and in 1976 another round of examination of the same youngsters now four to five years older was completed. Once again, fifty-eight of the original sixty families were reached. The experience of these children within the divorcing families provide a main source of the information presented here.

## Initial Responses of Children to the Marital Rupture

Children and adolescents alike experienced the parental separation and its aftermath as the most stressful period of their lives. The family rupture evoked an acute sense of shock, intense fear, worry, and grieving that the children found overwhelming. Only a small number of the children and adolescents were relieved by the divorce decision, perhaps 10%, and these were mainly older youngsters who had seen physical fighting between their parents and were fearful about such recurrences, either on their own behalf or on behalf of one of their parents.

The children's early responses were not governed by a balanced understanding of the issues that led their parents to the divorce decision. Most children have a great deal of difficulty in identifying with the needs of a particular parent or in understanding the adult issues that led their parents to divorce, even though they may be well aware of one or both parents' anger, unhappiness, or loneliness, nor were the children much, if at all, affected by the high incidence of divorce in the community. It appears that each child considers his/her own situation uniquely and is not comforted by the misery of friends or neighbors. In fact, the high incidence of divorce in the community can also frighten children whose parents are not divorcing. School teachers have reported children coming to school in acute anxiety because their parents fought the preceding night, worrying whether the parental quarrel meant that there would be a divorce forthcoming in their family.

At the time of the parental separation, the child's attention is riveted entirely on the disruptive process itself in his or her family and is intensely worried about what will happen to him. Whatever its shortcomings, the family is perceived by the child as having provided the support and protection he needed and will continue to need. The divorce signifies for him the collapse of that structure, and he is likely to feel alone and very frightened.

### *Who Helps the Child?*

For many American children, the crisis at the time of the divorce is exacerbated by the relative unavailability of the extended family or support within the community. In the population studied, less than 25% of the 131 youngsters were comforted or helped by grandparents, aunts or uncles, or other members of the extended family. In the main, they were remarkably unsupported by other adults. Less than 10% recalled the kindness and compassion of an adult who intervened at a critical time in their lives. In general, we and others have been concerned with the loneliness of the child in the divorcing family and the limited support available in the schools, in the church, in the community, among adults who generally have contact with the family as physician, teacher, or minister in the community. Thus, the child is doubly burdened by his or her own fear of the collapse of the family and by the relative absence of support in the social surround. Like the nursery school rhyme "the child stands alone"—or relatively alone—when the parents divorce.

### *Diminished Capacity to Parent*

Contributing significantly to the widespread distress of the children was the fact that many children and adolescents faced the tensions and sorrow of divorce with very little help from their parents. During the critical months following the separation, the adults, who were occupied with the crisis in their own lives and the many decisions they faced, provided diminished parental care to children who were already upset by visible family disruptions. Parents are not necessarily less loving or less concerned with their children during divorce, but changes in their lives direct their attention elsewhere into their own preoccupations and problems.

The many practical changes in their lives take their toll and diminish the time and the attention available for the children. Custodial parents are likely to seek full time employment, and children are left with new sitters in strange homes or child care settings. Many children come home to empty houses after their day at school. Noncustodial parents often have housing that is inadequate for extended visiting and see their children on the run. New love relationships take on special importance. There is often a flurry of social and sexual activity immediately following the marital breakup as parents seek new companions during weekends that customarily had been spent in the company of the children.

Moreover, many adults are depressed, angry, and humiliated following the decision to dissolve the marriage, and there is an understandable connection between the adult's unhappiness and deterioration in the capacity to provide emotional support to children. The diminished parenting set children who were accustomed to good parental care adrift and rendered them more vulnerable to their fears of being abandoned by both parents. Children who had long suffered the neglect of their parents experienced the diminished care at the time of the divorce as a reinforcement of the parents' limited interest in their welfare.

A very vivid example of the diminished parenting was the grave difficulty many parents experienced in telling their children about their decision to divorce and the failure of many to explain the divorce to the children. Parents confessed to us that they did not know how much to tell, how many details of their intimacy to reveal, whether to elaborate on one partner's infidelity or another's frigidity. They could not decide where or when to tell the children, or how long before one parent departed the household. Many were apprehensive that their children would be unhappy, frightened, or angered by their decision. Often they explained the divorce decision clumsily and in ways that inflicted the most suffering on the children, saying "he left *us*!", or "She does *not* love *us*!", or "The divorce will not make any difference." Thus, in many families there was an awkwardness in communication or a silence between parent and child at the height of the child's need for support. In fact, no single family in our experience provided the children with an *adequate* opportunity to express their concerns, to recognize with them what the divorce really was about, that there was indeed a family crisis, and that things would be difficult for a while with the realistic expectation that life would gradually improve.

The parent's diminished capacity to be helpful to their children at this time undoubtedly contributed to the intensity of the children's response and particularly to their fearfulness. Furthermore, the parents' inability to provide the support the children needed continued for an extended period of time—often for several years following the marital breakup. From the particular perspective of the court, it is important to bear in mind that the diminished capacity to parent, which we found to be widespread, is also reflected in the impaired judgment of many parents and their difficulty in separating their own needs from the needs and best interests of their own children at the time of crisis.

## The Trajectory of the Dissolution Process

The timetable of the divorcing process is considerably longer than most people realize. Certainly, the multiple changes in the individual lives of the adults and the children in their relationship with each other that were set into motion by the decision to divorce exceeded our own expectation in their drama, in their complexity, and in their widening effects. The period of disequilibrium in the lives of the children often lasted several years. At five years following the marital separation it was obvious that for many children and adults the divorce-related issues remained infused with strong feelings. Perhaps this extended timetable is realistic and to be expected, and we and others have been naive in expecting quicker integrations of the major changes precipitated by the family breakup.

It is possible to distinguish several stages in the trajectory of the divorcing process: (a) the initial acute phase, (b) the transitional phase, and (c) the restabilized family. The acute initial period following the decision to divorce is characterized by high expression of anger, by frequency of depression, and by the diminished capacity to parent, which we have described. By the end of the first year to one and one-half years following the separation, acute responses among the children began to subside or to disappear altogether. The transition period often lasted two to three years and is marked by many external moves as well as by changed family circumstances. Finally, the third stage of the divorcing process is that of the early years within the restabilized, post-divorce family or the new marriage. By the five-year mark some of the families had succeeded in creating a stable home and in improving the quality of life for the family members in comparison with the predivorce family. At the other end of the wide spectrum, the adults or the children or both together were unhappy or were no happier than they had been during the failing marriage.

There are significant differences in the experiences of adults and children during each of these three phases of the divorcing process. Although the initial breakup of the family is profoundly stressful, the eventual outcome depends in large measure not only on what has been lost but also on what has been constructed to take the place of the failed marriage. The effect of the divorce ultimately reflects the success or failure of the participants, parents and children, to master the immediate disruption, to negotiate the transition successfully, and to create a more gratifying family to replace the family that failed. The goal of society therefore is not only to facilitate or permit the dissolution of the unhappy marriage but also to lay the foundation for the emerging postdivorce family, which will protect the psychological and economic needs of the children during their growing up years.

### Parent-Child Relationships Following Divorce

There is considerable evidence that the relationship between the child in the divorced family and both of his or her parents does not diminish in emotional importance within the postdivorce family. Although the mother's caretaking and psychological role became increasingly central in families where the mother had sole custody, the father's psychological significance did not correspondingly decline. Even within the remarriages, at least during the early years of these remarriages where the stepfather often became a prominent figure to the children very quickly, the biological father's emotional significance did not disappear or diminish markedly. It has in fact been strikingly apparent through the years that, where the child maintained frequent or infrequent contact with the noncustodial parent, the children would have considered the term "one parent family" as a misnomer. Where children have been reared in a two parent family their self-image appears to be firmly tied to the relationship with both parents.

Taken as a whole, our findings point to the desirability of the child's continuing relationship with both parents during the postdivorce years in an arrangement that enables each parent to be responsible for and genuinely concerned about the well-being of the children. Families in which the children had a good outcome at five years were those who were able to restabilize and restore the parenting after the initial dip during the crisis of the marital breakup. Children who did well had a custodial and a noncustodial parent who, separately or in cooperation with each other, retained or strengthened their parental commitment, or at the least these children who did well were well parented by one parent and did not feel rejected by the other. Improvement also occurred when the divorce separated a child from a psychologically destructive or abusive parent. Of course, some children benefitted from the new parental relations of the remarriage. In families where the children did well, the friction between parents had mostly dissipated. In those arrangements that promoted beneficial development, the child or adolescent enjoyed parental support and a sense of being loved and valued by one parent and not demeaned or rejected by the other. Those who enjoyed the sense of continuity with both parents felt that the divorce had contributed to the quality of their life by removing the stress and continuing the important gratifications. Occasionally, it appeared to us that the child's self-esteem was even enhanced in that he or she felt especially valued in recognition of the obstacles to maintaining the relationship that needed to be overcome in the divorced family. Children and adolescents were generally aware of the ease with which appointments could be forgotten or plans postponed by the visiting parent. Similarly, children were often aware of the burdens of the custodial parent. They could be profoundly appreciative of the efforts that entered into maintaining the household and the demands of working and carrying responsibility for the family, and they were often sensitive to the worries and responsibilities the custodial parent carried alone.

At the other end of the spectrum, children who felt rejected or neglected by the custodial and/or noncustodial parent were likely to be stressed and troubled. Parallel to the finding that a good father-child relationship supported over the years by visiting appropriate to the child's wishes and needs was correlated with high self-esteem is the complementary finding that a poor father-child relationship within the context of inappropriate, infrequent, or unreliable visiting was significantly linked to depression in children. The child's experience of being repeatedly disappointed because of the infrequency or the unreliability of the father's visiting or the disinterest or insensitivity of the father to his children during the visits caused the children grave unhappiness, which did not seem to diminish over the years. Despite repeated disappointment and the passage of time most children did not give up the hope that the father would eventually fulfill their expectations. Only a few children developed immunity to repeated disappointments and were able to overcome the hurt of the father's rejection. Those who did so had the help of unusually sensitive mothering and/or step-parenting as well as their own considerable inner resources.

Children who remained in the custody of a lonely, depressed, or emotionally disturbed mother were also likely to do poorly. The additional stresses of the divorce on the emotionally disturbed or vulnerable parent often led to deteriorated parenting, which was no longer mitigated by the buffering presence of the other marital partner. Children who were in the custody of a chronically troubled mother were more likely to go downhill than during the failing marriage where they had two parents to maintain them despite the unhappiness between the parents.

## Failure of the Divorce

A central cause of poor outcome at the five-year mark among the children and adolescents was the failure of the divorce to provide the remedy for which it was intended. When one or both parents continued to be distressed, when the parent or parents experienced no relief, where the quality of family life deteriorated, the children felt unable to master the stress and the psychic pain.

Similarly when the parents continued to fight bitterly with each other as they had during the marriage or where the bitterness following the divorce exceeded the bitterness of the marital conflict, children were seriously hindered in their efforts at mastery. We were startled to discover that 30% of the children whom we studied were aware of great tension and continued bitterness between their parents at the five-year mark. This continued fighting was significantly related to poor psychological adjustment among the children.

Continued friction between parents who had long ago divorced reflected psychological instability and especially loneliness and social isolation in one or both adults. The children in these troubled families were adversely affected both by the continued quarreling between the parents and by the psychological disturbance and lonely, unhappy feelings of one or both parents. For these families the divorce has failed, as had the marriage, and the children were bewildered, angry, and unable to understand or justify the continued stress within the family. Moreover, they had been deprived of the adult help children need in order to get on with the postdivorce family and to close the chapter of the divorce.

## The Visiting Relationship

We have made the erroneous assumption that the visiting relationship is continuous with the predivorce relationship between parent and child. Actually, the visiting relationship has no counterpart in the intact family. In a very real sense it is a new parent-child relationship that needs to be created and maintained following the divorce. We were startled to discover that there was no correlation between the pattern or frequency of the fathers' visits postdivorce and the predivorce father-child relationship. We were led by this discovery to recognize the complexity of the visiting relationship and some of the burdens it imposes on the adults and the children.

There are many reasons for the difficulties that attach to

developing the visiting relationship. Actually a parent-child relationship rests upon a continuity of contact within a thousand situations that mark each day and each successive year. The feelings of mutuality are forged out of a thousand moments of caring, of approval, or disapproval, of anger, of forgiveness. These feelings must all be compressed into the funnel that represents the visit. It is not easy to do. The logistics of caring for children, especially children of different ages, outside a home base are formidable for most adults. Parent and child often find themselves with no place to go and no idea what to do together. Furthermore the visit itself evokes the echoes of the dying marriage with its angers, its jealousies, its love, and its longing. People can behave dreadfully to each other at such times because they are stimulated by their memories. All of these combine to generate severe stress during the visit.

In addition visiting parents, whether fathers or mothers, who sometimes feel depressed and rejected after the divorce often feel more depressed after they visit their children. The parting from the children is particularly painful, and parents sometimes develop exacerbated depressed and unhappy feelings after a particularly loving visit. Visiting parents who feel guilty at having left a child in the care of a less competent parent, or who left the marriage to pursue a love affair, have trouble maintaining their visiting since their guilt is ignited anew following each visit. Thus, a great many factors affect the visiting relation that have little to do with the parents' attachment to his or her children. The parent who does not visit may love his or her children deeply, or he may not. The visiting pattern is not a good barometer of the father's interest.

Unfortunately, children do not understand the complexity of the factors that affect the father's visiting. They do understand with considerable generosity of spirit factors of geographical distance and financial constraints, but they do suffer very much when the parent that can visit fails to appear. Often they conclude that they are not only unloved but unlovable. It is this continued disappointment that erodes the youngsters' self-esteem so drastically.

The visiting relationship is fragile and needs encouragement and protection, particularly following the marital breakup when it is especially vulnerable to attrition. Therefore, court orders that restrict or direct visitation need to be considered and evaluated in their total impact on the child and the family. Visiting disputes touch multiple aspects of the family's life in the present and well into the future. Perhaps parents may behave differently if they can be helped to recognize that continuity in the visiting relationship and the sense of not feeling rejected by the visiting parent are central in the child's postdivorce psychological well-being.

Furthermore, if the goal is to establish and maintain a parenting relationship that will be helpful to the child in growing up, then the format of one weekend during each fortnight, which attorneys often designate as reasonable or expectable, is probably insufficient. Actually, most children below the age of nine prefer to see the visiting parent at least weekly and many children yearn for contact several times weekly where this is possible. Young children may suffer if the visits are infrequent because they fear that the visiting parent will disappear. The appearance of the father for the young child often acquires a jack-in-the-box quality, which may contribute to the symptomatic behaviors that custodial parents report following the visits. The presence of symptomatic behaviors following a visit may reflect the child's difficulty in returning and a fear of not seeing that parent again as much as a disturbance in the visiting relationship.

## Joint Custody

The increasing interest in the sharing of legal and physical custody of the children has reflected the growing recognition that the child can maintain his or her relationship with both parents after divorce. This model may indeed have wider applicability than has been previously recognized. In our own sample of 131 children, one-quarter of these youngsters had two committed parents during the failing and conflicted marriage. This group of parents who were able to maintain cooperation around the rearing and care of the children during the unhappy marriage provide a pool of likely candidates for joint custody following the divorce.

Generally, although we still lack a great deal of the information we need about all custodial arrangements including joint custody, it is reasonable to suggest that when parents are able to give their continued parenting priority in their lives and in their major decisions, where they are not in conflict over the children, where they are psychologically stable people, and where they both participated in the care of the children during the marriage, shared physical custody in the postdivorce family would appear as a viable option. Even these parents, however, are likely to need psychological counseling in order to set up arrangements appropriate to the individual personality and age of the children. Some children are able to deal better with change than others and such determination is difficult to make in the absence of an experience that could demonstrate the child's flexibility in changing routines. There is some evidence that elementary school age children are able to make use of joint custody arrangements, even those that involve changing from fathers' to mothers' homes within each week, but that adolescents and very young children find such changes stressful.

Joint custody is very taxing on parents. It requires a commitment to the children and a mutual respect for the other partner as a parent. It is important to note that the child's continuity with both parents can take place within the custody of the single parent if both parents recognize the child's need and right to continuity. The legal structure influences but clearly does not determine relationships within the family.

## The Angry Parent and the Child

The fighting between parents for the possession and presence of their children is likely to have tangled roots within the relation between the parents. Often the struggle for the children embodies the intense, unresolved conflicts and angers of the failed marriage. The struggle may reflect the parents' need for a supporter and ally in the marital battle. Beyond these issues, however, the fighting over the children can have its roots in the parents' dependence on the child. The intense dependence of parents on children, sometimes very young children, is not uncommon at the time of the divorce crisis. A considerable number of parents in our study indicated, too, that the physical presence of the children kept them going and effectively staved off depression and psychological disorganization. One of the issues that surfaced in regard to custody and visitation disputes was the parents' dread of being alone following the divorce.

Jealous, angry, or distraught parents cast their children into a great many roles in the marital battles ranging from that of audience whose presence appeared sometimes as a necessary backdrop to the parental fighting to that of committed battle allies. The children, in their turn, ranged in their participation from astonished, frightened observers to denunciatory Greek chorus and ultimately, in some instances, to full alignment with one parent against the other. The participaton of children in a relationship with one parent that was aimed at humiliating the other parent occurred particularly among those who were between nine and thirteen years old at the separation as well as among a considerable number of the adolescents. Approximately one-fifth of the 131 children in our study entered the fray actively within the family circle on the side of one parent, most often on the side of the parent who opposed the divorce.

## At What Age Should Children's Preferences Be Followed?

Although the wishes of children always merit careful consideration, our work suggests that children below adolescence are not reliable judges of their own best interest. The attitudes at the time of the divorce crisis may derive from the crisis itself and may be very much at odds with their usual feelings and inclinations.

The anger of the children at the parent whom they held responsible for the divorce, the eagerness of some to be coopted into the parental battling, and the willingness to take sides often against a parent to whom they were tenderly attached during the intact marriage were recurrent phenomena in the behavior of the nine- to twelve-year-olds. On the other side of the ledger and equally disconcerting in another way was the passionate commitment of some of the youngsters in this age group to rescue a depressed or suicidal parent. Their loyalty, while commendable, was sometimes to their own detriment when they took over the parenting of the unhappy parent long before they had the maturity or the capacity to do so. Furthermore, their propensity to split the parents into "good parent" and "bad parent," which was often at odds with the role of the respective parents over the years, led us to doubt their capacity to make informed judgment about their own best interests. These observations, together with the fact that several of the youngsters with the most passionate convictions at the time of breakup later came shamefacedly to regret their vehement statements at that time, have increased our misgivings about relying entirely on the expressed preferences below adolescence in deciding issues that arise in divorce related litigation.

## The Task of the Court

One task of the judge is to help the disputing family to establish the legal, psychological, and economic foundations for the postdivorce family, which can provide a solid base for the child during his or her growing up years. In fulfilling this complex task the court operates under certain grave constraints. The first constraint is that of time. The pressures of the court calendar limit the time and attention available for each family. In consideration of the complexity of the human issues presented by families brought before the court, the time is almost always insufficient.

An additional constraint is related to the timetable of the court intervention. We learn from crisis theory that there are critical times in the life of the family when relationships are in flux and are therefore more amenable to intervention and influence from the outside. This fluid time in the divorcing process is likely to be immediately after the relationships of the predivorce family have broken loose from their customary moorings. Thus, during the acute phase of the marital breakup—immediately after the separation, before positions have hardened and before decisions about the many issues the divorcing couple confront have been made—is the maximum time for intervention. The court calendar timetable operates independently of this major intervention timetable and thereby constrains the efficacy of the court intervention.

A third constraint on the judge is the lack or insufficient availability of the essential tools for intervention within the family dispute, namely, competent well-trained counselors in sufficient supply. The complex problems we have delineated are unlikely to resolve with a court order. It is unlikely that a court order can address the fragility of the emerging visiting relationship, and it is equally unlikely that an order can reduce friction between the marital partners. These complex psychological issues can be driven underground or they can be forced into another area, but there is no argument that suggests that the order itself would address the psychological conflict which underlies the legal dispute.

It seems evident that the task of the judge on the Family Court bench can only be done effectively with the help and appropriate deployment of well-trained counselors who can, at his instigation, move in at the appropriate time in the family dispute to alleviate tension and build towards the postdivorce family, which can indeed safeguard the best interests of the child. Unfortunately, both the powerful judge and the powerless child within the divorcing family lack the constituency that will create the structure they both need.

## References

Hetherington, E. Mavis. Effects of father absence on personality development in adolescent daughters. *Developmental Psychology*, 1972, *7*, 313-326.

Hetherington, E. Mavis, Cox, Martha, & Cox, Roger. Divorced fathers. *The Family Coordinator*, 1976, *25*, 417-428.

Hetherington, E. Mavis, Cox, Martha, & Cox, Roger. The aftermath of divorce. In J.H. Steven, Jr., & M. Matthews (Eds.), *Mother-child, father-child relations*. Washington, D.C.: National Association for Childhood Education, 1978.

Jacobson, D. The impact of marital separation/divorce on children: Parent child separation and child adjustment. *Journal of Divorce*, 1978, *4*, 341-360.

Kelly, J., & Wallerstein, J. The effects of parental divorce: Experiences of the child in early latency. *American Journal of Orthopsychiatry*, 1976, *1*(1), 20-32.

Kelly, J., & Wallerstein, J. Part-time parent, part-time child: Visiting after divorce. *Journal of Clinical Psychology*, 1977, *VI*, 51-54.

McDermott, J. Parental divorce in early childhood. *American Journal of Psychiatry*, 1968, *124*, 1424-1432.

McDermott, J. Divorce and its psychiatric sequelae in children. *Archives of General Psychiatry*, 1970, *23*, 421-427.

Wallerstein, J. Responses of the pre-school child to divorce: Those who cope. In M.F. McMillan and S. Henao (Eds.), *Child psychiatry: Treatment and research.* New York: Brunner/Mazel, 1977, p. 269-292.

Wallerstein, J., & Kelly, J. The effects of parental divorce: The adolescent experience. In E.J. Anthony & C. Koupernik, (Eds.), *The child in his family*, Vol. 3. New York: Wiley and Sons, 1974, p. 479-505.

Wallerstein, J., & Kelly, J. The effects of parental divorce: Experiences of the preschool child. *Journal of American Academy of Child Psychiatry*, 1975, *XIV*(3), 600-616.

Wallerstein, J., & Kelly, J. The effects of parental divorce: Experiences of the child in later latency. *American Journal of Orthopsychiatry*, 1976, *46*(2), 256-269.

Wallerstein, J., & Kelly, J. *Surviving the breakup: How children and parents cope with divorce.* New York: Basic Books, Inc., 1980.

Chapter 6

# CHILD CUSTODY DETERMINATION

SHELDON G. KIRSHNER

THE SATISFACTORY SETTLEMENT of disputes stemming from intrafamily relationships has presented one of the most serious challenges to the judicial process in our recent history. Little doubt remains that the most difficult of all these challenges has been child custody determination. Some of the more strident critics have even asserted that the breakdown in this field has demonstrated the total bankruptcy of the traditional dispute settlement techniques.[1] In order to understand the complexities of custody dispute resolution an understanding of legal concepts and awareness of law-related and social service factors is necessary. In addition to the presentation on child custody determination this chapter provides a legal-social service integrative approach and methodology as an alternative to the present system.

## HOW CUSTODY IS DETERMINED

When divorcing or separating parents determine they cannot agree as to custodial arrangements for their children, they usually contact a lawyer. At best, the attorney counsels his[2] client as to

This chapter contains materials reprinted from *Journal of Family Law*, 1978-79 *17*(2), with the permission of the editors.

[1]*E.g.*, Gardner, *Children of Divorce—Some Legal and Psychological Considerations*, VI(2) J. CLIN. CHILD PSYCHOLOGY 3 (1977); Henning & Oldham, *Children of Divorce: Legal and Psychological Crises*, VI(2) J. CLIN. CHILD PSYCHOLOGY 55 (1977).

[2]Reference to the male pronoun includes the female gender as well.

legal decisions, provides sensitivity concerning related life decisions, encourages reasonableness and negotiation where appropriate, and serves as an adversary representing his client's interests. At less than best, he serves solely as an adversary representing the declared interests of his client.

Among the factors that determine the tone of what follows contact with the attorneys are: the character and personality of the clients and the requests they make of their attorneys; each client's relations with his spouse; the character and personality of the attorneys and their prior relations, if any; and how each attorney views the strong and weak points of his client's case.

## The Law and its Application

If the attorneys as between themselves, and the clients as between themselves, cannot negotiate a custody resolution, then the matter goes to trial.[3] Typically, custody trials are unpleasant, with each attorney attempting to harass, humiliate, and degrade his client's spouse.

At the conclusion of the trial, and at all other times, as a matter of law, the "best interests of the child" determines who shall have custody.[4] Most states provide for this by statute,[5] often articulating the variables to be considered in a "best interests" determination: moral character and prudence of the parents[6]; age and sex of the child[7]; wishes of the parent[8]; wishes of the child[9]; interaction and interrelationship of the child with parents, siblings, and any

[3]Courts tend to accept any custodial arrangements concluded by the parties, although they are not bound to do so. *See* Ford v. Ford, 371 U.S. 187 (1962).

[4]The other party, absent the most extreme circumstances will have visitation. *E.g.*, Alaska Stat. §09.55.205 (Supp. 1979); Ariz. Rev. Stat. §25-332 (Supp. 1973); Fla. Stat. §61.13 (2b) (1979); Ind. Code §31-1-11.5-21(a)(Supp.1979); Minn. Stat. §518.17(1) (Supp.1979).

[5]*E.g.*, Fla. Stat. §61.3(f)(1979), *but see* Utah Code Ann. §30-3-10-(1969): "the court shall consider the best interests of the child and past conduct and demonstrated moral standards of each of the parties."

[6]*E.g.*, Code of Ala., Tit. §30-3-1(1975) moral fitness of the parents; Fla. Stat. §61.13 (1979).

[7]*E.g.*, Code of Ala., Tit. §34, 35(1958); Ind. Code 31-1-11.5-21(a)(Supp.1979).

[8]Virtually all states.

[9]Virtually all states.

other persons significantly affecting the child's best interests[10]; interest of the parties in, and attitude toward, the child[11]; love, affection, and other emotional ties existing between the parent and the child[12]; the capacity and disposition of the parents to give the child love, affection, and guidance and to continue education of the child[13]; mental and physical health of all individuals involved[14]; general health, welfare, and social behavior of the children[15]; causes for dissolution of the marriage or legal separation[16]; child's adjustment to his home, school, and community[17]; length of time child has lived in a stable, satisfactory environment, and the desirability of maintaining continuity[18]; the permanence, as a family unit, of the existing or proposed custodial home[19]; the cultural background of the child[20]; and the capacity and disposition of the parents to provide the child with food, clothing, medical care, or other remedial care.[21] Most statutes also contain a proviso that the court may consider whatever other information it deems relevant.[22]

Certain of these variables are given more weight than others,[23] the most stressed being which parent is best able to provide emotionally for the child.[24] This often overcomes evidence of sexual indiscretions, which may offend community morals.[25]

---

[10]*E.g.*, Colo. Rev. Stat. §14-10-124(1979); Ind. Code §31-1-11.5-21(a)(Supp.1979).

[11]*E.g.*, Ore. Rev. Stat. §107.137(b)(1979).

[12]*E.g.*, Fla. Stat. §61.13(a)(1979); Ore. Rev. Stat. §107.137(1979)(and other family members).

[13]E.g., Fla. Stat. §61.13(b)(1979); Minn. Stat. §518.17 (Supp. 1979).

[14]*E.g.*, Colo. Rev. Stat. §14-10-124(e)(1979).

[15]*E.g.*, Neb. Rev. Stat. §42-364(c)(1978).

[16]*E.g.*, Conn. Gen. Stat. §46(b)-56(b)(1978).

[17]*E.g.*, Fla. Stat. §61.13-3(H)(1979).

[18]*E.g.*, Fla. Stat. §61.13-3(D)(1979); Minn. Stat. §518.17(d)(Supp.1979); Ore. Rev. Stat. §107.137(c)(1975)(existing relationship).

[19]*E.g.*, Fla. Stat. §61.13-3(e)(1979).

[20]*E.g.*,Minn. Stat. §518.17(i)(Supp.1979).

[21]*E.g.*, Fla. Stat. §61.13-3(c)(1979).

[22]*E.g.*, Ill. Rev. Stat §Ch.40(1979).

[23]Oster, *Child Proceeding: A Study of Vague and Indefinite Standards*, 5 J. FAM. LAW 21 (1965).

[24]*Id.*

[25]*E.g.*, Howland v. Howland, 337 N.E. 2d 555 (1975) (Ind.); Watkins v. Watkins, 221 Ind. 293, 47 N.E.2d 606 (1943); *In re* Rice, 236 N.W.2d 40 (1975) (Iowa); *but see* Jarrett v. Jarrett, 440 N.E. 2d 421 (1979) (Ill.).

The preference of the child is also carefully considered when the child has a meaningful basis (age and maturity) for a preference, not the parent who provides the child with the most toys or fewest restrictions.[26] The consideration of either parent being better able to provide financially for the child is viewed in context of the Court's power to make support orders.[27]

In addition to the variables and their weighting, there are two presumptions that are at times present; first, that mothers are better parents than fathers[28]; second, if not always, then usually with respect to young children,[29] particularly female children.[30] These presumptions, which have been repudiated in a number of jurisdictions resulting in a greater likelihood that a father will get custody following litigation, are probably nonetheless often followed by trial judges.

There is presently a growing trend toward "joint custody," which has resulted in legislation in some states dictating a preference for a "joint custody" award unless the child's best interests indicate otherwise.[31] Although not uniformly defined, "joint custody" generally refers to both parents sharing responsibility for major decision making concerning the child, as well as his physical custody. This is differentiated from the traditional custody award wherein there is a custodial parent who has physical custody and who exercises authority over decision making concerning the child. The confines of custody awards are however quite broad and may include an *order* of "joint custody," with physical custody to one parent and visitation by the other, but with responsibility for major decision making concerning the child shared by both parents.

---

[26]*E.g.*, Pierce v. Pierce, 213 La. 475, 35 So. 2d 22 (1948); Edwards v. Edwards, 23 Ky. 1051, 64 S.W. 726 (1901), *but see* Ga. Code 30-127 (1962); A child of 14 has the right to determine the parent with whom he will live. Conclusive unless parent is determined not to be a fit and proper person to have custody.

[27]*E.g.*, Miss. Code Ann. §93-5-23(1979). (Virtually all states.)

[28]*E.g.*, Harper v. Harper, 229 S.E.2d 875 (Va.)(1976).

[29]*E.g.*, *supra* note 28; *but see* Likovich v. Likovich, 220 Pa. Super. 202, 287 A.2d 156 (1971): tender years doctrine will not control where mother is guilty of unchaste or improper conduct detrimental to the welfare of the child.

[30]*E.g.*, Ross v. Ross, 89 Colo. 536, 5 P.2d 246 (1931); *but see* Davis v. Davis, 254 S.W.2d 270 (1953)(Mo.).

[31]Cal. Civ. C. Sec. 4600.5 (1979).

The difficulty with the implementation of a "joint custody" *order* is that greater cooperation and flexibility between the parents is required than under the more typical custody arrangements. Divorcing parties usually are cool toward one another, at best, and although the author is aware of no definitive study, it seems likely that "joint custody" would be in the "best interests of the child" atypically rather than typically.

## Law-Related Factors

Having given consideration to the "best interests" legal concept, and in order to provide insights into what the outcome of a custody trial might be, the following factors must also be considered: the ability of the parties to sustain fees; the lawyers; the judge; where the litigation takes place; the witnesses, including the parties and the children; and the facts.

### *The Ability of the Parties to Pay Fees*

Custody litigation is time-consuming and fees are usually considerable. Examples of exceptions, with respect to fees, are *pro bono* work on behalf of indigents as public service, and nonprofit legal services. Custody litigation usually requires thirty to 100 or more hours of a lawyer's time. Unexceptionally, custody work is performed by attorneys who charge substantially and require nonrefundable retainers to cover twenty hours or more of their time. Attorney fees vary depending upon the skill and reputation of the attorney, and complexity of the case, and the locale. The fees of an individual of experience in a major metropolitan area might be twice per hour of that of his small town coequal; reflecting the disparity in overhead expense and cost of living. In either setting, lesser experienced attorneys may charge as little as half the fees of their more experienced and well-known counterparts.

As for families who cannot afford fees, they are often required to use their own resources in affecting whatever custody determinations are made. These may include Court sanctioned or informal agreements; resulting from discussions, various types of threats or harassments including child snatching, or promises of reward. If one spouse can afford fees and the other not, the attorney fees of the spouse without necessary finances may be assessed in whole or part against the more able counterpart.

### *The Judge*

As law-trained professionals, judges bring legal expertise to the task of custody determination. Although rarely social service trained, they are required to evaluate evidence relating to social service matters, and judges traditionally report that custody decisions are the most difficult to make.[32]

As individuals, each judge brings to each case a unique complexity of the following qualities: intelligence, experience, wisdom, interest in the matter before him, and concern for the particular parties involved, impartial and judicial temperament, attitudes about social norms, prior experience with counsel and parties, and legal expertise. Further complicating their decision making, they bring to each case certain philosophical, sociological, and psychological preconceptions concerning appropriate behavior, family relationships, and the needs of children at various stages in their development.

### *Where the Trial Takes Place*

Due to the prevalence of child snatching and, additionally, the parties moving to differing locales, what follows is a discussion of the "local counsel rule." The rule states that when a lawyer is to try a case outside of his own locale, and always when he is in another state, he should hire a local lawyer to assist him. This is not, so the author believes, to give local lawyers more business, but rather to even up the contest. For example, when a lawyer comes from a large metropolitan area to appear before a small town judge, he is considered an outsider. He is often regarded as a "city slicker," and his racial, ethnic, or religious background may weigh heavily against him. When the local attorney appears before the judge, he may carry the reputation of personal and professional integrity. This is a difficult matter for an outsider to

[32] *E.g.*, Levin, *Guardian Ad Litem in a Family Court*, 34 MD. L. REV. 341 (1974).

overcome and is made doubly difficult if the local lawyer represents a local client and the non-local lawyer represents a non-local client. At times getting local counsel can be problematic. The author can recall not being able to find recommended counsel within twenty-five miles of where a case was heard, because of the stigma of representing an outsider against a local person whose family was well regarded. A corollary to the foregoing is that an attorney, particularly in a small town, will tend not to want to represent an action directed against another attorney, that is, where the opposing attorney's client is an attorney.

### *Credibility of Witnesses*

Who is to be believed and to what extent is critical to the determination of facts. It is of little consequence that a witness is testifying truthfully if he appears to the judge to be biased, unsure of his facts, or dishonest. The expert witness, who is usually a psychiatrist or psychologist, may be excellent at therapy or diagnosis. If, however, he does not testify convincingly or is less convincing than an opposing expert, or his credentials are less impressive than those of his counterpart, the weight and credibility of his testimony will be diminished. Here, too, experts who testify regularly before a judge, and who are credible, may be given an edge by the Court. However, as social service professionals can frequently be found to bolster opposite sides of conflicting positions or to testify in mitigation of what would normally appear to be outrageous behavior, judges also take this into consideration.

### *The Facts*

The facts, as any individual knows them, are not the keystone to a custody determination; but rather what they appear to be to the judge after testimony, cross-examination, and argument. Perspective, extenuating circumstances, and outright contradiction often change the contour of "facts," particularly in the hands of a skilled attorney and credible witnesses.

## Difficult Cases

The traditional tool employed by courts in resolving difficult factual questions so that the best interests of the child may be served is the *guardian ad litem.*[33] The *guardian ad litem,* or attorney[34] representing the child, aids the court by gathering information and then presenting evidence and/or making recommendations as to custody and visitation.[35] A number of states by statute provide for the discretionary appointment of a *guardian ad litem* or attorney to represent the child,[36] although courts have the inherent power to appoint *guardians.*[37] The statutes provide for a fairly wide range of activities open to the *guardian ad litem* in carrying out his responsibilities.[38] He may *inter alia* interview the parties, the children, neighbors, or relatives; examine school records; or request a social work or psychological evaluation.[39]

Is there a need for the *guardian ad litem* to be an attorney? A legal proceeding is a highly specialized form of dispute resolution. There are many rules that govern the conduct of all concerned, and not to be represented by one who is expert at those rules is to be at a disadvantage. The *guardian ad litem,* therefore, who represents the child should be an attorney.

---

[33]*E.g.,* Carle v. Carle, 503 P.2d 1050 (1972)(Alaska); Minn. Stat. §518.165 (Supp. 1979); N.H. Rev. Stat. Ann § 458.17-a (Supp. 1979); W.S.A. 1.01 §247.045 (Supp. 1979).

[34]*E.g.,* Ariz. Rev. Stat. § 25-321 (Supp. 1979); Colo. Rev. Stat. § 14-10-116 (1979); Mont. Rev. Codes Ann. § 48-324 (Supp. 1977); Ore. Rev. Stat. § 107.425 (2) (b) (1979); Wash. Rev. Code § 26.09.110 (Supp. 1979). Most *guardians ad litem* are attorneys.

[35]*E.g.,* "The *guardian ad litem* shall advise the court with respect to custody and visitation." Minn. Stat. 518.165 (Supp. 1979); "counsel shall be heard upon all matters pertaining to the interests of . . . the . . . child or children, including the custody." Conn. Gen. Stat. § 46 (b)-54 (Supp. 1979); Iowa Code § 598.12 (Supp. 1979).

[36]*Supra* notes 31 and 32.

[37]Jenkins v. Whyte, 62 Md. 427 (1884); *cf.* Bush v. Linthicum, 59 Md. 344 (1883); Tatum v. Wright, 139 Md. 20, 28-29, 114 A. 836, 839 (1921); *see* Wendland v. Wendland, 29 Wis. 2d 145, 138 N.W.2d 185 (1965); Barth v. Barth, 12 Ohio Misc. 141, 225 N.E.2d 866 (1967); Zinni v. Zinni, 103 R.I. 417, 238 A.2d 373 (1968); Utah Copper Co. v. Indus. Commission, 57 Utah 118, 193 P. 24 (1920).

[38]*E.g.,* Ky. Rev. Stat. § 403.090 (3) (Supp. 1976) (friend of the court); Mo. Rev. Stat. § 452.390 (Supp. 1979).

[39]*E.g.,* Mo. Rev. Stat. § 452.390 (1976).

## LEGAL SOCIAL SERVICE INTEGRATIVE APPROACH AND METHODOLOGY

Recognizing that a custody decision is based on the best interests of the child, the approach begins with the proposition that a child has three sets of interests: emotional, educational and developmental, and economic. It is asserted that these interests may be in conflict with those of the parents or other potential guardians and that consequently there needs to be independent representation of the child through a *guardian ad litem* who is an attorney. It is further asserted that the *guardian* is competent to evaluate only the child's economic interests and that social service professionals are required to evaluate his emotional, and educational and developmental, interests. The guardian, it is recommended, should be responsible for seeing that there is an evaluation of the appropriate interests by the social service professionals, followed by their recommendations as to all matters relating to custody (including visitation) and that he evaluate the economic interests and recommend thereon. These evaluations are to be presented by the guardian to the court in the form of a Child Environmental Impact Statement. This is a document (or the evidentiary basis therefore, as required) which indicates the probable impact on the child, based on the evaluation of his interests, of a change from his present environment to the environment to be provided by each of the proposed guardians. A Model Child Custody Act is provided below, as is a Model Child Environmental Kidnapping Act, which is designed to serve as a deterrent to child snatching.

### *Emotional interests*

The child has an interest both in his own emotional health and stability and in the emotional health and stability of the parent awarded custody.[40] The literature indicates that children whose parents divorce or separate typically experience emotional reactions such as denial, depression, grief, guilt, rage, and anxiety as a reflection of the initial impact of the separation of their parents

---

[40] *E.g.*, Fla. Stat. § 61.13 (g) (1979); Minn. Stat. § 518.17 (Supp. 1979).

and the loss of the substantial parentage of either their father or mother.[41] They often require outpatient therapy.[42] This is followed by the problems of the development of, and adjustment to, a life-style that recognizes the parental and custodial arrangement adopted by the parents.[43] As 80% of divorced parents remarry, usually within three years,[44] there is then the adjustment to the remarriage of either or both the custodial or noncustodial parent,[45] with the attendant problems of stepparents and stepsibs.[46] Finally, there is the need to adjust to the confrontations surrounding petitions for changes in custody and visitation rights or their enforcement as well as child snatching and the use of the child as a weapon against, or to spy on, the other parent.[47] The subject of the psychological impact of divorce and separation is further covered in the chapter by Judith Wallerstein.

### *Educational and Developmental Interests*

The interests of the child require the better educational and developmental environment. It seems hardly necessary to assert the importance of education in obtaining social and economic benefits, particularly in these times of greater social mobility and professional opportunity for women and minorities. The interests of the child also entitle him to develop in an environment that will best prepare him for eventual entry and participation in an adult society wherein he is likely to have a family and children of

---

[41] *E.g.*, Grollman & Grollman, *How to Tell Children About Divorce*, VI (2) J. CLIN. CHILD PSYCHOLOGY 35 (1977); Dlugokinski, note 43 *infra*; Kelly & Wallerstein, *The Effects of Parental Divorce: Experiences of the Child in Early Latency*, 46 AMER. J. ORTHOPSYCHIATRY 20 (1976).

[42] *E.g.*, Kalter, *Children of Divorce in Outpatient Psychiatric Populations*, 47 AMER. J. ORTHOPSYCHIATRY 40 (1977).

[43] *E.g.*, Dlugokinski, *A Developmental Approach to Coping with Divorce*, VI (2) J. CLIN. CHILD PSYCHOLOGY 27 (1977).

[44] Westoff, L.A. *Two-Time Winners*, NEW YORK TIMES MAGAZINE, Aug. 10, 1975, at 10-13.

[45] *E.g.*, Thies, *Beyond Divorce: The Impact of Remarriage on Children*, VI (2) J. CLIN. CHILD PSYCHOLOGY 59 (1977).

[46] *Id.*

[47] *E.g.*, Kelly & Wallerstein, *supra* note 41, at 29.

his own. In the required growing up process, this environment should provide a positive resource through the various stages of his development, helping him through the difficulties of growing up as well as helping him to understand his changing relationships with others and his changing role in society.

There are two components of primary importance in the education environment. One is the school and peer environment and the other is the family environment. Concerning the school environment, inquiry must be made as to the quality of the school the child will be attending with each of the proposed custodians. For example, is one a school well known for its quality of education where many of its graduates, if it is a high school, go on to college, and the other not? Also important is whether the child has demonstrated educational abilities and motivations such that transferring him to a relatively poor school would have a deleterious effect. Concerning the family environment, the importance of the child's education to each potential guardian must be assessed.

"Developmental" implies growing up.[48] Each stage of life has its peculiar problems,[49] and one of the parental functions is to aid the child in dealing with these problems in the growing up process.[50] A knowledge of the day-to-day relationship between the child and potential guardian is therefore important in assessing the prospective developmental impact of that individual. Any preference of the child for a parent, with an understanding of the basis and implications of that preference, is also of importance.

PROPER USE OF PERSONNEL: The application of facts to rules of law is a standard task of the attorney. Unfortunately, as a number of law review articles have pointed out,[51] the basis for com-

---

[48]*E.g.*, see R. JOHNSON & G. MEDINNUS, CHILD PSYCHOLOGY: BEHAVIOR AND DEVELOPMENT 263 (2d. ed. 1968); L. LONGSTRETH, PSYCHOLOGICAL DEVELOPMENT OF THE CHILD (1969).

[49]*E.g.*, J. COLEMAN, ABNORMAL PSYCHOLOGY AND MODERN LIFE 14 (3d ed. 1964); *see* G. CAPLAN, PREVENTION OF MENTAL DISORDERS IN CHILDREN (1961).

[50]*E.g.*, *see* L. LONGSTRETH, *supra* note 48; R. JOHNSON & G. MEDINNUS, *supra* note 48.

[51]*E.g.*, Levin, *Guardian Ad Litem in a Family Court*, 34 MD. L. REV. 341, 363 (1974); Foster & Freed, *Child Custody (Part II)*, 39 N.Y.U. L. REV. 615 (1964).

prehending meaningful social work and psychological facts exceeds the training and experience of the attorney and requires psychologists and social workers. Paradoxically, under the present system the screening as to serious psychological impairment is by the *guardian ad litem* or judge who uses the social service professional to validate or invalidate his own intuitions or conclusions. Through this method, some of the most dramatically disturbed parents and children are probably detected, the less bizarre but as profoundly disturbed are probably not. There have been suggestions[52] that what is required is an attorney with a background in child development, or psychoanalytic child development. This is both wide[53] and short of the mark. Exposure to a few social work or child psychology courses does not provide the basis for conducting a professional evaluation in the child mental health area.

### *Economic Interests*

The child's economic interests other than in immediate support generally require long-range planning. A college education is costly. A child may already have shown academic abilities and interests, or he may be young, with his educational background, abilities, and plans undeveloped. Whenever possible, the financing of his higher education should, under these circumstances, be protected through trusts, insurance, and other devices. If the sale of the family home, for example, produces a profit of $36,000 and a traditional agreement splits the money between the parents with an understanding that the father will help to pay the child's college expenses, the child may eventually be left to his own devices. This is particularly true if the child is young and the mother remarries, as the father may attempt to rid himself of responsibility and hope that the ex-wife's current husband will

---

[52]*E.g., see* Levin, *supra* note 51, citing Sadoff, *Civil Law and Psychiatry: New Dimensions*, 56 A.B.A. J. 165 (1970).

[53]It is very questionable whether a large majority (or even a majority) of the social science community, particularly psychologists, would agree that a background solely in psychoanalytic child development was what one needed to evaluate children (What about the evaluation of parents?).

assume it. This may also be very much the case where visitation has been infrequent or has been hampered by the mother attempting to get at the father through the child, so that the emotional ties between father and child are weak. In the division of the property, some might be split three ways instead of two.

A second important area of economic interest requiring planning involves children who have substantial medical, dental, psychiatric, physical, or cosmetic disabilities where substantial funds may be required to address these difficulties. As with the child's education, protection should be afforded when possible.

## Related Matters

### *Motives and Interests of Parents*

In most cases, the parents decide matters of custody between themselves. The parties, through their attorneys, present their agreement as a *fait accompli* and it is generally accepted. There are, however, a number of possible conflicts between the motives or interests of parents and the best interests of their children.

As the child is frequently viewed consciously or subconsciously as an extension of the individual,[54] a parent may seek custody of the child for narcissistic reasons.

Custody by one parent, particularly over a child who is the favorite of the other parent, may be sought in order to punish the other parent.[55] The problem may not come to the attention of the attorneys or the court but may be handled as an intrafamily matter with threats of recrimination and offers of property settlement as part of the scenario.[56]

Custody to the mother generally means for her a higher support figure, while custody to the father means a lower, if any, support figure.[57] It is not uncommon, therefore, for fathers to contest custody formally or as an intrafamily matter in order that they may withdraw from the contest in exchange for the mother

---

[54]*E.g.*, O FENICHEL, THE PSYCHOANALYTIC THEORY OF NEUROSES (1945).

[55]Personal communications with psychotherapists treating divorcing parents and their children, 1974-80, Chicago, Illinois; Personal communications with attorneys practicing matrimonial law, 1976-80 Chicago, Illinois, and elsewhere.

[56]*Supra* note 55.

[57]*Supra* note 55.

agreeing to less support.[58] A proposed large settlement, or substantial item of property such as a house, may be the factor determining whether custody is contested.[59]

The mother, to prevent her children from thinking she does not care for them,[60] may attempt to obtain custody even though she feels she is not the better parent and in fact does not want custody.

The father may believe that he is the better custodial parent but that he will not be able to meet his career responsibilities and properly care for his children if he is awarded custody. He may, therefore, indicate that the mother is the better parent.[61]

### *Child Environmental Impact Statement (CEIS)*

A mandatory CEIS (see Model Child Custody Act below) would help to alleviate groundless petitions for changes in custody. If each jurisdiction required a copy of the most recent CEIS, or testimony as to its recommendations and the basis therefore, to be placed in a child's file and then compared with a new or updated CEIS, the presence or absence of meaningful change in the child's emotional, educational and developmental, and economic interests would be more readily apparent. Part of the present problem is that there is no meaningful, if any, record for the court to examine in determining whether subsequent changes have warranted a change in custody.

### *Criminal Sanctions Against Child Snatching*

The problem of child snatching within a jurisdiction does not present the difficulties that removal of the child to a second jurisdiction presents, because of a court's contempt powers over individuals within its jurisdiction. There may be reluctance on the part of a second jurisdiction to provide criminal sanction against individuals who unlawfully remove children to that jurisdiction. Perhaps this is because the second jurisdiction often awards custody to the removing party. To then provide criminal

---

[58]*Supra* note 55.
[59]*Supra* note 55.
[60]*Supra* note 55.
[61]*Supra* note 55.

sanction for the removal would appear to create a conflict with its decrees concerning the welfare of the child. A Federal Child Environmental Kidnapping Statute, presented below, might therefore be desirable. Parents have historically been excluded from liability under the present Federal Kidnapping Statutes.[62] Very recent legislation has addressed this matter, but its effectiveness is currently unknown.[63]

## MODEL ACTS

### Model Child Custody Act

At the inception of every divorce, separation, and custody matter, the Child Environmental Impact Statement and Federal Child Environmental Kidnapping Act are required to be explained to each of the parties by their attorneys. If they are not represented by counsel, the court shall assume the task.

GUARDIAN AD LITEM

1. In all cases wherein the custody of a child is to be determined or where there is a petition for a change or modification in custody, or where visitation rights are applied for or there is a petition requesting a modification of visitation rights, a *guardian ad litem* who is an attorney shall be appointed on behalf of the minor child.

2. The *guardian ad litem* shall see that a Child Environmental Impact Statement (CEIS) is prepared or updated. He shall prepare those aspects of the CEIS that deal with the economic interests of the child. He shall further see that the emotional, and educational and developmental, interests of the child are evaluated by a qualified social service agency and that the social service agency prepares those aspects of the CEIS that relate to their evaluation.

3. The CEIS shall be presented to the counsel for the parties who may stipulate either as to the facts or recommendations contained therein or indicate with particularity which facts

---

[62] 18 U.S.C.A. 1201 (Supp. 1977); Brooks v. United States, 199 F 2d 336 (4th Cir. 1952).

[63] 28 U.S.C.A. 1738A (Supp. 1981), and the application of 18 U.S.C.A. 1073 (Supp. 1981).

and/or recommendations they dispute. To the extent that the facts and recommendations are not stipulated to, counsel for the parties shall first present expert testimony on the matter in dispute. The *guardian ad litem* shall cross-examine as necessary. The *guardian ad litem* shall then present the testimony of those who prepared the report relative to matter in dispute, which testimony shall be subject to cross-examination by the parties. The *guardian ad litem* shall make motions, present testimony, and engage in other activities as necessary.

4. The CEIS shall remain in the court's files as shall a copy of all testimony concerning parts of it that were disputed.

5. The costs of the *guardian ad litem* and CEIS shall be assessed against the proposed custodians in proportion to their abilities to pay. To the extent that they are unable to pay, the court shall assess fees against the county.

QUALIFIED SOCIAL SERVICE AGENCY

A qualified social service agency is one whose members are, or are operating under the direction and supervision of, a State licensed psychologist or Board Certified psychiatrist and a State licensed social worker.

CHILD ENVIRONMENTAL IMPACT STATEMENT (CEIS)

In this report produced in part by the *guardian ad litem* and in part by a qualified social service agency, the social service agency shall evaluate the emotional, and educational and developmental, interests of the child in terms of the various proposed custodial environments and based on its evaluations make custody and custody-related recommendations, including alternatives not suggested by the parties. The social service agency shall indicate the factual basis for its recommendations. The social service professional in charge shall discuss the CEIS with the parties as it relates to the emotional, and educational and developmental, interests of the child, to attempt to minimize the detrimental impact of the divorce and/or separation. The *guardian ad litem* shall evaluate the economic interests of the child and make recommendations concerning those interests. He shall indicate the factual basis for his recommendations.

## Federal Child Environmental Kidnapping Act

The willful seizing, confining, inveigling, decoying, or carrying away of a minor under the age of fourteen resulting in the transport of that minor in interstate commerce,

A. by a (1) parent adjudicated not to have custodial rights in the the state most recently determining custody, or whose custodial rights in that state are such that removal to another state is unauthorized; or
(2) former legal custodian adjudicated not to have custody rights in the state most recently determining custody; or
(3) de facto custodian for a continuous prior period of six months or more; or
(4) relative of child within the following categories: grandparents, aunts and uncles

B. without a court order from the court in which custody rights were most recently adjudicated permitting such transport or written consent of the most recently adjudicated custodian, shall result in imprisonment for forty-five days.

It shall be a defense that (1) the minor was taken in interstate commerce for reasons of medical, including psychiatric, emergency and placed under the medical care of a licensed medical professional or psychologist within twelve hours and (2) that the custodial parent or his attorney or the *guardian ad litem* for the child was notified, with twenty-four hours of the abduction, of the whereabouts of the child by the person(s) referred to in (A).

It shall be no defense that subsequent to the child being transported in interstate commerce a custody adjudication resulted in custody being awarded to the person referred to in (A).

## Screening Alternative to Model Child Custody Act

While it is believed that the mandatory CEIS is the most meaningful way to deal with the child custody problem, it may be politically too difficult to realize in the form of legislation. Many people may find unacceptable the notion that parents are incapable of providing for the best interests of their children. This is not to suppose that a custody arrangement operating in the best interests of the child will not be concluded initially by the parents but rather that such positive arrangements will be haphazard at best. Some minimal scrutiny would therefore seem not only desirable but perhaps even required by fourteenth and first amendment rights.[64]

STAGE ONE: In those cases wherein there is no custody dispute or apparent need for independent representation of the child as determined by the court, there should be an interview by a court or private mental health specialist with each proposed guardian and the child (where reasonable, e.g., not infants). This serves two functions: (1) to determine whether the custody and visitation arrangements proposed raise reasonable questions as to whether they might be detrimental to the welfare of the child; (2) if they do not, to discuss with the parents the probable detrimental impact of the divorce and separation on their children and ways of reducing and dealing with that impact.

STAGE TWO: When the proposed arrangements raise reasonable questions as referred to above, a CEIS should be developed.

The weakness of the Screening Alternative is that much of the flexibility that the mandatory CEIS provides, in terms of alternatives the parents had not considered, is eliminated. Subtle but important factors concerning the relationship between each parent and each child are not examined, and their impact for the present and the future not dealt with.

An inherent weakness, in terms of acceptance by a state legislature, of a mandatory CEIS or the Screening Alternative is that if either is accepted it must be available to indigents, with costs being borne by the State.

## EXAMPLE CUSTODY MATTERS ANALYZED

The following fact patterns are analyzed first using the traditional approach followed by an analysis using the legal-social service integrative approach and methodology.

### Fact Pattern I

A family of four presents itself to the court, the parents with

[64]U.S. CONST., amend. I, XIV.

counsel having determined between themselves all matters of custody, child support, alimony, and property settlement. (Traditional analysis: the Court adopts the agreements of the parties in its orders.)

VARIATION: Same as above in all respects except that each parent wants custody, contending that he is the better parent but conceding that the other parent is a good parent.

### *Fact Pattern I Analyzed*

Applying the traditional approach to Fact Pattern I (Variation), a *guardian ad litem* might be appointed and would at best interview the parents and the children, and visit their home. He would find both parents to be reasonable people concerned about their children and adequate as parents. He would also find that both children would prefer to be with their mother and would probably base his recommendation on that fact: custody to the mother, reasonable visitation to the father.

Application of the legal-social service integrative approach and methodology to this fact pattern might result in the following abridged Child Environmental Impact Statement (CEIS):

EMOTIONAL & EDUCATIONAL & DEVELOPMENTAL INTERESTS

Family: Robert A., Father; Age 42, Attorney
Janice A., Mother; Age 35, Nurse
Alan; Age 14
Susan; Age 13

The following psychological instruments might be administered and evaluated by a state licensed psychologist:

Personal Opinion Inventory (Zaks)
Thematic Apperception Test
Draw a Person Test Battery
Rorschach Ink Blot Test
Weschler Adult Intelligence Scale (Weschler Intelligence Scale for Children)
Bender Visual Motor Gestalt Test
Standard Illusions Test
Graphic Tridimensionality Test (Zaks)

A complementary social work screening would be supplied by a state-licensed social worker, including home visits and the evaluation of present and potential school environments. The psychologist would interview each family member and discuss the results of his testing and interviews and the social work screening with them.

*Recommendation:* Although the father and son would very much like to relate well to one another, they do not. There are certain conflicts that if resolved at this time will aid them considerably in ensuring improved relations between them for the long-term future. Failure to resolve them at this time will make their relations more distressing and their problems more difficult to resolve. This has been discussed with them and they have agreed to participate in counseling. Toward this end it is recommended that Alan be placed in the custody of his father with the understanding that he maintain their Chicago suburban home until Alan finishes high school. The father has also agreed to change his work schedule so that he can have dinner with his son and be available in the early evening hours as well. A room in their home is to be set aside as a study. It is further recommended that if the foregoing is implemented, their situation should be reevaluated after six months.

It is recommended that Susan, who is an eighth grade, second semester student complete the balance of the semester in the school where she is enrolled and then transfer to a private high school with an excellent reputation located in the downtown Chicago area, where her mother plans to reside. Maternal custody should begin in August.

As Susan may have difficulty meeting girls her own age until school begins, it is recommended that she stay in the family home under the custody of her father during the remaining summer months. Until that time she should be permitted to stay with her mother as often and for as long as she likes and every effort should be made to accommodate her wishes in this regard.

During all the above periods it is recommended that the parent without custody be permitted liberal visitation.

ECONOMIC INTERESTS PREPARED BY A MEMBER OF THE ILLINOIS BAR: The family assets have been evaluated and it has been determined that the family, in addition to having approximately $40,000 in equity in a home in Highland Park, Illinois, has approximately $54,000 in cash and stocks.

*Recommendations:*

1. That a sum of $12,000 be placed in trust for each child to be used for his college education with accumulation of interest on the $24,000 in trust.

2. The existing life insurance on father, presently in effect with death benefits of $100,000 and with Janice A. listed as beneficiary, should be changed to list each child as a beneficiary in the amount of $50,000. An amount sufficient to pay the premium for the eight years until Susan is twenty-one, $9,210, should be placed in trust for that purpose with the interest on that sum to pour over into the children's educational trust on equal shares.

3. Health insurance, of not less coverage than is now in force, should be maintained by the father for each child until each reaches the age of twenty-one.

4. Funds for parts one and two of this recommendation should be derived from other assets, such as cash and stocks, and not through the sale of the house.

## Fact Pattern II

Husband (H) and Wife (W) have two children aged nine and twelve and live in Illinois, County A.

(1) June, 1974: W takes both children and moves with her boyfriend to County B.

(2) September 1974: H, having located W, files a *habeas corpus* petition[65] in County B and requests custody of the children. W appears, contests H's petition and also requests custody. October, 1974: The court appoints a *guardian ad litem* on behalf of the children. November 1974: The *guardian* recommends, and the court so orders, that custody be given to W with liberal visitation for H. No report is filed by the *guardian*.

(3) January 1975: W, having decided that she needed some time away from the children to "get herself together," turns the children over to H. March 1975: H files for divorce in County A, wherein he resides, and requests a change in custody to himself.

---

[65]An action in which it is alleged that someone is improperly detained and wherein the relief sought is that the person detained be produced.

The Sheriff presents W with the petition for divorce and change of custody, but she does not subsequently appear in person or through an attorney at the trial and her whereabouts are unknown. October 1975: The trial: the court grants H a divorce and awards him sole custody.

(4) November 1975: In October, 1975, W having married her boyfriend, moved with him to Lincoln, Nebraska intending permanent residence therein. She now returns to Illinois and petitions the court in County A to permit the children to stay with her over the summer months. This is contested by H. December 1975: The court reappoints the *guardian.* January 1976: The *guardian* recommends, and the court orders, that W's request be granted if she posts a $3,000 bond guaranteeing return of the children. No report is filed by the *guardian.*

(5) February 1976: W, unwilling to wait or post bond, removes the children from school and immediately boards a plane for Lincoln, Nebraska.

(6) March 1976: W petitions the Nebraska court for a change in custody,[66] claiming that the children had not been properly cared for by H, who she testifies is, and has been for many years, an alcoholic. She alleges that while in his custody her children often went to school without breakfast, unclean, with inadequate and dirty clothes, and were generally without supervision during the evening hours and on weekends. She also alleges that the children have been the subject of unusually severe corporal punishment by their father. The children, under duress from their mother, affirm through false testimony. He is personally served with notice in Illinois, but being without funds and feeling that the situation is hopeless, does not participate in the proceedings. May 1976: W is granted sole custody of the children.

(7) June 1976: The older child runs away to live with his grandparents in Wisconsin. The grandparents refuse to return

[66]In virtually all states, custody awards are not usually modified unless there has been a "material" change of circumstances affecting the best interests of the child. In situations where more than one state may have an interest in the outcome, the widely adopted Uniform Child Custody Jurisdiction Act provides rules to help determine which state should decide custody. There are, however, U.S. Constitutional requirements such as *full faith and credit* that must be considered before applying the UCCJA (U.S. CONST. art. IV).

the child to either parent, and in September 1976, petition for his custody. October 1976: Both parents are served in their respective states, although neither responds personally or through counsel. The court appoints a *guardian* to see that an investigation is conducted and to make recommendation to the court. November 1976: The *guardian* recommends custody to the grandparents, and the court so orders.

(8) February 1977: W files a *habeas corpus* petition in Wisconsin seeking to enforce the Nebraska decree, which awarded her custody. H, having gotten some money together, files similar actions in Wisconsin and Nebraska seeking to enforce the Illinois decree, which awarded him custody. March 1977: The Wisconsin court denies W's petition, relying on the Supreme Court decision in *May v. Anderson*,[67] and indicating that the Nebraska decree was not entitled to enforcement (through full faith and credit) in a sister state as to H or the grandparents since the Nebraska court lacked *in personam* jurisdiction[68] over the parties. Concerning H's petitions, both the Nebraska and Wisconsin courts hold that since there was *in personam* jurisdiction over W in Illinois, the Illinois decree was final. The Courts also hold, however, that under the Supreme Court decisions in *Halvey v. Halvey*[69] and *Kovacs v. Brewer*,[70] the decree was entitled to enforcement (pursuant to full faith and credit) as to the original facts only. As the presence of new material facts would provide a basis for readjudication in Illinois, and as such facts are present, the Illinois decree is not enforceable. It is a standoff.

### *Fact Pattern II Analyzed*

The following differences could be predicted from the use of the CEIS and enforcement of the Child Environmental Kidnapping Act at the various stages of Fact Pattern II:

Point (2). A CEIS would be developed. It is possible in the development of the Impact Statement that the likelihood of

---

[67] 345 U.S. 528 (1953).

[68] Authority to order them to do or not to do something (i.e., to relinquish physical control over children).

[69] 330 U.S. 610 (1947).

[70] 356 U.S. 604 (1958).

future problems would be foreseen and various alternatives discussed with the parties. Some or all of the later problems that occur in the fact pattern might therefore have been eliminated or ameliorated.

Point (3). The CEIS is transferred to the court wherein the divorce proceedings are taking place. It is examined to determine whether the father should now be awarded custody (March 1975).

Point (4). In November 1975, when W appears requesting reasonable visitation, the CEIS is examined. It is updated if there is a claim that conditions have changed so that W should no longer be entitled to visitation.

Point (5). W is imprisoned for forty-five days. The children are returned to H following W's apprehension and remain with him during her imprisonment.

Point (6). A copy of the CEIS will immediately be required by and sent to the Nebraska court for their examination. The false claims of the mother will be exposed and the children will be spared giving false testimony against their father. The Nebraska court might determine it has the less significant contacts and refuse jurisdiction.

Point (7). The most recent version of the CEIS is sent to Wisconsin. It is updated, then being a relatively complete picture of what has transpired since June 1974 and considered by the court.

## SUMMARY

Child custody determination is a phenomenon that addresses human relations and social service problems in a legal forum. It is therefore a difficult matter. Since desirable results require flexibility, skill, patience, and good will of all concerned, much less than one might hope for, is often the outcome.

In this chapter the author has tried to provide an overview of child custody determination. Legal concepts and law-related and social service factors are considered, and examples of custody matters are presented and analyzed using the traditional methods and a proposed legal-social service integrative approach and methodology.

Chapter 7

# CROSS-CULTURAL PERCEPTIONS OF CHILDREN'S RIGHTS

TERU L. MORTON, RICHARD A. DUBANOSKI, AND DANIEL D. BLAINE

IN 1959, THE GENERAL ASSEMBLY of the United Nations unanimously adopted its Declaration of the Rights of the Child. This declaration called for international recognition of such basic human rights as entitlement from birth to a name and nationality; the right to adequate nutrition, housing, recreation, and medical services; the right to free and compulsory education; and the right to freedom from neglect, cruelty, and exploitation. The adoption of this Declaration was a remarkable step in the child rights movement, for it represented international acknowledgement of children and their rights and needs.

Although representatives of widely different countries did agree *in principle* on what children's rights should be, Burgess (1979) has pointed out that the emphases of specific societies might be quite different. Thus, in some societies, the emphasis may be on political or individual rights, such as equal protection under the law or trial by jury. Other societies may emphasize economic and social human rights to a greater extent, including the right to employment or adequate standards of living. Although one may argue about the different needs and rights of

We are grateful to Cindy Ikenaga and Lynn Yoshida for their contributions as research assistants. This research was supported by Grant 21/C/79/350/F/727/B/314 from the University of Hawaii.

children from culture to culture, it appears that the needs of children throughout all countries are still unmet. The daily hunger of some children around the world is one example of the unkept promises of the Declaration of the Rights of the Child.

The United Nations General Assembly concluded much the same thing when it declared 1979, the twentieth anniversary of the original Declaration, to be the "International Year of the Child." Among the worldwide goals for this year were to increase understanding of what a child needs in order to develop full potential, to increase sympathy for unmet needs, to develop programs for action in order to improve conditions, and ultimately, to bring about a commitment to children on the national and international level strong enough to produce necessary changes. It seems that while the U.N. Declaration of the Rights of the Child was a landmark document in terms of social and political philosophy, it did not create much actual change in concern for the welfare of children throughout the world.

Within this country there has been considerable controversy concerning the interpretation, extension, and application of the basic rights recognized in the original 1959 U.N. Declaration. There are some who wish to use it to protect the undeveloped or unsophisticated child, and others who wish to use it to liberate children and expand their rights. Farson (1974), for example, has identified two classes of child advocates—those interested in protecting children, and those interested in protecting children's rights. This classification is paralleled by Worsfold (1974), who distinguished between the paternalistic view of children and children's rights to fair treatment. It is reflected again in the two dimensions of child rights proposed by Rogers and Wrightsman (1978), rights to nurturance and rights to self-determination, and by Feshbach and Feshbach (1978), who distinguish between a child's needs and a child's rights.

Others, such as Annes and Healey (cited in Beyer, 1974), have conceptualized "rights" on a continuum, with recognized legal rights at one end and philosophical or political statements of what the law ought to be at the other. It is thus held that the middle of the continuum, those "rights" that would probably be recognized in a court of law if such an occasion arose, represents the "gray area" in which prevailing cultural orientations toward children and the disposition of Family Court judges, child advocates, and teachers may have the greatest impact. It is this arena of child rights that is most controversial, where establishment of public sentiment is most fruitful, and where the impact of such efforts as the International Year of the Child and other child advocacy actions should be most apparent over time.

The controversy concerning what child rights are or should be is also a function of disagreement concerning the division of rights and responsibilities between the parent, the child, and the state, as enacted by the Family Court system in this country. If a child is to be responsible for his or her own actions (self-determination), then the parents are no longer responsible. If a child is mistreated by parents, then the state (via the courts) may intervene in "the best interests of the child." If the rights of a child are changed, then there is a concomitant change in the rights of the parents (Baumrind, 1978). If parental rights and responsibilities are decreased, then the role of social institutions in what was once the province of the family will increase (Levy, 1976). This balance of power between parent, child, and state is a difficult and emotionally laden issue on which there is great controversy, not only among legal philosophers, but also among lay citizens increasingly aware of the child advocacy movement.

At present, there are a finite set of rather generally worded laws protecting children in this country, and also restricting their rights to certain adult freedoms. Most decisions affecting children are actually made by their parents, with teachers only occasionally, and judges and juries even more rarely, participating. While courts and child advocates presumably act in the best interests of the child, parents and other socializing agents must operate in protection of their own interests as well. The emergence of activism to protect children from abuse from parents and other adults stands in bewildering contrast to the new demands for corporal punishment in the schools; and while the legal age of adulthood in most states is eighteen, eighteen-year-olds are still not granted full adult status vis-à-vis sexual freedom, occupational choice, and work hours in many places (Rogers & Wrightsman, 1978). Thus, there is still much that is unclear and inconsistent in the way in which our society orients toward children and their rights, responsibilities, and privileges.

The picture becomes even more blurred when one considers such attitudes concerning children and their rights across various cultures. It is known that different cultures confer adult status at different ages (Barry, Bacon, & Child, 1957), that the reported incidence of child abuse varies across cultures and even within the subcultures of the United States (Dubanoski & Snyder, 1979), and that parenting styles and attitudes about children differentiate, once again, among our world cultures and also among our own American ethnic groups (Munroe & Munroe, 1975). Feshbach and Feshbach (1978) assert that children's rights, such as the right to privacy and the right to an individual versus a group-based choice, are intimately related to the specific legal and social structure of a society, while children's needs are more universal and less subject to negotiation, e.g., such things as the need for food, shelter, caring, and protection from physical and psychological abuse. Careful consideration of cultural norms and values affecting children's needs and rights is thus absolutely necessary since rights are centrally placed in a culture or society, and needs are in priority on the basis of cultural values, norms, and resources. As Feshbach stated, "[t]he specific context or cultures of a society is [a] significant perspective from which child rights must be evaluated" (1978, p. 14).

There is a paucity of empirical research on attitudes toward child rights even within our own culture, and of course even less comparing such attitudes across cultures. Most of the writing to date has been non-data-based, and those most visible in the child advocacy movement in this country have been, for the most part, adults of European ancestry probably raised in a middle or upper middle class setting. With the lack of consensual orientation even among this group toward issues of child rights, it would be expected that cultures and subcultures would reflect even greater disagreement. The present research was begun with the recognition that more information was needed concerning the perceptions of children's rights, needs, and privileges by various cultures. By understanding the cultural parameters of such issues as acceptable disciplining strategies, the place of court intervention in family disputes, and the responsibility of parents for their children's actions, the needs of children may be more skillfully met, and children's rights may be better protected.

One approach to researching people's conceptions of child rights is simply to ask them what they think child rights are, or should be. Such questions, however, may merely invoke the moral-philosophical truisms and noncontroversial platitudes found on earlier bills of child rights. The present line of research sought to diminish this problem by addressing specific issues concerning the application of norms and values pertaining to a child's needs, rights, and responsibilities. It was felt that it is this level of attitudinal analysis that will permit the most sensitive index of practical everyday orientations to children among our respondents.

Our earlier work has been based on a sixty-four-item questionnaire consisting of attitude statements constructed from the existing literature on child rights in the legal and social science fields. The statements covered such areas as attitudes toward child versus parental responsibilities, school problems, court intervention, discipline, and decision making by the child (Dubanoski & Morton, 1978). This questionnaire was administered to over 1000 subjects of both sexes, various ethnic groups, and a wide range of ages. Earlier analyses (Morton, Dubanoski, & Blaine, 1979) have indicated that some child rights and privileges are highly endorsed regardless of the child's age (e.g., right to legal protection and basic resources such as food, shelter, and medical care), while others are endorsed differentially as the child matures (e.g., a child's right to independent choice and to responsibility for self increase with the child's age, whereas the adult's responsibility for providing a basic socialization for the child decreases as the child's age advances). These age-dependent rights, needs, and responsibilities have been factored into four clusters—the Child's Right to Independent Choice, the Child's Responsibility for Self, the Adult's Responsibility for Basic Socialization, and the Adult's Right to Discipline and Punish, where each factor represents a group of attitudes toward child rights which increased or decreased together as the child matures from toddler to teenager (Morton et al., 1979). For example, the factor labeled the Child's Right to Independent Choice consisted of statements related to the child's right to choose his or her own home, church, schooling, diet, and friends.

Our earlier exploratory work has established that respondents' age, sex, and ethnicity all differentially influence their orientation toward children, their rights, and needs. For instance, ethnic differences between Japanese Americans and European Americans were assessed (Dubanoski, Morton, & Blaine, 1979). Initially, an attempt was made to determine whether ethnic differences could be characterized by different conceptualizations, i.e., different factor structures. The results of factoring the Japanese American and European American samples separately did not result in structures different enough to warrant a conclusion of different conceptualizations of child rights by the two ethnic groups. Consequently, differences between ethnic groups were compared on the scale resulting from the factor structure discussed above. Among the findings was the greater endorsement by the Japanese of the scale labeled the Adult's Responsibility for Providing Basic Socialization to the Child. This result is in accord with previous cross-cultural research on childrearing attitudes (e.g., Shizuru, Dubanoski, & Marsella, 1974).

In the present study, the influence of culture on perceptions of child rights was also assessed. The respondents in this sample were Japanese Americans, European Americans, and Marshall Islanders from Micronesia, the Trust Territories of the United States. The first two cultural groups were chosen for a number of reasons, the primary one being that each represents a major subcultural group within Hawaii's multicultural society, and each has maintained some ethnic identity regarding childrearing attitudes and behavior patterns. Comparison of subcultures bounded by a larger societal structure provides valuable information to individuals within that society concerning cultural variegation in interpreting laws and policies, in resisting court intervention, and in support of new policies and institutionalized services. Such information would be helpful when decisions concerning children of various cultural groups, as in Hawaii, must be made so that the best interests of various children can be considered. It must be remembered that judgments of a child's best interests, of a parent's fitness, and of what constitutes abuse must take into careful consideration the specific cultural norm and values; otherwise, ideological hegemony and institutionalized ethnocentrism can potentially create greater problems for the child with intervention into intact cultural supports of both the family and the individual.

Similar reasons were important for the inclusion of the Marshallese sample. This country is in a state of transition regarding many aspects of its life because of the increasing influence of outside cultures, and traditional views of child-rearing, education, and the role of the state as *parens patriae* are changing rapidly. The decisions that must be made concerning the children of Micronesia must reflect these changing perceptions. It was felt that comparing this sample of Marshall Islanders to a group more acculturated toward Western values (Japanese Americans) and to a group representing the Western values per se (European American) would provide some interesting contrasts.

No specific predictions were advanced concerning cultural differences in perceptions of child rights in the three cultural groups. Since European Americans, Japanese Americans, and the Marshallese represent decreasing degrees of "mainstream" or "Americanized" values and norms, it was expected that there would be some similarity, reflecting this influence of Western philosophy. At the same time, however, the three cultures are thought to be different in some notable ways. European American families tend toward nuclear units while Japanese American individuals typically identify with a more extended family network. Perhaps because of the greater intrafamilial resources, Japanese Americans are very underrepresented in publically available statistics on crime, violence, mental illness, and abuse—they are rarely seen in agencies designed to provide extrafamilial assistance in such matters (Kinzie & Furukawa, 1974; Kitano, 1969). In contrast, European Americans are overrepresented in the courts and correctional and mental health facilities, and in incidence of child abuse (Hansen & Markoff, 1974; Kinzie, 1974). European Americans have often been held to be more laissez-faire than Japanese Americans, who are characterized as more authoritarian and controlling in the parent-child relationship. All of this would suggest that perceptions of the needs, rights, and privileges of the child would differ somewhat between these two groups.

Less has been documented concerning the Marshallese population, whose culture over the past decades has been influenced by both Japanese and American cultures, and whose entire society is undergoing rapid transition. Traditionally, the Marshallese have been quite controlling in parent-child relationships, but most discipline is rigorously confined to within-family networks.* Disciplinary strategy is largely through giving and taking away of pleasurable commodities, with little physical punishment until a parent or custodial elder becomes quite upset. In the traditional context, there was little transiency, but well-established extended kinship networks. If substantial difficulty occurred within a parent-child relationship, a child was commonly adopted by a more congenial blood relative in the network. A child was initiated into adult life at approximately age twelve, with full sexual rights and the endowment of the right/responsibility for duties in the familial copra-making enterprise. With recent acceleration of American involvement in Micronesia, the Marshallese have become more mobile and the life-style more transient, as they have left home islands in search of jobs, education, and the pleasures to be found in the more densely populated areas. As old ways fracture and Western, modern ways erode the Pacific Islanders' traditions, more modern or American approaches to what children need or deserve are emerging. These appear to be more laissez-faire attitudes toward discipline and control, and greater interest in larger societal institutions such as schooling and civil service. It is a society at a crossroads, and as the Marshall Islands inevitably and rapidly develop, their leaders are attempting to cull the best of American values and norms, without adopting those aspects that are culturally dissonant. The successful development of systems of law, health, education, and welfare will require much sensitive comparison of the Marshallese

*Most of the information on the Marshallese was obtained by one of the authors (R.A.D.) in an interview with Mr. Charles Eko, a long-term resident of the Marshall Islands and an adopted son in a Marshallese family.

traditions with the norms and values of modern technological cultures such as that of the United States.

## Method

### *Subjects*

Originally, 411 subjects, all university students, were recruited from essentially equivalent psychology courses at the college level to participate in the present study. Of these, fifty-eight were dropped from the sample because of failure to complete all questionnaire items, leaving a total of 353 participants. This sample consisted of 118 Japanese Americans from the University of Hawaii, 203 European Americans from both the University of Hawaii and the University of New Mexico, and thirty-two Marshallese from University of Hawaii extension college courses in Majuro, Marshall Islands. All subjects were of middle socioeconomic status relative to their sociocultural context, with the average years of post-high school education being approximately two years for the Japanese Americans and European Americans, and one year for the Marshallese. The age range sampled was great, eighteen to fifty-nine years, with an overall mean age of twenty-four years. The mean ages of the ethnic groups were twenty-seven for the Japanese Americans, twenty-two for the European Americans, and thirty for the Marshallese. Males constituted 33% of the overall sample, 29% of the Japanese American, 30% of the European American, and 69% of the Marshallese samples.

Overall, 80% of the sample was childless, although this variable, like age, was not equally distributed across the three ethnic groups; 32% of the Japanese Americans, 4% of the European Americans, and 78% of the Marshallese were parents. These apparent nonequivalences are in actuality representative reflections of the ethnically differentiated demographic profiles of college attenders in these three groups. European Americans delay families the longest, or choose to remain childless altogether the most, and typically enter college immediately after high school. The Marshallese have families earliest of these three ethnic groups, and typically take time before continuing with college courses, if indeed college is attended at all.

### *Procedure*

A questionnaire concerning attitudes towards children's rights was distributed to students in college courses who volunteered to serve as respondents. Instructions were held constant through a written face sheet and through verbal paraphrasing of these instructions. The questionnaire consisted of requests for general demographic information, the open-ended question, "At what age does a child become an adult?", and sixty-four additional attitude statements, each accompanied by a seven point scale on which subjects indicated their degree of agreement. A score of one indicated strongly disagree, a score of seven indicated strongly agree, and a score of four indicated neither disagree nor agree. While each attitude statement was rated four times for four child age groups (0-5, 6-11, 12-14, and 15-17 years), the present interest was in overall endorsement of various attitude statements, irrespective of the age of the child being considered. Therefore a subject's average rating for a given statement was the measure of interest. Respondents were given as much time as needed to complete the questionnaire, with American subjects completing it in approximately thirty to forty minutes and the Marshallese subjects taking forty to sixty minutes. Additional verbal paraphrasing of items was offered to these subjects where clarification of meaning was requested.

On the basis of earlier findings regarding this questionnaire, fourteen attitude statements were selected for the present study. These were chosen to represent a range of attitudes towards child rights, as reflected in prior factor analyses to determine the principle dimensions of child rights (Morton et al., 1979), and also because they appeared to have relatively high face validity. That is, they were felt to be most relevant to actual decision making in law and social policy and action, and by the same token, the most valid items in terms of congruence of meaning across the three cultures. These selected attitude statements and an open-ended opinion question concerning the age of majority are listed in Table 7-1.

**TABLE 7-1**
ATTITUDES TOWARDS CHILDREN'S RIGHTS

1. At what age does a child become an adult?
2. Parents should not leave a child at home alone without adult supervision.
3. Duties should be given to children so that they learn responsibility.
4. A parent should keep their child at home so the child won't get into trouble.
5. It is fine for a parent to go through a child's possessions to get an idea of what the child is doing.
6. A child should be allowed to quit school whenever he or she wants to.
7. Children should report to authorities when they feel their well-being is threatened by parents or school personnel.
8. Teachers should use physical punishment when the child is a "real problem."
9. Parents should not direct their anger or aggression toward their children.
10. A child should be silenced if he/she interrupts an adult conversation.
11. A child should be guaranteed economic support from his or her parents.
12. Information about sexual matters should be freely and openly given to children.
13. The courts should not differentiate children from adults when they are accused of serious crimes such as murder or theft.
14. Withholding food is a reasonable method of disciplining the child.
15. A parent is wrong to interfere with their child's choice of friends.

## Results

To examine the influence of the ethnocultural factor on responses to the fifteen statements, while controlling for possible sex-related influences, each of these variables was subjected to a stepwise regression, with ethnicity as the last predictor variable to be entered. Thus, the effects of the sex times ethnicity interaction, and then the main effect of sex, were partialled out so that the effect of subjects' ethnicity, above and beyond any effects associated with their sex, might be examined. All statistically significant ethnicity effects were then subsequently assessed with Duncan's Multiple Range Test with Kramer's adjustment (1956) to determine where the significant differences between means existed. The mean scores for the three cultural groups, the F values for the effect of ethnicity on each of the attitude items, and the results of the means comparison are presented in Table 7-II.

It can be seen that there were no differences due to ethnicity in responses to the question "At what age does a child become an adult?" On average, respondents felt this age to be almost twenty

TABLE 7-II
Summary of Analyses

| Var | F-ratio[2] | Japanese American (N=118) | European American (N=203) | Marshallese (N=32) |
|---|---|---|---|---|
| | | Ethnic Group Means[1] | | |
| 1 | <1.00 | 19.50[a] | 19.61[a] | 19.91[a] |
| 2 | <1.00 | 4.63[a] | 4.74[a] | 4.88[a] |
| 3 | 19.78 † | 6.53[a] | 6.12[b] | 5.66[c] |
| 4 | 50.04 ‡ | 2.27[c] | 2.65[b] | 5.59[a] |
| 5 | 25.16 ‡ | 2.73[c] | 3.16[b] | 5.35[a] |
| 6 | 6.38 † | 1.49[b] | 1.65[b] | 2.31[a] |
| 7 | 18.07 ‡ | 6.13[a] | 6.16[a] | 4.26[b] |
| 8 | 2.08 | 2.05[a] | 2.45[a] | 2.63[a] |
| 9 | 3.52* | 6.48[a] | 6.58[a] | 5.97[b] |
| 10 | 5.66 † | 3.85[ab] | 3.49[b] | 4.45[a] |
| 11 | 5.11 † | 6.42[a] | 6.41[a] | 5.67[b] |
| 12 | 53.50 ‡ | 6.24[a] | 5.25[b] | 3.40[c] |
| 13 | 10.76 ‡ | 2.66[b] | 3.37[a] | 3.70[a] |
| 14 | 34.34 ‡ | 1.54[b] | 1.49[b] | 3.42[a] |
| 15 | 4.99 † | 3.87[b] | 4.31[a] | 3.93[ab] |

[1]The ethnic group means were compared using Duncan's Multiple Range Test ($\alpha = .05$, df = 347) adjusted for unequal *n*'s using Kramer's (1956) procedure. Means with the same superscript are not significantly different. The means for variable 1 represent years and the means for the remaining variables represent scores on a 7-point scale, with 1 = strongly disagree, 4 = neither agree nor disagree, and 7 = strongly agree.

[2]All F values are based on a SS for ethnicity with sex and ethnicity times sex partialled out; df in all cases = 2 and 347.

*$p < .05$
†$p < .01$
‡$p \leq .0001$

years old, but individual differences in responses were far greater than differences due to ethnicity.

No differences between ethnic groups were also found for two of the attitude statements. All three groups gave moderate endorsement to the statement, "Parents should not leave a child at home without adult supervision" and all disagreed somewhat with the proposition that "Teachers should use physical punishment when the child is a 'real problem'."

All groups agreed that "Duties should be given to children so that they learn responsibility." However, Japanese Americans gave the strongest endorsement, followed by European Americans, and lastly the Micronesians. This is consistent with the Japanese and Japanese American values of responsibility, dependability, self-control, and diligence which Kitano (1969) reports may make Japanese more "American middle class" in their values than the white mainstream American middle class itself. It is also congruent with the general Pacific Islanders' fabled valuing of play over work, particularly among children.

While the Micronesians were in moderate agreement with the statement, "A parent should keep their child at home so the child won't get into trouble," the Americans moderately disagreed, with the Japanese group in most disagreement. This may reflect the greater comfort with mobility among Americans, in contrast to the more parochical focus of the Marshallese. It could also reflect, however, culturally different definitions of "home," wherein it is an entire hamlet or island to a Marshall Islander, and merely a house to Americans.

The three cultural groups were also differentiated by their responses to the assertion that "It is fine for a parent to go through a child's possessions to get an idea of what the child is doing." Japanese Americans moderately disagreed, European Americans slightly disagreed, and Marshallese moderately agreed. This may well reflect cultural differences in valuing of privacy, in that Japanese Americans most prize and respect both physical and psychological privacy (Kinzie & Furukawa, 1974), while the Marshallese operate more from a sharing, communal basis, with family members often sharing the same sleeping quarters, for example.

There was also ethnicity differences in responses to the item "A child should be allowed to quit school whenever he or she wants to," with the American subjects disagreeing more strongly than the Marshallese respondents. Public schooling, which is both free and compulsory, is a relatively long-lived institution in this country, widely agreed to be a primary socializing experience necessary to citizenship and upward socioeconomic mobility. In the Marshall Islands, such an institution is quite recent and still not regarded as fully necessary for participation in the community, where primary socializing of children is the responsibility of the family.

"Children should report to authorities when they feel their

well-being is threatened by parents or school personnel" also received differential responses from the ethnic groups, with Japanese and European Americans more strongly endorsing this than the Marshallese. Once again, this would appear to reflect the greater emphasis on familial control and the greater alienation from supra-familial societal institutions of the Marshall Islanders, in contrast to the relatively greater acceptance of such institutions and authorities by Americans.

Both the Japanese American and European American groups were in stronger agreement with the statement "Parents should not direct their anger or aggression toward their children" than were the Micronesians. The American groups may have been more influenced by contemporary psychological thinking, which warns against such behavior. In addition, among Marshall Islanders, it is quite normative to discipline non-aggressively until a threshold of misbehavior is reached, at which time a more aggressive action is called for.

The Marshallese were in slight agreement with "A child should be silenced if he or she interrupts an adult conversation," while Japanese and European Americans were in slight disagreement; the significant difference was between the Marshallese and the European Americans. Again, this may reflect a differential view of child and adult relations among three cultures with the American emphasis on treating children with the same respect as adults. It is also likely that this difference reflects the greater encouragement of verbal discourse in more Western society.

While all ethnic groups were in agreement with the statement "A child should be guaranteed economic support from his or her parents," the Japanese Americans and European Americans were in strongest agreement. This would seem to reflect the economic realities—in this country, there is little alternative to parental support of children, while in Micronesian society, children may be adopted by another branch of the family relatively frequently.

A surprising finding was the differential responses to "Information about sexual matters should be freely and openly given to children." Japanese Americans gave this relatively strong endorsement, European Americans moderately endorsed this, and the Marshallese slightly disagreed. The reverse order was more expected. Perhaps responses to this attitude statement may best be interpreted in terms of the reactions of young adults to the orientation toward sexual matters of their parental generation. In this case, Japanese Americans, raised with little sexual knowledge except what they could acquire from age peers, would react with more wholehearted endorsement of this statement. In contrast, the Marshallese, raised in a sexually accepting culture, might reject this somewhat, feeling that a more controlled and conservative approach to the imparting of sexual information was called for. Thomas (1975) has observed that restrictions on sexual behavior occur in those islands in the South Pacific where there has been widespread missionary activity and where a low degree of privacy is combined with high face-to-face interaction; it is likely that the mild restriction of sexual information for children suggested by the Marshallese in this study reflects these conditions.

All groups disagreed with the statement "The courts should not differentiate children from adults when they are accused of serious crimes such as murder or theft," although Japanese Americans were in greatest disagreement. This is consistent with the greater inequality between child and adult in Japanese culture, and may also reflect in part the disproportionately low rate of such serious crimes among Japanese Americans generally, but especially by children.

"Withholding food is a reasonable method of disciplining the child" was disagreed with by all ethnic groups, but more so by the Japanese and European American groups. This quite likely reflects the Marshallese practice of rewarding good behavior with treats and sweets, and using removal of things for controlling the misbehavior of children.

Finally, an ethnic effect was found for the attitude statement "A parent is wrong to interfere with their child's choice of friends." European Americans agreed somewhat with this, Japanese Americans disagreed somewhat, and Marshallese fell in between. This is not surprising, given the relatively tight control of children and their peer group activities valued by Japanese Americans (Kitano, 1969), and the relatively laissez-faire orientation to a child's peer group characteristic of the European Americans.

## Discussion

The overall pattern of results suggests that the American ethnic groups of Japanese and European ancestry have more in common concerning attitudes towards child rights than either group has in common with Marshallese. The Marshall Islanders seem to feel less cohesiveness between the family and larger societal institutions, such as those of law, education, and social welfare. Furthermore, Marshallese seem relatively less concerned with a child's rights than with a child's needs. They would seem to uphold the protection of children from adult concerns, while ensuring that the environment is proper for children to be nurtured by, and to learn from, adult caretakers. In comparison, the European and Japanese Americans demonstrated a greater acceptance of, and comfort with, the larger societal institutions. They rely more heavily on such systems to carry on the socialization of children, the meeting of their needs, and the protecting of their rights. This essentially American middle class profile is extended by the apparent stress by these groups on the protection of children's rights, manifest in the psychological flexibility and permissiveness of the culturally ideal parent.

The similarity of the Japanese American and European American groups on the sampled indices of the American value system supports the conclusions of others (e.g., Iga, 1966) that Japanese Americans of this generation are, for most practical purposes, completely acculturated. That the Japanese Americans seem to value "Protestant" work ethic values and a child's right to privacy support the characterizations of this group as an "ethical culture," wherein the means toward an end are as important or more important than the end itself (Kitano, 1969), and as the "model minority" in this country (Peterson, 1966).

The results of this study must be treated rather tentatively, however. There is a dearth of pertinent cross-cultural research comparing these three groups, certainly on attitudes relevant to children's rights, and indeed a complete lack of pertinent research on Marshall Islanders. Without prior research findings to consolidate with the present study's results, broad generalization concerning the attitudes of these groups runs the grave risk of enhancing already existing but unfounded stereotypes.

Quite apart from this lack of germane literature, there are other reasons for caution in drawing conclusions. First, only a handful of attitudes were sampled, and much more information would be needed to establish any definitive profiles of a subject's orientation toward children. Second, these were small samples, especially in the Micronesian case, and conclusions must be correspondingly reserved. Third, the matter of equivalence across social and economic dimensions is difficult in this kind of cross-cultural comparison. While the three cultural groups were all generally equated in amount of education, corresponding to approximately equal socioeconomic status, they differed in the extent to which they had established families. As noted earlier, our sample may have been representative of college students in these three sociocultural groups—the Marshallese, and to some extent the Japanese Americans, in the sample were older and more likely to be parents than the European Americans. It is possible that another study that controlled for parental status across the various cultures might yield somewhat different conclusions; we would hope to examine this in future analyses. In short, the present investigation was exploratory and is insufficiently rigorous in terms of measurements, sample size, and validated representativeness of the sample to permit adamant generalizations concerning the specific cultures.

On the other hand, these findings do support the assertion that cultures do vary on attitudes and values pertinent to children's rights. All three of the cultural groups in the present study value children, and ostensibly the members of each group wish to be good parents, or to otherwise enhance the welfare of children. However, what a "good parent" does varies from culture to culture, as does the role of the child and the relative priority of various rights and needs. Outside judges, whether social scientists, policy makers, or service deliverers, must be extremely sensitive to this and ensure that evaluation consider the full cultural context of the child and his or her caretakers.

Burgess (1979) has argued that our affluent Western society emphasizes the protection of child rights, while poorer or less developed countries are more likely to emphasize the meeting of children's needs. Feshbach and Feshbach (1978) have posited that the route for enhancing rights is through the courts, while the route to meeting needs is through the legislature, school, family, and other major institutions of the larger society. In all probablity the Marshall Island society will continue to differ from American society, at least in the foreseeable future, in the structures functioning to protect and enhance the welfare of children.

It is doubtful that any one set of policies and procedures will perfectly fit all cultural groups, or indeed even one. It is more likely that appliers of policies and procedures can become sufficiently sensitive to the specific cultural context in question so that specific decisions affecting a given child will truly be in that child's best interests. Cultural differences have important implications for the kinds of court decisions that will be made, the power granted to educators, the quantity and quality of social services employed within a given sociocultural group, and the kind of child rights legislation that is supported.

Our research on cross-cultural comparisons of perceptions of children's rights is far from complete. Baumrind (1979) has recognized the reciprocal balance between the rights and responsibilities of parents and the rights and responsibilities of children. She has further asserted the importance of the child's developmental stage in this balance. Our overall research program in fact examines conceptualizations of age-dependent and age-independent rights and responsibilities of children and their parents. The present study has been a preliminary attempt to establish the degree of cultural variation. Futher studies must, and will, extend the concepts of reciprocal rights and responsibilities and the developmental perspective in cross-cultural comparisons. Only in this framework, it is felt, will the fullest understanding of children's rights across cultures be achieved.

## References

Barry, H., Baron, K., & Child, L. Cross-cultural survey of some sex differences in socialization. *Journal of Abnormal and Social Psychology*, 1957, *55*, 327-332.

Baumrind, D. The principle of reciprocity in the development of socially responsible behavior in children. Invited address for the symposium entitled, "Children's Rights and the Development of Social Responsibility," annual meeting of the American Psychological Association, New York, September 1979.

Baumrind, D. Reciprocal rights and responsibilities in parent-child relations. In N.D. Feshbach and S. Feshbach (Eds.), *The changing status of children: Rights, roles, and responsibilities. Journal of Social Issues*, 1978, *34*, 179-196.

Beyer, H.A. The child's right to refuse mental health treatment. Paper presented at the meeting of the American Psychological Association, New Orleans, September 1974.

Burgess, D.S. An international perspective on child rights. In P.A. Vardin and I.N. Brody (Eds.), *Children's rights: Contemporary perspectives*. New York: Teachers's College Press, 1979.

Dubanoski, R.A., & Morton, T.L. Conceptualizations of child rights in a cross-cultural context. Paper presented at the symposium entitled, "Children's Rights," annual Western Regional Meeting of the Society for Research in Child Development, San Jose, February 1978.

Dubanoski, R.A., Morton, T.L., & Blaine, D.D. A cross-cultural investigation of perceptions of child rights. Paper presented at the annual meeting of the American Psychological Association, New York, September 1979.

Dubanoski, R.A., & Snyder, K. Cultural patterns of child abuse and neglect. Paper presented at the annual meeting of the Western Psychological Association, San Diego, April 1979.

Farson, R. *Birthrights: A bill of rights for children*. New York: MacMillan, 1974.

Feshbach, N.D. Dimensions of child rights. Paper presented at the Conference on Children's Rights: Issues and Viewpoints, Florida State University, Tallahassee, Florida, 1978.

Feshbach, N.D., & Feshbach, S. Toward an historical, social, and developmental perspective on children's rights. In N.D. Feshbach and S. Feshbach (Eds.), *The changing status of children: Rights, roles, and responsibilities. Journal of Social Issues*, 1978, *34*, 1-7.

Iga, M. Changes in value orientation of Japanese-Americans. Paper presented at the annual meeting of the Western Psychological Association, Long Beach, California, April 1966.

Kitano, H.H. *Japanese Americans: The evolution of a subculture*. Englewood Cliffs, New Jersey: Prentice-Hall, 1969.

Kramer, C.Y. Extension of multiple range tests to group means with unequal numbers of replication. *Biometrics*, 1956, *12*, 307-310.

Levy, R.S. The rights of parents. *Brigham Young University Law Review*, 1976, 693-707.

Morton, T.L., Dubanoski, R.A., & Blaine, D.D. Perceptions of the rights of children: An exploratory investigation. Paper presented at the annual meeting of the Western Psychological Association, San Diego, April 1979.

Munroe, R.L., & Munroe, R.H. *Cross-cultural human development.* Monterey, California: Brooks/Cole Publishing Co., 1975.

Peterson, W. Success story: Japanese American style. *The New York Times,* January 9, 1966.

Rogers, C.M., & Wrightsman, L.S. The status of children's intellectual rights. In N.D. Feshbach and S. Feshbach (Eds.), *The changing status of children: Rights, roles, and responsibilities. Journal of Social Issues,* 1978, *34,* 59-68.

Shizuru, L., Dubanoski, R.A., & Marsella, A.J. Maternal attitudes as a function of generation and culture. Paper presented at the annual meeting of the Hawaii Psychological Association, Honolulu, May 1974.

Thomas, D.R. Authoritarianism, child-rearing practices, and ethnocentrism in seven Pacific Islands groups. *International Journal of Psychology,* 1975, *10,* 235-246.

Worsfold, V.L. A philosophical justification for children's rights. *Harvard Educational Review,* 1974, *44,* 142-157.

Chapter 8

# TEACHING CHILDREN ABOUT THEIR RIGHTS

GARY B. MELTON

ONE OF THE PERSISTENT tensions in the child advocacy movement has been that it often purports to represent children as consumers without directly involving them. As has been noted in historical analyses of the child-saving movement (Levine & Levine, 1970; Platt, 1977), child advocates have often ended further regulating the lives of children and adolescents in the guise of protecting them. On the other hand, "kiddie libbers" (Farson, 1974; Holt, 1974) have tended uncritically to accept children's capacity for self-determination without regard to developmental factors. In both instances, advocacy may be enriched if well-intentioned adults really listen to children's own concerns. This chapter is focused on issues in preparation of children for such participation.

Whether the rights espoused are exemplary of a "nurturance" (child-saving) or a "self-determination" (kiddie-lib) orientation (Rogers & Wrightsman, 1978), they may well be moot if children are unaware of them. The reality of children's rights is based at least partially on whether social institutions governing children, such as public schools, actually inform their clients of their rights and allow their expression without retribution (Bergman, 1979). Furthermore, self-determination realistically may require attention to developmental factors in comprehension and conceptualization of rights. To the extent to which such concepts are based on experience with rights, there is a clear implication that the possible degree of involvement by children in deciding their own fate is a function of the quality of moral and political education to which they are exposed.

## Children's Concepts of their Rights

In considering possible educational interventions in this area, it is useful to begin by examining children's concepts of their rights and factors involved in determining these concepts. Despite the obvious practical importance of this topic, available research is sparse (Tapp, 1976). In one of the few studies thus far, Melton (1980, in press) hypothesized that children's concepts of and attitudes toward their rights would be a function both of maturational factors and social class. In terms of maturational factors, it was hypothesized that children would develop mature concepts of rights only when egocentricity had been diminished to the point that the child was concerned with respect for others and that he perceived rights on some basis other than his concrete experience of what he can do or have. Furthermore, development of principled reasoning about rights would appear to require a degree of abstraction contingent on acquisition of formal operational thought. Such cognitive changes would appear necessary for development of mature concepts of rights, but they were hypothesized to be insufficient. Specifically, while rights are usually conceptualized as entitlements that exist independently of whether they are actually fulfilled (Friedman, 1977), some groups in our society are in reality more likely to experience "rights" than others. A conceptualization of rights as privileges bestowed at the whim of authority may be accurate for many lower class children.

Ninety children in the first, third, fifth, and seventh grades from the Boston area were administered a semi-structured interview concerning twelve vignettes involving interpersonal conflict in which a child might assert a right. Stories involved, for examples, censorship of the school newspaper, parents' reading a girl's diary, a child's seeking treatment independently, punishment in school without due process, access to school records, etc. Children's judgments concerning these vignettes were found to develop along a three-level sequence similar to that postulated by Tapp and Levine (1974) in their theory of legal development. Briefly, Level 1 reasoning involves a confusion of rights with what one can in fact do or have. By such a conceptualization, children have rights only if adults allow them. Level 2 involves a confusion of rights with privileges associated with being "nice" or accorded by one's role, physical competence, or social status. Finally, Level 3 concepts of rights are based on abstract ethical principles, such as freedom of the press and right to privacy. In such a framework, rights may exist "naturally" without respect to their legal recognition because of their logical necessity for maintenance of human dignity. Perhaps the best known example of such thinking was Jefferson's declaration of the "unalienable rights" of "life, liberty, and the pursuit of happiness." In keeping with the hypotheses, school grade contributed highly significantly to the variance in concepts of rights, with social class having a highly significant effect on the rate of progression.

First graders, regardless of class, tended to give Level 1 responses to the vignettes. They tended to determine whether a child has a right in a given situation by examining whether he would be punished for its assertion. They were acutely aware of who was "boss" in a given context, down to the caretaker in a park. Exemplary of this view was a first grader's conclusion that whether a child should be able to vote should be decided by a panel of the police, George Washington, and Jimmy Carter. Another Level 1 response to the question of whether children should be able to vote follows:

> No! (?) Because they've not the right to vote in the voting booth. Once we went in with my mother, but we didn't touch anything. That's what you shouldn't do. Don't touch any levers. (?) No. (?) Because their mothers won't let them.

Most high-socioeconomic status (high-SES) youngsters (those from an affluent suburb) reached predominantly Level 2 reasoning by third grade, while children in the low-socioeconomic status (low-SES) sample (a working-class suburb) on the average did not achieve this level of conceptualization of rights until at least a couple of years later. To children at Level 2, the primary determinant of whether one had a right in a given situation was *fairness* associated with being "good" and maintenance of the social order. Level 2 thinking about rights is shown in the following opinion about whether a principal should be able to censor a student's uncomplimentary editorial about the school rules:

> No, because his story would probably be interesting, and everybody would want to look at it and see how it is. (?) He just won't let him print it, and the boy would probably say, "Why? It's a good story, and the other kids might like it." (Anything to do with rights?) Yeah, he should let him try and print his story and see if the kids like it.

Thus, this boy was concerned not with maintenance of freedom of expression but rather with being polite or fair. It should be noted that youngsters sometimes reached different conclusions using this reasoning. High-SES early adolescents tended to identify with the authority figures in the vignettes and to interpret the rights conflicts in terms of fairness to the authorities. One child suggested that, before a story is written that might embarrass the principal, a signed release like the ones *Candid Camera* producers seek from their "victims" should be obtained.

Level 3 reasoning was not pervasive for any of the participants in the study, although such concepts of rights were revealed in a few isolated vignettes by some of the seventh graders in the sample. It is not surprising that this level of reasoning about rights was seldom achieved even among bright, affluent seventh graders, given both the level of cognitive development necessary for principled moral reasoning and the relative scarcity of such reasoning among the adult American population (Kohlberg, 1969). Data from older adolescents were not collected in the study, but Level 3 reasoning might have been much more common in a somewhat older high-SES sample. While interpretations must be considered equivocal because of small cell size, there was some tendency for high-SES seventh graders to begin to give a Level 3 answer but then to say in essence that it is not nice to assert such rights. This mixture of logic may be exemplary of a transition from Level 2 to Level 3 conceptualization. This transition may be prolonged because of a recognition that "rights" often do not represent entitlement on a practical level. The following response to the censorship vignette by a girl in the high-SES seventh grade sample is a clear example of the conflict resulting from such inconsistency:

> There's two sides to it. Here's the first side. There's freedom of the press. In the school newspaper you're supposed to print what's happening and what you think. If you can't print it, why have a newspaper? Then, the other side from the principal's point of view: If one kid says it, then everybody is going to come up to the principal and try to get the rules changed even though they're still good. (How would you resolve it?) I'd say you couldn't. (Anything to do with rights?) Well, maybe in a town newspaper you could write but not in a school newspaper. (?) Well, I gotta give you an example. Last year these kids thought that—There was a big auction, and all the people in the school donated things. It was for buses to go on a camping trip. We raised more than we needed. So the kids got up a petition that it should go to us, and the teachers said that it should go to the other grades that didn't go on the camping trip. And the kids had to stay after school because they didn't listen to the teachers explain. That's probably what would happen if Mark complained—everybody would. (?) I don't think they should have had to stay after school, but it was kinda dumb. We had a good deal. It was only about $35 for the whole week. We had a deal. It was really kinda selfish. They didn't want the money to go to the other kids.

One of the real dilemmas in teaching children about their rights, discussed in more detail later in this chapter, is that what children actually *experience* is that they have very limited rights. Thus, the girl quoted above had some concept of the significance of freedom of expression, but she had also learned that its place, even in a relatively progressive suburban middle school, is questionable for children. In some schools, usually in lower-class neighborhoods, there is an openly repressive environment. For example, when they were asked an open-ended question about what rights children actually have, some of the children in the low-SES school thought for a while and then said that they have the right to go to the bathroom. Three of ten seventh graders interviewed in an inner-city Boston middle school spontaneously mentioned freedom from fear: "They should be able to move about freely and not be tense....Like some kids walk around tense. A kid threatens him and says, 'I'm going to beat you up.'" Obviously, in such an environment rights may seem quite ephemeral.

It is possible, though, that middle-class institutions actually do a more effective albeit more subtle job of socializing "conventional," expedient (Level 2) views of rights. With less direct emphasis on external control and avoidance of punishment, middle-class children learn the rules by which the system functions. The inconsistency between the espoused values of free speech and free press and the reality of repression of alternative views creates dissonance for the adolescent with his newly discovered capacity for hypothetico-deductive reasoning (Kagan, 1971). One of the ways of dealing with such inconsistency is simply to rationalize it as necessary for the preservation of order. In his sensitive clinical study of children in wealthy families, Coles (1977) cited cases in which youngsters were outraged by injustice and inequality, such as the treatment of migrant workers, but learned eventually that their own privileged status was "proper" and efficacious. They arrived at a position of social Darwinism in which the social order was viewed as a *fait accompli.* Put colloquially, "some got it, and some ain't." Affluent youngsters experience a sense of entitlement but often without its being extended to people generally.

In short, while there are strong developmental trends in acquisition of concepts of rights, the experiences that children actually have within the political system (broadly defined) affect the rate and end point of such development. To the extent to which it is important that children develop a sense of participation in the political system and of potential for self-determination and self-actualization, it seems valuable to provide educational experiences that will facilitate psycholegal development.

## Significance of Rights Education

The most obvious applied significance of teaching children about their rights is in terms of providing a basis for a reasoned exercise of their newly acquired legal rights. In 1967 the Supreme Court delivered an opinion (*In re Gault*) that had a dramatic effect on the structure and process of juvenile courts. Prior to that time, juvenile court judges functioned in a grandfatherly role, in which they reached decisions based on their subjective perceptions of the child's best interests. Delinquency proceedings were conceptualized as a noncriminal exercise of the state's protective role as *parens patriae*. Therefore, the usual due process protections were not deemed relevant.

In *Gault*, however, the Court ruled that "neither the Fourteenth Amendment nor the Bill of Rights is for adults alone." Most of the traditional rights to due process in criminal proceedings were accorded to juveniles accused of crimes: notice of the charges, right to counsel, right to confrontation and cross-examination, and the privilege against self-incrimination. The major problem concerns determination of competency of juveniles to waive rights. If children do not understand what a right is, how can they make a "knowing and intelligent" waiver of rights? If the child believes he has no alternative to conformity to authority, can he reasonably be expected to tell a policeman or a judge that he does not wish to answer their questions? Should a child's attorney follow his client's wishes when the child may not understand an attorney's function?

Grisso and his colleagues (Grisso & Lovinguth, 1979; Grisso & Manoogian, 1980; Grisso & Pomicter, 1977) have examined juveniles' understanding of the *Miranda* warning. Developmental considerations, such as those identified in Melton's (1980, in press) study, have been found to affect juveniles' willingness to waive their rights. In a survey of juvenile suspects in the Saint Louis area, it was found that adolescent suspects, as compared to younger juveniles, were less likely to waive their rights. However, interviews of juvenile offenders revealed generally that they have difficulty in applying abstract legal rights to their own situations. About two-thirds of Grisso's sample understood rights as privileges bestowed at the whim of authority rather than as entitlements that are inviolable. For example, Grisso and Lovinguth asked delinquents to describe the meaning of the following statement from the *Miranda* warning: "You do not have to make a statement and have the right to remain silent." Most of the participants in the study were able to give an accurate definition of the right to silence. However, when they were asked if they were required to "talk" if instructed to do so by a judge, 60% replied affirmatively. Thus, the majority of the participants were unable to apply the Fifth Amendment; they understood the right to silence as revocable by authority. As Grisso and his colleagues have pointed out, their data imply that special procedural safeguards may be necessary in juvenile court. Furthermore, for our purposes here, it is implicit that youngsters need to be educated in the application of legal rights to "real-life" situations. Even though they may be able to define the right to silence to the satisfaction of a court, it is questionable whether the waiver of rights by juveniles whose psycholegal development is immature is meaningful.

There are noncriminal proceedings as well in which competency to exercise rights is an issue. In some instances, the courts have invoked a "mature minor rule" as an attempt to deal with the issue. Under such a rule, the minor, regardless of age, can make a decision independently, *provided* that he or she understands its consequences and makes it for the minor's own benefit. This subjective standard was applied, for example, in the Supreme Court's highly publicized decision on the right of minor women to abortions (*Planned Parenthood of Central Missouri v. Danforth*, 1976). Similarly, minors' potential for participation in decisions concerning themselves has been increased in such spheres as custody (Siegel & Hurley, 1977), placement in special education* (*P.L. 94-142*), and acquisition of contraceptives (*Carey v. Population Services International*, 1977). Children's potential for self-determination and protection has also been increasing in terms of "everyday" interaction with the health care system (Melton, 1978) as well as dramatic events, such as decisions concerning organ transplants (Saks, 1978). In each of these instances, children need to know and be able to apply the concept of a right as well as to understand enough about the specific situation to be able to make an informed judgment. Again, children need education in the possible ramifications of assertion of a right and information concerning the potential to apply it to a real-life situation. Without such programs, the rights that have been extended to children will exist more on paper than in practice.

More generally, though, rights education may be useful in

*Children's right to participate in educational planning for themselves under Public Law 94-142 is a qualified one. The law requires such participation "when appropriate."

preparing youngsters to be full participants in the law and to use the law effectively as a means of enhancing the quality of life. Tapp and Levine (1974) have expressed this view eloquently:

> ...The socialization of conceptions of rights, justice, and claims-consciousness is essential if individuals are to develop their capacities as creators as well as consumers of law. As persons develop greater experience in mobilizing the law, other legal behaviors beyond simple legal compliance are stressed. In providing a legitimate mechanism for participation and conflict, the law demonstrates a potential for stimulating just, humane, and autonomous modes of legal reasoning. Furthermore, to the extent that the law functions as a mobility belt, it can have a crucial impact on socializing a more pervasive sense of competence in individuals—especially among the variously "poor" (p. 8).

As conceptualized here, higher levels of legal reasoning are based on individual conscience and moral principles and not on the rewards and punishments that follow given judgments and behaviors. Furthermore, as an individual thinks increasingly abstractly about the *principles* underlying the law, then he will be increasingly inclined to perceive the potential of the law for creating a climate of justice. Thus, legal development would appear to induce a recognition of a possibility of social change. On an individual level, self-determination and self-actualization could be viewed not only as possibilites but as entitlements.

Friedman (1977) has written sensitively of the socializing functions of rights consciousness. Such a viewpoint has provided the moral and legal bases for the changes in the status and range of life chances of women and minorities in recent years. In that sense, as Tapp and Levine noted, the law does indeed function as a "mobility belt." Friedman has argued that claims of right offer an orderly form for sometimes dramatic social change:

> When claims of right...are asserted suddenly and in great volume and intensity so that the institutions that normally supply the rights cannot handle the demand, a gap appears between socialized values and social realities. It is fruitful of conflict, since the legitimate expectations of individuals may be frustrated or totally denied. A whole social system has grown up on the hidden assumption that some rights—even those that everyone concedes in theory—will not in practice be claimed. Ironically, to claim them now may have a devastating effect, although the claims themselves are simple, obviously just, and have in theory always been treated as valid (pp. 72-73).

While sometimes setting in motion sweeping changes in social practices, claims of rights are fundamentally conservative and indicative of significant socialization. As Friedman has argued, blacks in the civil rights movement did not ask whites to *grant* them equality but rather to fulfill rights already guaranteed under the Constitution. Still more basically, moral claims were made on the bases of a spirit of human equality and brotherhood and of a respect for persons underlying Judeo-Christian society. In a real sense, rights claims are based on an affirmation of personhood and human dignity.

This association of rights consciousness with personal ego strength and with social conscience makes education about rights particularly significant. Given the finding cited earlier that poor children tend to be slow in acquiring a concept of rights as entitlements, justice demands that efforts be made to increase their sense of just claim and of potential for assertion of personal and group autonomy. Essentially, the implication is that "underprivileged" children start not only with a relative lack of opportunities but also (as a result) with no sense of entitlement to demand such opportunities. While it obviously will not eradicate inequality, rights education might be useful in giving "victims" the psychological and moral weapons with which to fight back.

## Principles of Rights Education

Given the potential significance of teaching children about their rights, the question becomes one of how to do it effectively. In that context, it may be useful to think of rights education as a subset of moral education. Much of the existing literature on moral development is based on children's reasoning about rules (Piaget, 1932/1965). As Friedman (1977) has noted, one of the principle characteristics of a right is that it is a "claim against or through authority" (p. 72). A rule is in some ways the opposite; it is an obligation that authority places against the individual. Because both concepts involve relationships to authority as well as ethical judgments in their degree of goodness and inviolability, it might be expected, and indeed the empirical data suggest, that the concepts follow a similar developmental progression. Given the absence of evaluation research on rights education itself, the existing moral education literature will be used to suggest the development of curricula about rights.

It is important to stimulate both vertical and horizontal development of moral and legal reasoning. That is, one hopes to induce successively higher level *structures* of moral and legal judgment. At the same time, as transitions occur to higher levels, it is desirable to extend the new level of reasoning to continually broader ranges of concerns. Thus, rights education may be conceptualized both as a means of exposing children to higher levels of reasoning and as providing an opportunity to extend existing reasoning to a concept that has important implications for full participation in a democratic society.

Tapp and Levine (1974); Levine and Tapp (1977) have suggested four strategies of legal socialization: legal knowledge, mismatch and conflict, participation, and legal continuity. This conceptualization will be used to organize ideas about teaching rights specifically.

## *Legal Knowledge*

It is the view of most psychologists with a cognitive-developmental or interactionist orientation that simply teaching rights in list fashion is insufficient for development of mature reasoning about the law and about rights specifically. From such a perspective, development of new cognitive structures or schemata is more significant than mere acquisition of information or memorization of facts. While rights are theoretically absolute, in practice the application even of legal rights requires much more complex cognitive processes than simply "knowing" the law. While natural rights obviously involve complex abstractions, legal rights also require high level judgments. As Freund (1977) has noted, there is a danger that an emphasis on learning the rules of law will result in a neglect of the dialectical process by which such rules are developed, tested, and revised. Freund has aptly described the cognitive process involved:

> Rules of law are often accommodations between right and right rather than condemnations of obvious wrong. Legal thinking strives to resolve

> in an acceptably fair way, and in specific contexts, the great antinomies of freedom and constraint, privacy and the right to know, free press and fair trial, security of acquisitions and freedom of transactions, national citizenship and local autonomy, blame-worthiness and compensation for harm. For example, the last-mentioned antinomy is inherent in the problem of compensating highway accident victims: Should the outcome turn on the fault of those involved, or should it be resolved irrespective of fault, as in the case of fire or casualty insurance? Is there a way of incorporating elements of fault in the solution without sacrificing the end of compensation to the victim? These are hard questions of justice that challenge the powers of creativity. It is precisely with such issues that the study of law differs crucially from the art of debating. While both call for the confrontation of claims with counterclaims, legal thinking requires a resolution in the individual mind and encourages the finding of solutions that transcend, as by a synthesis, the polar opposites of a debate (p. 159).

Furthermore, exposure to legal dicta will not in and of itself create higher-level legal reasoning. For example, most law students do not exhibit post-conventional legal reasoning (Levine & Tapp, 1977; Tapp & Levine, 1974).

Nonetheless, without a basic knowledge of what rights are and of procedures for their assertion, even a principled thinker may not be able to apply (or create) the law. As noted earlier, if children, and perhaps parents, do not know their rights, then children's rights may in fact be moot. The Supreme Court made similar assumptions in its famous ruling that suspects must be informed of their rights prior to interrogation if confessions are to be considered voluntary and therefore admissible (*Miranda v. Arizona*, 1966).

It should be noted that even this basic spoon-feeding approach to rights education may be threatening to many adults, a point that will be discussed in more detail later in this chapter. It is hard to imagine many principals telling students that they are free to express political opinions by wearing armbands or writing controversial articles in the school newspaper. Similarly, many may find it objectionable to tell students that they have the right to access to school records, or as some courts have ruled, that their lockers are private and subject to search only if the authorities have a warrant. Doubtlessly many would view telling minor women about their rights to contraception and abortion as unconscionable. The point is that, although they do not mesh with other principles to be discussed here, purely didactic approaches to teaching rights may themselves represent major steps for many school systems and individual educators.

Traditionally "civics" classes have dealt with such topics as the process by which a bill becomes law and the separation of powers among governmental branches. Few curricula have examined individuals' daily interaction with the political system or the system's obligations to its citizens. Where rights have been discussed, the discussions have tended to consist of platitudes about the Bill of Rights without attention to its concrete applications, especially in the lives of children. "Free press" is seldom applied in classwork to the work of the student press. "Due process" is not likely to be discussed in terms of school disciplinary procedures. The functioning of the judicial system is unlikely to be explained in terms of cases of consumers' small claims against unscrupulous businessmen. While there are now many "legal education" programs, most have emphasized responsibilities and obedience to authority rather than rights (Levine & Tapp, 1977). Inclusion of material about rights within social studies curricula, even in a purely didactic, non-participatory format, is likely to require striking changes in the curricula and probably in many educators' attitudes toward their students.

### *Mismatch and Conflict*

From both cognitive-developmental and social-learning perspectives, exposure to conflict is thought to heighten moral development. Cognitive developmentalists emphasize conflict as stimulating the process of equilibration in moral development (Turiel, 1979). Essentially, cognitive stage theorists (Piaget, 1956/1971; Pinard & Laurendeau, 1969) understand development as occurring when the child discovers new ways of thinking that conflict with existing schemata. Change happens when the child actively accommodates to new experiences. The implication is that advanced reasoning about rights will occur only when disequilibrium is induced by exposure to conflicting value orientations about rights.

It is clear from such a perspective that including behavioral conformity through conventional moral instruction will not result in significant moral development. The classical finding is that moral instruction, such as exhortation not to cheat, does not work in inducing consistent moral behavior (Hartshorne & May, 1928-1930). Kohlberg (1966) has argued that this failure is the result of emphasizing situational and expediency factors rather than presenting reasons for moral behavior (for example, trust as a motivator not to cheat). Such concrete exhortations are also seen to be ineffective because they involve instruction at a level that is often actually beneath the conceptual level of the child. The assumption is that children will reject "talking down" to them. In any case, they would not be expected to profit from overly concrete moral education; no new ways of thinking are presented in such a curriculum.

Social-learning theorists have also emphasized the role of conflict in enhancing moral development. The process of development is viewed as involving the interaction between cognitive competencies and experience, particularly observations of models (Mischel & Mischel, 1976). Increasingly well-developed moral formulations are likely to be preceded or accompanied by increasingly complex modeling of such judgments and behavior. Obviously, one cannot be expected to give high level reasons if he has not been exposed at all to such reasoning. The kind of conflict that social-learning theorists emphasize is not between cognitive structures per se. Rather, there is an emphasis on *pluralism*, which is thought to induce acceptance and understanding of diverse points of view (Garbarino & Bronfenbrenner, 1976). Essentially, ability to make nonabsolutist moral judgments requires exposure to models in a variety of roles. Simplistic judgments would be expected in cultures or subcultures where there is a monolithic pattern of socialization.

While the literature concerning factors affecting attitudes toward children's rights is still sparse, the available literature on attitudes toward civil rights generally confirms the importance of exposure to conflicting points of view. There is broad concensus among adults in favor of democratic principles like freedom of speech (Erskine & Siegel, 1975; Prothro & Grigg, 1960; Wilson, 1975; Zellman, 1975). However, that consensus breaks down when opinion is gathered concerning concrete applications of the principles (i.e., whether a Communist should be allowed to give a public speech). The best demographic predictor of whether an individual will espouse civil liberties in specific situations is educational level (Montero, 1975; Prothro & Grigg, 1960; Wilson, 1975; Zellman, 1975). Prothro & Grigg (1960) found, for example, that regional and income differences in attitudes toward civil liberties disappeared when education was held constant.

The most common explanation of such findings is that higher education results in exposure to diverse points of view and increases tolerance for them. Education is thought to reduce tendencies to see issues in black and white. As students explore issues in depth, they come to appreciate their complexity and to understand how people can reach different conclusions. Furthermore, as people become more sophisticated in their thinking, illogical reasoning may arouse more dissonance for them. Educated people may be less likely to tolerate the inconsistency in advocating free speech for all and then denying it to an unpopular group.

Of course, the causality may be in the opposite direction. That is, rather than education inducing libertarian ideas, it may be that libertarian people are more likely to seek diverse experiences, such as within education. Even with education and other demographic variables held constant, Zalkind, Gaugler, and Schwartz (1975) found flexibility, independence, and self-reliance to correlate positively with libertarian attitudes. In a study of fifth through ninth graders, Zellman and Sears (1971) found attitudes toward free speech to be positively related to "divergent thinking self-esteem." Thus, confidence in one's ability to generate novel ideas is positively related to tolerance for free speech. Even if these personality variables do result in a self-selection factor in the education-libertarianism relationship, the implication still is that exposure to diverse points of view is important in development of positive attitudes toward civil rights. Authoritarian people tend to come from families in which they are exposed to rigid world views and punished for any deviation (Adorno, Frenkel-Brunswick, Levinson, & Sanford, 1950). Thus, they have minimal experience in handling conflict.

Given that the presence of conflict would be predicted to be useful in stimulating higher level reasoning about rights, the question is one of how to induce significant conflict. Cognitive developmentalists have tended to recommend presenting a mismatch with the child's reasoning, but not too much of a mismatch. The usual recommendation (Kohlberg, 1966) has been to provide reasoning to a child which is one stage (in Kohlberg's six-stage formulation) above the child's own. This advise is based on a study by Turiel (1966) in which children were presented with reasoning two levels above, one level above, or one level below the child's own. The most absorption of the experimenter's moral judgments occurred when the reasoning was +1.

Rest (1974) has criticized the idea that +1 modeling is essential to change. He made two basic points: "first, cognitive developmentalists, including Piaget, usually describe the acquisition of new structures in terms of the single individual trying to reorganize his thoughts, not learning from a model; and second, new cognitive structures can be evolved in the absence of higher stage models (Who was +1 for Socrates?)" (p. 246). Beyond the conceptual issues that Rest raised, though, there is a practical critique that may be more compelling. It is probably unrealistic to expect teachers to assess the reasoning of each of their pupils individually. Such assessments also require a significant amount of knowledge and skill in moral development and education. Finally, and perhaps more importantly, the available data on the typical legal reasoning of teachers, and for that matter most adults, suggest that their reasoning is not sufficiently disparate from their students' to provide much conflict (Levine & Tapp, 1977; Tapp & Levine, 1974). Rights education probably has to begin with teachers, therefore. Regardless, the general principle is that rights education will be most effective if the student is presented with ideas that will foster a dialectic. At the same time, the ideas presented must not be so advanced that the student cannot assimilate them.

***Participation***

Cognitive developmentalists regard role-taking as a mediating step between cognitive and moral development (Selman, 1976). That is, social cognition requires a certain level of cognitive development; at the same time, advanced levels of moral development are dependent upon an awareness of the circumstances and needs of others and the interdependence of people. Specifically with regard to concepts of children's rights, a knowledge of the requisites for orderly interaction among people is necessary for Level 2 reasoning. Level 3 reasoning would appear to require still more complete understanding of the conditions necessary for people to experience their full humanity and to have the satisfaction of living in a just society.

The implication of such a view is that psychologal development is facilitated by the child's actually *experiencing* rights and participating in roles that allow for some degree of self-determination. Free press is likely to have a distant, empty quality to students in schools where the newspaper is censored. Students are likely to have little conception of their own potential for self-governance when the student "government" is limited to planning dances in the school gymnasium. Morally absolutist judgments about rights receive confirmation when school authorities can invade the personal space of students and search their lockers or mandate dress styles. In addition to allowing discussion of rights in the classroom, rights education requires attention to the entire atmosphere of the school. It is this aspect of a rights-education program that, while probably the most effective component, is probably most likely to produce a defensive reaction from school officials.

Restrictive practices stem from a belief system that has some aspects of "victim blaming" (Ryan, 1971). The basic notion is that children cannot be trusted. This view is likely to be most pronounced in schools that have a high percentage of poor and minority-group children. For example, in the research by Melton (1980, in press) discussed earlier, several teachers in the low-SES school apologized to the researcher for the level of intellect of their students

It is noteworthy that student participation yields additional rewards beyond enhanced legal and moral development, at least with adolescents. Trickett (1978) examined the social ecology of five types of public schools: urban, rural, suburban, vocational, and alternative. Alternative schools were by far the highest on all three relationship dimensions measured: involvement, affiliation, and teacher support. Interestingly, alternative schools were also high on system maintenance dimensions (order and organization, rule clarity), although quite low in teacher control and quite high in innovative practices. Apparently, openness to new ideas and high respect for students is accompanied both by a high degree of relatedness and by a high degree of orderliness. Although Trickett did not test such a hypothesis, these social rewards may be the behavioral result of increased moral development stemming from increased student participation.

Level of participation may also be positively correlated with a sense of personal competence and efficacy. Gump (1965) found that "undermanned" environments which demand high levels of active participation (experience as "operatives") yield satisfactions associated with "being important," meeting challenges, and improving personal capacities. In keeping with the formulation of rights-concept development presented here, it is probable that students will be increasingly prone to claim rights for themselves as they experience their "importance."

### *Legal Continuity*

Tapp and Levine (1974; Levine & Tapp, 1977) argued that the probability of children's becoming full participants in law creation is increased by socialization strategies that inculcate a view of the law as applicable to multiple social systems. Essentially, the idea is that the law should be thought of in a broader perspective than as applying just to the "legal system" of governmental regulation. As conceptualized here, "rights" are relevant to a wide variety of conflicts among child and police, child and teacher, child and parent, and child and peer. Given such a view, the teacher may in fact use the group process in the classroom for concrete examples in teaching about rights.

Weyrauch (1977) has described the "basic law" of one small group, which may be a useful starting point for thinking about other groups.

Levine & Tapp (1977) have described the advantages of such a strategy of "legal continuity":

> The advantage of socializing strategies that reflect a broad conception of law is substantial. Such a perspective should increase the probability of one's using complementary, yet diverse "legal" alternatives to redress grievances, accommodate interests, or secure rights. For example, an individual can reason whether to press a claim through formal or informal "law" or through adversary or conciliatory techniques. Further, continuity enhances a conception of the individual as instrumental in determining the nature of the network of "legal" activity, as opposed to passively receiving an externally imposed set of regulations. Thus, the individual is more likely to develop an ethical legality, and the law is more likely to be, or to become, an expressive, participatory institution (p. 176).

It should be noted that, while Levine and Tapp's argument is intuitively sound, the hypothesized effects of a strategy of legal continuity are just that, hypotheses. Research is needed to validate the assumption that legal education will have an impact on behavior in diverse settings.

## Educators' Knowledge of Rights

It has already been suggested that a rights-education program should begin with the teachers. One survey of teachers and education students illustrates this principle starkly. Weiser and Hayes (1966) found that two-thirds of their sample agreed that "the government should prohibit some people from making speeches," and more than two-thirds did not believe in the right of free petition of authorities for redress of grievances. Pluralities favored permitting police to give suspects the "third degree" and to censor books they found objectionable. Thus, many teachers have negative attitudes toward expression of civil liberties generally.

These antilibertarian attitudes are likely to be particularly aroused when children begin to assert rights. Zellman (1975) has speculated that willingness to permit expression of unpopular views is related to the degree of threat which the individual experiences when hearing these views. For teachers who lack confidence in their own ability to maintain respect through means other than punitive control, assertion of rights by children would be expected to be particularly threatening. Such threats would be likely to arouse considerable reactance (Brehm, 1966) or emotional response to the perceived threats to their own freedom to exercise authority. The implication is that teaching children about their rights without adequately preparing teachers and other adults who work with children is likely to put children into a bind. If they were to assert their newly discovered rights, they might invoke the wrath of those who realistically have authority over them. Furthermore, such contingencies would be likely to render rights moot. Even if children are able to *conceptualize* rights well, their *behavior* may appear to reflect a Level 1 understanding if the reality is that any expression of entitlement would be likely to be punished or at least unrewarded.

Developing positive attitudes toward children's rights is not sufficient for teachers charged with implementing curricula about rights. At least basic legal knowledge is also required. While the most important aspects of knowledge about rights probably have to do with actually experiencing rights in the schools and other institutions, certain factual knowledge is also useful and perhaps necessary for full legal participation, as discussed previously in this chapter. Survey research indicates that most adults lack basic knowledge about their rights in such areas as criminal and consumer law (Note, 1973; Williams & Hall, 1972). This problem as it applies to teachers, though, should be easily remediable through in-service training and teacher education. The more difficult issue is the attitudinal one discussed above. It is possible that psychological consultants in the schools could be helpful in reducing hostile or fearful attitudes about instructing children about their rights.

## Materials about Rights

Although "civics" classes do not usually begin until secondary school, elementary schools have social studies programs into which materials about rights could be inserted. Most elementary school social studies curricula follow a sequence of expanding world views in their foci: first grade, the family; second grade, the neighborhood; third grade, the city; fourth grade, the state; fifth grade, the nation; sixth grade, the world. While existing curricula are notably bereft of materials about rights, the teacher could easily include discussions of rights issues at each of these levels. For example, first grade teachers could elicit discussions about privacy in the family. Similarly, sixth graders might discuss the applications of the UN Declaration of the Rights of the Child (United Nations, 1979).* The general point is as outlined in the principles of "participation" and "legal continuity." That is, efforts should be made to expand children's awareness of the relevance of rights to everyday situations that have an impact on their own lives. One way to proceed would be to stimulate discussion of vignettes like those used in the study of rights concepts discussed previously.

At the secondary school level, real cases that have involved applications of the Bill of Rights could be presented. There is a series of pamphlets available in the Xerox Public Issues Series that does an excellent presentation of cases in which students can be expected to have a personal investment (Cutler & Schwach, 1975; Oliver & Newman, 1968; Pearson & Cutler, 1975). For example, case law with respect to school dress codes and town curfews is discussed. Here again, though, the enterprising teacher could assemble vignettes for discussion that might deal with current school or community issues affecting teenagers. In presenting such topics for discussion the teacher should, of course, attempt to present different points of view, especially at a higher level of reasoning.

## Conclusion

Some general guidelines for programs in rights education have been presented with attention to the available literature in legal and moral development. It is useful in conclusion, though, to

*The United States Committee for UNICEF has teacher's materials and audiovisual aids available for teaching about children's rights, including slides illustrating the Declaration of the Rights of the Child.

return to a discussion of the importance of initiating such a program. There is the obvious implication of helping to give children the tools necessary to serve, at least in part, as their own advocates. Perhaps the most compelling ethical basis for rights education is from a long-term perspective, though. Research was presented which indicates that poor children are relatively slow to acquire a view of rights as having any relevance to themselves. There is also evidence that adults of low socioeconomic status, particularly those from minority groups, are relatively ignorant of their legal rights. What is more disturbing about this research is that it indicates an ignorance of the legal and moral means of social change. Such ignorance has the effect of reinforcing discrimination, which is in actuality illegal. For example, 40% of low-income blacks and 52% of low-income Mexican-Americans in a Texas study believed that "Texas law prohibits Negroes from teaching white children in the schools" (Williams & Hall, 1972). Similarly, in a Michigan study (Note, 1973), 25% of blacks (compared to 11% of whites) said that they believed that, "under Michigan law, a school board can require blacks and whites to go to separate schools, as long as they are of equal quality." An incorrect belief that interracial marriage is illegal was held by 18% of blacks, compared to 6% of whites.

Programs of rights education are not likely to rectify completely this discrepancy in knowledge of civil rights and specifically of children's rights. As argued in the discussion of development of concepts of rights, a belief in limited rights may reflect the social, if not the legal or ethical, reality of life for disadvantaged groups in our society. Nonetheless, efforts to increase a sense of entitlement and an awareness of legal rights might aid in the "mobility belt" which Tapp and Levine (1974) described.

## References

Adorno, T.W., Frenkel-Brunswik, E., Levinson, D.J., & Sanford, R.N. *The authoritarian personality*. New York: Harper & Row, 1950.

Bergman, J.L. *Student rights and responsibilities: An analysis of student, teacher, and administrator knowledge in a school system where a well established policy exists*. Unpublished doctoral dissertation proposal, University of Maryland, 1979.

Brehm, J.W. *A theory of psychological reactance.* New York: Academic Press, 1966.

Carey v. Population Services International, 431 U.S. 678 (1977).

Coles, R. *Privileged ones. Vol. 5 of Children in crisis.* Boston: Little, Brown, 1977.

Cutler, C.L., & Schwach, H.J. *Juveniles and the law.* Middletown, Conn.: Xerox Educational Publications, 1975.

Erskine, H., & Siegel, R.L. Civil liberties and the American public. *Journal of Social Issues,* 1975, *31*(2), 13-30.

Farson, R. *Birthrights.* New York: Macmillan, 1974.

Freund, P.A. Law in the schools. In J.L. Tapp & F.J. Levine (Eds.), *Law, justice, and the individual in society: Psychological and legal issues.* New York: Holt, Rinehart & Winston, 1977.

Friedman, L.M. The idea of right as a social and legal concept. In J.L. Tapp & F.J. Levine (Eds.), *Law, justice, and the individual in society: Psychological and legal issues.* New York: Holt, Rinehart & Winston, 1977.

Garbarino, J., & Bronfenbrenner, U. The socialization of moral judgment and behavior in cross-cultural perspective. In T. Lickona (Ed.), *Moral development and behavior: Theory, research, and social issues.* New York: Holt, Rinehart & Winston, 1976.

Grisso, T., & Lovinguth, T. *Juveniles' definition of legal defense and right to silence.* Paper presented at the meeting of the American Psychological Association, New York, September, 1979.

Grisso, T., & Manoogian, S. Juveniles' comprehension of *Miranda* rights. In P.D. Lipsitt & B.D. Sales (Eds.), *New directions in psycholegal research.* New York: Van Nostrand Reinhold, 1980.

Grisso, T., & Pomicter, C. Interrogation of juveniles: An empirical study of procedures, safeguards, and rights waiver. *Law and Human Behavior,* 1977, *1,* 312-342.

Gump, P.V. *Big schools—Small schools.* Moravia, N.Y.: Chronical Guidance Publications, 1965.

Hartshorne, H., & May, M.A. *Studies in the nature of character* (Vol. 3). New York: Macmillan, 1928-1930.

Holt, J. *Escape from childhood: The needs and rights of children.* New York: E.P. Dutton, 1974.

*In re* Gault, 387 U.S. 1 (1967).

Kagan, J. A conception of early adolescence. In J. Kagan & R. Coles (Eds.), *Twelve to sixteen: Early adolescence.* New York: Norton, 1971.

Kohlberg, L. Moral education in the schools: A developmental view. *School Review,* 1966, *74,* 1-30.

Kohlberg, L. Stage and sequence: The cognitive-developmental approach to socialization. In D.A. Goslin (Ed.), *Handbook of socialization theory and research.* New York: Rand McNally, 1969.

Levine, F.J., & Tapp, J.L. The dialectic of legal socialization in community and school. In J.L. Tapp & F.J. Levine (Eds.), *Law, justice, and the individual in society: Psychological and legal issues.* New York: Holt, Rinehart & Winston, 1977.

Levine, M., & Levine, A. *A social history of the helping services: Court, clinic, school, and community.* New York: Appleton-Century-Crofts, 1970.

Melton, G.B. Children's right to treatment. *Journal of Clinical Child Psychology,* 1978, *7,* 200-202.

Melton, G.B. Children's concepts of their rights. *Journal of Clinical Child Psychology,* 1980, *9,* 186-190.

Melton, G.B. *Child advocacy: Psychological issues and intervention.* New York: Plenum, in press.

Miranda v. Arizona, 384 U.S. 436 (1966).

Mischel, W., & Mischel, H.N. A cognitive social-learning approach to morality and self-regulation. In T. Lickona (Ed.), *Moral development and behavior: Theory, research, and social issues.* New York: Holt, Rinehart & Winston, 1976.

Montero, D. Support for civil liberties among a cohort of high school graduates and college students. *Journal of Social Issues,* 1975, *31*(2), 123-136.

Note. Legal knowledge of Michigan citizens. *Michigan Law Review,* 1973, *71,* 1463-1486.

Oliver, D.W., & Newman, F.M. *Rights of the accused: Criminal procedure and public security.* Middletown, Conn.: Xerox Educational Publications, 1975.

Pearson, C., & Cutler, C. *Liberty under law: Case studies of the basic principles of the Bill of Rights.* Middletown, Conn.: Xerox Educational Publications, 1975.

Piaget, J. *The moral judgment of the child.* New York: Free Press, 1965. (Originally published, 1932.)

Piaget, J. The general problems of the psychobiological development of the child. In J.M. Tanner & B. Inhelder (Eds.), *Discussions on child development.* New York: International Universities Press, 1971. (Proceedings of the World Health Organization study group, 1956.)

Pinard, A., & Laurendeau, M. "Stage" in Piaget's cognitive-developmental theory: Exegesis of a concept. In D. Elkind & J.H. Flavell (Eds.), *Studies of cognitive development: Essays in honor of Jean Piaget.* New York: Oxford University Press, 1969.

Planned Parenthood of Central Missouri v. Danforth, 428 U.S. 52, (1976).

Platt, A.M. *The child savers: The invention of delinquency* (2nd ed.). Chicago: University of Chicago Press, 1977.

Prothro, J.W., & Grigg, C.W. Fundamental principles of democracy: Bases of agreement and disagreement. *Journal of Politics,* 1960, *22,* 276-294.

Rest, J. Developmental psychology as a guide to value education: A review of "Kohlbergian" programs. *Review of Educational Research,* 1974, *44,* 241-259.

Rogers, C.M., & Wrightsman, L.S. Attitudes toward children's rights: Nurturance or self-determination. *Journal of Social Issues,* 1978, *34,* 59-68.

Ryan, W. *Blaming the victim.* New York: Vintage, 1971.

Saks, M.J. Social psychological contributions to a legislative subcommittee on organ and tissue transplants. *American Psychologist,* 1978, *33,* 680-690.

Selman, R.L. Social-cognitive understanding: A guide to educational and clinical practice. In T. Lickona (Ed.), *Moral development and behavior: Theory, research, and social issues.* New York: Holt, Rinehart & Winston, 1976.

Siegel, D.M., & Hurley, S. The role of the child's preference in custody proceedings. *Family Law Quarterly,* 1977, *11,* 1-58.

Tapp, J.L. Psychology and the Law: An overture. *Annual Review of Psychology,* 1976, 359-404.

Tapp, J.L., & Levine, F.J. Legal socialization: Strategies for an ethical legality. *Stanford Law Review,* 1974, *27,* 1-72.

Trickett, E.J. Toward a social-ecological conception of adolescent socialization: Normative data on contrasting types of public school classrooms. *Child Development,* 1978, *49,* 408-414.

Turiel, E. An experimental test of the sequentiality of developmental stages in the child's moral judgments. *Journal of Personality and Social Psychology,* 1966, *3,* 611-618.

Turiel, E. Developmental processes in the child's moral thinking. In P. Mussen, J. Langer, & M. Covington (Eds.), *Trends and issues in developmental psychology.* New York: Holt, Rinehart & Winston, 1969.

United Nations. *Declaration of the rights of the child.* Resolution adopted by the General Assembly, November, 1979.

Weiser, J.C., & Hayes, J.E. Democratic attitudes of teachers and prospective teachers. *Phi Delta Kappan,* 1966, *47,* 476-481.

Weyrauch, W.O. The "basic law" or "constitution" of a small group. In J.L. Tapp & F.J. Levine (Eds.), *Law, justice and the individual in society: Psychological and legal issues.* New York: Holt, Rinehart & Winston, 1977.

Williams, M., & Hall, J. Knowledge of the law in Texas: Socioeconomic and ethnic differences. *Law and Society Review,* 7, 99-118.

Wilson, W.C. Belief in freedom of speech and press. *Journal of Social Issues,* 1975, *31,* 69-76.

Zalkind, S.S., Gaugler, E.A., & Schwartz, R.M. Civil liberties attitudes and personality measures: Some exploratory research. *Journal of Social Issues,* 1975, *31,* 77-92.

Zellman, G.L. Antidemocratic beliefs: A survey and some explanations. *Journal of Social Issues,* 1975, *31,* 31-54.

Zellman, G.L., & Sears, D.O. Childhood origins of tolerance for dissent. *Journal of Social Issues,* 1971, *27,* 109-136.

Chapter 9

# CHILDREN AS RESEARCH SUBJECTS: PROBLEMS OF COMPETENCY AND CONSENT

DONALD N. BERSOFF

THE USE OF CHILDREN as participants in psychological (and biomedical) research raises questions far beyond the apparently restricted scope of the topic. Children are, in the main, considered developmentally restricted in their ability to comprehend and respond meaningfully to requests for participation in what may be technically complex experiments. Thus, they are judged to be incapable of giving legally sufficient informed consent and, as a result, are enrolled as subjects by proxies—third parties, usually parents—who consent for them. The philosopher-ethicist Paul Ramsey (1970) asserts that no one possesses the right to conscript children in research that is not of direct benefit to them. In response to arguments that such a position severely restricts the accumulation of scientific knowledge, Ramsey contends that the moral progress of the human race transcends the benefits of such research. In that light, the "testing of children is the paradigm instance that at times it may be necessary to choose between morality and knowledge even though we normally assume that we do not have to choose between them" (Hauerwas, 1980).

Undoubtedly, then, the justification for including children in research evokes concerns that are ethical as well as legal (for general reviews of the literature that consider these issues, see Annas, Glantz, & Katz, 1977; Bersoff, 1978; Cooke, 1980; National Commission for the Protection of Human Subjects of Biomedical and Behavioral Research [hereinafter, National Commission] [Appendix], 1977; Sardello, 1978). This chapter, however, is more delimited in its goal. It aims to explore only the complex legal problems of using children as participants in research. The chapter begins with an exploration of the concepts of consent and competency, then reviews the National Commission's recommendations concerning research involving children (1977) and the proposed regulations promulgated by the Department of Health, Education, and Welfare (1978), and concludes with a lengthy evaluation of these proposals in the context of the legal rights of children generally.

## Consent and Competency

It is now universally accepted, though not always honored, that human participants must give their informed consent before they may be used as subjects of research (Katz, 1972). The underlying legal and philosophical premise of the informed consent doctrine is the notion of "thoroughgoing self-determination" *(Natanson v. Kline,* 1960, p. 406). This doctrine, grounded in the respect society has for subjects as persons, emerged as a rule of law in the context of physician-patient malpractice suits. The first clear expression of the rule was delineated over seventy-five years ago:

> [U]nder a free government, at least, the free citizen's first and greatest right, which underlies all others—the right to the inviolability of his person, in other words, his rights to himself—is the subject of universal acquiescence, and this right necessarily forbids a physician or surgeon . . . to violate without permission the bodily integrity of his patient by a major or capital operation . . . without his consent or knowledge (*Pratt v. Davis,* 1905, p. 166).

However, there was no reason for the informed consent doctrine to be limited to treatment relationships. In many ways the insensitivity of behavioral and medical researchers to the interests of those they studied matched that of the physicians. In 1954 a group of professors from law and the social sciences recorded and studied the deliberations of juries with "bugging devices." The researchers obtained the approval of the judges and lawyers involved but neither the jurors nor the litigants were aware that microphones had been concealed in the jury room. In 1963 three scientists injected "live cancer cells" into twenty-two chronically ill patients at a New York hospital with the approval of the institution's director of medicine but without the fully informed consent of those injected. In 1972 the American public was finally told that for forty years the United States Public Health Service directed and funded a continuing study of the effects of untreated syphillis in approximately 400 black males in Alabama. There was no evidence that consent for participation had even been obtained. At about the same time, the media publicized the fact that mentally retarded residents at Willowbrook State School in New York had been the subjects of an experiment in which researchers attempted to find a vaccine for fecally borne hepatitis. Although parents consented, the conditions under which it was secured were suspect and many of the children became ill. Of overriding influence as far as the scrutiny of behavioral research is concerned was Milgram's (1963) study of obedience. Central to the startling results was the deception, by the experimenter, of the subjects involved who thought they were administering dangerous electrical shocks to others.

These disclosures either evoked or heightened sensitivity to the right of research subjects to become full and informed participants and led eventually, as we shall see, to government regulation of the informed consent process. While consent is, therefore, crucial to much of what is to follow, it must be recognized that informed consent (or, alternatively, the duty to disclose) may be more of a principle than a consensually defined concept, as there is considerable dispute as to its meaning. Nevertheless, it is generally accepted that the doctrine of informed consent comprises three basic characteristics.

KNOWLEDGE: The person seeking consent must disclose sufficient information in a manner that can be understood by the person from whom the consent is sought. However, as the definition implies, the duty to disclose is not absolute. It is tempered by what may be called the materiality rule. Researchers need only disclose those risks that a reasonable person would need to make an intelligent decision to accept or reject the proposed involvement. Only if a prudent subject would have foregone participation when apprised of an undisclosed fact or risk is that fact or risk considered material.

VOLUNTARINESS: Communicating all necessary information in a comprehensible manner does not guarantee that consent is voluntary. Consent must be obtained in the absence of coercion, duress, misrepresentation, or undue inducement. In short, the person consenting must do so freely. From a philosophical perspective, it may be impossible to judge whether any decision is made voluntarily and from a behaviorist's perspective it is antithetical to theory to even conceive of free (or more, properly, undetermined) choice. As a practical matter, voluntariness implies decisions made without unacceptable influence or interference by the researcher.

CAPACITY: Persons must be legally competent to give consent. While all adults are considered capable of making legally binding decisions (unless they have been adjudicated incompetent in a formal proceeding), children are not. The consequence of a presumption or adjudication of incompetence is that others may be substituted as a decision maker. With children, given their purported cognitive and affective immaturity and the law's presumption of incompetency, the component of informal consent perceived as least satisfied is capacity. As such, it deserves some extended attention.

The notion of competency is not unidimensional. In law, it arises in both the criminal and civil arenas. Standards for determining competency change as the context in which it is considered changes. For example, the legal system has developed somewhat dissimilar rules for determining competency of adults to stand trial, to plead guilty, to make enforceable contracts, or to make a will. The same is true of children. While children cannot vote or marry or become independent parties to a lawsuit, they may seek, in some cases, an abortion, psychiatric counseling, or treatment for venereal disease without parental consent. Recently the New Jersey Supreme Court *(State in the Interest of R.R.,* 1979) ruled that a four-year-old child was competent to testify as a witness in a delinquency adjudication against an adolescent who had allegedly subjected him to sodomous acts. The court refused to rule that age per se rendered any proposed witness incompetent. Rather, the court looked at two narrow factors—whether the child consciously recognized the duty to tell the truth and whether he had the ability to understand questions and to frame an intelligent answer. Despite the fact the child sometimes responded in gestures and needed his mother's help to interpret his verbal answers, he was deemed to have met these two tests and the court upheld the admission of his testimony (for a discussion of this case, see Comment, 1980). As we shall see, the ability to express oneself does not qualify a child to accept or reject participation as a research subject.

How one defines competency, therefore, assumes great significance. A judgment that a person is incompetent permits others to exercise the right of informed consent that would otherwise be left to the individual. "Neglecting to seek informed consent . . . [from the participant] indicates a . . . failure to recognize the autonomy and hence, the humanity of the subject" (Macklin & Sherwin, 1975, p. 443). The Supreme Court has recognized the principle of autonomy in two correlative strands of cases—one upholding the individual's right to self-determination and the other protecting assaults on bodily integrity (see e.g., *Carey v. Population Services International,* 1977; *Schmerber v. California,* 1966; see generally Schwartz, 1975). The ultimate question, then, is not whether there is a right to autonomy but the extent that its exercise will be enforced.

In most cases, whether one will be permitted to act independently is tied to a judgment concerning rationality. Like competency, there are several possible meanings to the term. It can be viewed as that distinguishing feature which separates humans from all other entities; it can denote the capacity of persons to use their reason to maximize chosen or accepted ends; or it may refer to the ends themselves. In this latter meaning, chosen means are not the criterion; it is the ends themselves that confer rationality (Macklin & Sherwin, 1975). How courts and legislatures view rationality may determine whether children will be capable of consenting for themselves. Friedman (1975) has provided a helpful analysis in this regard:

> 1. Some courts define competency as the capacity to reach a decision based on rational reasons. Here the judge determines whether the person

has the ability to understand the nature of the procedure, to weigh its risks and benefits, and come to a reasonable determination. In essence, the court expresses a value preference for a particular mode of thinking.

2. Other courts define competency as reaching a reasonable result. This approach requires the judge to decide whether the result of the person's decision is one which a reasonably competent person might have made. Thus, when persons, who as a consequence of mental illness, retardation, brain dysfunction, or immaturity are likely to make decisions that result in substantial damage to their mental or physical well-being, the court employing this standard will consider the person incompetent.

3. Finally, a minority of courts define competency as the capacity to make a decision. This approach avoids the difficulties inherent in evaluating whether a person's thinking is rational or irrational but would preclude the apparent consent of those clearly out of touch with reality. The judge under this standard would merely decide whether the person has sufficient understanding of the nature of the procedures, its risks and benefits, and possible alternatives. If so, any decision, provided there is a decision, will be honored.

Some legal commentators have offered the more radical proposal that standards concerning competency either be abolished or established at a very low threshold. For example, Friedman (1975) describes a rule in which there would be no concern at all about the individual's ability to understand. Rather, the inquiry would simply focus on whether persons were able to hear the question and were able to answer questions concerning their willingness to consent affirmatively or negatively. As long as these conditions existed, all answers would be honored, despite the fact that they might have been evoked by reality distortions or stated in a perseverative manner, e.g., "No, no, no," to any and all questions. Goldstein (1977) suggests a similar test, not as an option, but as a requirement:

> The burden in law for incompetence should be very high. No evidence other than a showing that the patient is comatose should ordinarily be accepted as proof of incompetence. . . . Respect for human dignity should not lessen according to an individual's mental health. But practice does undercut that respect by making provision for "substituted consent" by a legal representative who may be forced upon them without their "informed consent." To accept such proxy consents is to authorize invasions of person and personality without regard to the wishes of the research subject—that is to deny them freedom to choose without saying so.

No courts have quite adopted either Goldstein's or Friedman's proposals. However, in *Wyatt v. Aderhold* (1974) the court may be said to have approached the use of such a standard. In ordering new procedures with regard to the sterilization of incompetent mentally retarded residents it required a review committee to determine whether the residents merely "formed, without coercion, a genuine desire to be sterilized," (p. 1385) not whether they understood the procedure nor arrived at a "rational" decision. Although not precisely alike, there are similarities to this position and that of the New Jersey Supreme Court's standard in admitting the testimony of the four-year-old child witness.

## Children's Consent to Research: The Federal Government's Perspective

As a result of the series of disclosures concerning the questionable, if not unethical, research practices in the years between 1950 and the early 1970s, the federal government began to carefully scrutinize the conduct of biomedical and behavioral scientists. The year 1974 may be viewed as the watershed in that respect.

In May 1974 DHEW published regulations regarding the protection of human subjects. These regulations govern the activities of those organizations who receive research funds or are accountable to DHEW (now the Department of Health and Human Services [DHHS]. First published in the Federal Register (39 Federal Register 18917, May 30, 1974) and now codified as federal regulations (45 C.F. R. § 46.101 *et seq.)*, the rules explicitly declare the Department's policy that "no activity involving human subjects to be supported by DHEW grants or contracts shall be undertaken unless a committee of the organization has reviewed and approved such activity and the organization has submitted to DHEW a certification of such review and approval. . . ." (45 C.F.R. § 46.102 (a)). These institutional review boards (IRBs) are to make four major determinations.

1. Whether the risks to the subject are outweighed by both the benefit to the individual and the importance of the knowledge to be gained so as to warrant a decision to allow the subject to accept these risks.

2. Whether the rights and welfare of these persons—called "subjects at risk"—will be adequately protected.

3. Whether legally effective informed consent can be obtained by appropriate and adequate methods.

4. Whether the design calls for periodic review of the research.

Two definitions made part of the regulations are pertinent here. One is the meaning of "subject at risk." The term includes:

> [A]ny individual who may be exposed to the possibility of injury including physical, psychological, or social injury as a consequence of participation as a subject in any research, development or related activity which departs from the application of those established and accepted methods necessary to meet his needs, or which increases the ordinary risks of daily life (45 C.F.R. § 46.103 (b)).

The other definition is the Department's attempt to conceptualize informed consent. Broadly defined, it is conceived as the "knowing consent of an individual or his legally authorized representative so situated as to be able to exercise free power of choice without undue inducement or any element of force, fraud, deceit, duress, or other form of constraint or coercion" (45 C.F.R. § 46.103 (c)). More specifically, the elements comprising consent include:

1. Fair explanation of the procedures to be followed, and their purposes, including identification of any procedures that are experimental.

2. Description of any attendant discomforts and risks reasonably to be expected.

3. Description of any benefits reasonably to be expected.

4. Disclosure of any appropriate alternative procedures that might be advantageous to the subject.

5. An offer to answer any inquiries concerning the procedure.

6. An instruction that the person is free to withdraw consent and to discontinue participating in the project or activity without prejudice.

7. Information regarding the availability of compensation for subjects injured as a result of participating in research.

Soon after DHEW published these regulations, Congress

passed the National Research Act, Title II of which is called "Protection of Human Subjects of Biomedical and Behavioral Research." Its primary purpose was to establish a national commission whose major task was to identify basic ethical principles that underlie the conduct of human research. The Commission, whose three year mandate has now ended, was composed of eleven persons from medicine, law, ethics, theology, the physical and social sciences, philosophy, and public affairs, of whom several were actively engaged in biomedical and behavioral research with human subjects. Its work has largely been taken over by DHHS's Ethical Advisory Board and the President's Commission for the Study of Ethical Problems in Medicine and Biomedical and Behavioral Research.

As an advisory body, the Commission did not have the power to make regulations. In the three years of its existence it was limited to recommending ethical principles and guidelines to the secretary of the then DHEW and to Congress. The secretary could adopt the recommendations as written, modify them, or reject them. In almost all instances where DHEW published either final or proposed rules the Commission's work has been revised. Table 9-I indicates the current status of rules governing research.

One of the final products of the National Commission was its recommendations concerning the operation and scope of IRBs (1978). For the most part DHEW accepted the Commission's recommendations when it published its proposed regulations (1979) amending its basic policy adopted in 1974 already described above. Among many of the amendments, a few are of direct relevance to psychologists. One proposal is to require IRB review and approval for research involving human subjects even if not supported by DHEW (now DHHS) funds as long as it is conducted at or supported by an institution receiving money from the Department. Almost every university and mental health facility in the United States receives financial support from DHHS. Second, the proposed rules would require scrutiny of human subject research irrespective of risk. Third, certain research would not have to undergo full scale IRB review. These kinds of research would include the use of survey instruments, the observation of public behavior, and the study of documents and

**TABLE 9-I**
PRESENT STATUS OF RULES REGULATING RESEARCH WITH HUMAN SUBJECTS

| Subject Population/Topic | Nat'l Comm. for the Protection of Human Subjects of Biomedical and Behavioral Research Recommendations Published | DHEW Action |
|---|---|---|
| Basic DHEW Policy[1] | ........................ | Rules Published 45 C.F.R. §§46.101-.122 Proposed Amendments Published 44 Fed. Reg. 47692 (August 14, 1979) |
| Fetuses, Pregnant Women and in Vitro Fertilization | 40 Fed. Reg. 33,530 (August 8, 1975) amended 40 Fed. Reg. 51,638 (November 6, 1975); 43 Fed. Reg. 1,759 (January 11, 1978) | Rules Published 45 C.F.R. §§46.201-211 (1978) Ethical Advisory Board Recommendations to Amend Rules Published 44 Fed. Reg. 35,033 (June 18, 1979) and 44 Fed. Reg. 47,732 (August 14, 1979) |
| Prisoners | 42 Fed. Reg. 3,076 (January 14, 1977) | Proposed Rules Published 43 Fed. Reg. 1,050 (January 5, 1978) (to be codified in 45 C.F.R. §§46.301-.306). |
| Psychosurgery | 42 Fed. Reg. 26,318 (May 23, 1977) | Response Published 43 Fed. Reg. 53,242 (November 15, 1978) |
| Children | 43 Fed. Reg. 2,084 (January 13, 1978) | Proposed Rules Published 43 Fed. Reg. 31,786 (July 21, 1978) (to be codified in 45 C.F.R. §§46.401-.410) |
| Institutionalized Mentally Disabled | 43 Fed. Reg. 11,328 (March 17, 1978) | Proposed Rules Published 43 Fed. Reg. 53,950 (November 17, 1978) (to be codified in 45 C.F.R. §§46,501-.508) |
| Institutional Review Boards | 43 Fed. Reg. 56,174 (November 30, 1978) | Response Published 44 Fed. Reg. 47,688 (August 14, 1979) |

[1]Final regulations amending basic DHHS Policy for the protection of human research subjects were published on January 26, 1981, effective July 27, 1981, in Federal Register, 1981, 46, 8366-8392. These amendments substantially reduce the scope of the existing DHHS regulatory coverage by exempting broad categories of research which normally present little or no risk of harm to subjects. They were published too late to allow inclusion in this Chapter but readers should refer to them to discern the latest binding policy.

records. Perhaps most important to readers, the proposal would *exempt* review of the following:

> Research conducted in established or commonly accepted educational settings, involving normal educational practices, such as (A) research or regular and special education instructional strategies, or (B) research on the effectiveness among instructional techniques, curriculum, or classroom management.
>
> Research involving solely the use of standard educational diagnostic, aptitude, or achievement tests, if information taken from these sources is recorded in such a manner that subjects cannot be reasonably identified, directly or through identifiers linked to the subjects (DHEW, 1979).

Thus, a great deal of what psychologists do as researchers would be exempt from DHHS regulation and IRB review. Readers should be cautioned that these are but proposals not yet adopted as controlling law (as of September, 1980).[2]

One earlier but perhaps more pertinent aspect of the National Commission's work was to identify the requirements of informed consent for those persons whose capacity for giving consent was either absent or limited. In this category are prisoners, children, and those institutionalized as mentally disabled. To accomplish this task the Commission was to consider the adequacy of information given to such persons about research, the risks, discomforts, and anticipated benefits from the research, as well as the competence and freedom of these subjects to make a choice for or against their involvement.

For present readers, the most relevant work of the federal government in this area are the National Commission's recommendations (1977) and DHEW proposed rules (1978) regarding research with children. The question of children's involvement in the consent process arises here in significant ways. The Commission believed that a child's objection to act as a research subject should be binding unless the experimental procedure holds out the prospect of direct benefit important to the health or well-being of the child and this benefit is available only in the context of research. In addition, while the Commission concluded that only parents could give formal and legally sufficient consent, it urged that children over seven years of age be allowed

---

[2]These proposals are now DHHS policy. *See* Footnote 1.

to "assent," that is, affirmatively agree to participate. However, DHEW's proposed regulations modified these recommendations and it may be helpful to provide a somewhat detailed summary of these rules as they pertain to consent.

First, DHEW gives Institutional Review Boards overall responsibility for determining that adequate provisions are made for soliciting the assent of children should they determine that children are capable of doing so. In deciding whether children are capable of assenting, the IRB is to take into account the age and maturity of the children involved. Thus, the right to assent may be abrogated in two situations: (1) If the IRB determines that children are incapable of being consulted and (2) if the research is directly beneficial to them and that benefit is available only in a research mode. However, there is a trade-off. If the IRB concludes that assent need not be obtained, it must then decide if an advocate should be appointed for the child. The advocate's role is to advise the IRB, researchers, and parents of any concern he or she may have about the child's participation.

With regard to parents' involvement, in less than minimally risky or in risky but directly beneficial research, the consent of only one parent would normally be required. In risky but not directly beneficial research the consent of both parents would be necessary. The proposed rules also take into account two special conditions. Parental permission is not considered a reasonable requirement if neglected or abused children are asked to participate as research subjects. In those cases, DHEW recommends that children be protected by appropriate alternative mechanisms whose precise nature is to be defined by state or local law. The second special condition concerns children who are wards of the state, as is the case with many institutionalized or adjudicated youth. In minimally risky and in risky but directly beneficial research the ward must assent if capable, the legal guardian must consent, and the IRB must appoint an advocate. In risky, nondirectly beneficial research children whose parents no longer have custody may be included only if the study is related to their status as a ward or it is conducted in settings like schools or camps where the majority of children are not wards. Here, too, the appointment of an advocate is required. Finally, if wards object to participation but the IRB determines they are incapable of assenting, they may still be enrolled as subject, although only with the approval of both the legal guardian and the advocate.

In sum, while both the Commission and DHEW reports do not satisfy those child advocates who believe that children should have the full panoply of adult rights and others who have serious concerns about the implementation of the proposals, they do signify an advance over the usual treatment of children as research subjects. Whether they go far enough is a question we now begin to explore.

## Balancing the Interests at Stake: The Developing and Chaotic Law of Children's Right to Independent Decision Making

One legal scholar (Kleinfeld, 1970) has distinguished between the right of persons to make various choices and the right of persons to be protected from the choices or initiatives of others. For the most part, the child advocacy movement has secured advances falling within the latter category. Children remain, like Ralph Ellison's hero, Invisible Persons whose views are infrequently evoked and whose wishes are rarely controlling. Involving children in the research consent process does represent a salutary attempt to promote rights of the first kind—the right to make choices—but much of the proposed rules represent advocacy of the second kind. Everyone is asked to serve children's best interest, even if that means overriding their refusal to participate when adults believe children will benefit.

There is also a great deal of representation of children in these rules by IRBs, parents, advocates, and ultimately the courts. But those who simply advocate greater representation for children fail to acknowledge the complexity of the concept. To "represent" is not to engage in an unidimensional activity. Parents as custodians, the state as protector, and advocates who seek to act in what they perceive to be in the best interests of children represent only in the sense of taking care of another. They may be said to act merely "*in* behalf of," that is, in the interest of or for the benefit of another. Those who act "in behalf of" are under no obligation to consult with their beneficiaries or abide by their wishes. They do what they think best in the light of their trust obligations. Such a rule is different than acting "*on* behalf of," which connotes that the advocate is acting on the part of, in the name of another, or as the one represented might act (Pitkin, 1967). If we are to genuinely urge the expanded rights of children, such advocacy must include the right of children to full-fledged participation in the decision-making process when their significant interests and future hang in the balance.

Whether children will ever exercise the independent right to consent to involvement in research depends a great deal on how the courts allocate power among parents, children, and various arms of federal and state government. That issue has received considered attention from legal scholars (e.g., Bersoff, 1982; Developments in the Law, 1980; Kleinfeld, 1970, 1971; Mnookin, 1978; M. Wald, 1979; P. Wald, 1974) and from the courts. It is to an analysis of that issue that we now turn.

Historically, both parents and the state have exerted inordinate control over children. Under ancient Roman law, fathers had the power of life and death over their offspring and infanticide was not uncommon (especially if children were female or deformed). Before the Norman Conquest, English fathers were able to murder newborns and sell children under seven years of age into slavery. It was not uncommon during the beginning of this century for parents to place children in jails without trials. In upholding this practice, one court reasoned:

> The petitioner was a minor between fifteen and seventeen years of age. Her father, as her natural guardian, had the legal right to regulate her conduct, to restrain her liberty within all reasonable bounds, and to direct her training and education. She was not entitled to general freedom of action, but was under his tutelage. He had the legal right to confine her within limits, to select her associates, and to commit her to the restraint of an institution for training and education during her minority, without her consent.
>
> The child herself, having no right to control her own action or select her own course of life, had no legal right to be heard in these proceedings (*Rule v. Geddes*, 1904, p. 35).

The modern manifestation of this control is the right of parents to commit their sons and daughters to mental hospitals. The Supreme Court, in a case we shall discuss more fully, has recently upheld this "volunteering of children" (Ellis, 1974) with only minor protections to reduce erroneous classification or unnecessary institutionalization (*Parham v. J.L.*, 1979).

The legal systems' solicitude for the family unit and the primacy of parental control does not mean, of course, that children are at the mercy of their mothers and fathers. "Parents may be free to become martyrs themselves. But it does not follow they are free... to make martyrs of their children" (*Prince v. Massachusetts*, 1944, p. 170). Courts will override parental prerogatives when parents are unable or refuse to care for their children's physical, medical, or emotional needs, when there is an abuse of parental authority, or when protectable property interests of children (e.g., inheritances) conflict with those of their parents. The most clear-cut example of state interference in family life is the passage of child abuse laws in all fifty of the United States (see Katz, Howe, & McGrath, 1975). The perceived consequences of all this benevolent intrusion by parents and the state in behalf of children has been summarized by one commentator:

> In this continuing struggle, the child has always been the pawn. Neither philosophically nor legally has he been recognized as having a right to *do* anything about the vicissitudes of his life, but only to await the action of others in his behalf or in his best interests. He is in a state of powerlessness, and for that reason, the institution of childhood has been seriously compared to the institution of slavery. It has been called the "last legal relic of feudalism" (Wald, 1974 p. 15).

As the more egregious and cruder forms of discrimination against minorities have been ameliorated in the past two decades, attention has turned to the plight of other groups who have not been afforded the full and equal protection of the laws. Those who have sought to enhance the status of children and to broaden their rights under the Constitution and federal and state laws have done so within what has been called the child advocacy movement. The result of their activity has been a significant alteration of the balance of power in child-populated, adult-dominated institutions. Most conspicuously, in juvenile courts, mental hospitals, and schools, older persons have found it more difficult to make unilateral decisions when those decisions directly involve important and often fundamental interests of children.

This recent burgec ting of concern and litigation with regard to children's rights can be traced to fifteen-year-old Gerald Gault's obscene phone call to an Arizona woman in the mid 1960s. As a result of his conduct Gault was brought before the juvenile court. Because at that time proceedings before such courts were considered rehabilitative and noncriminal, no records were kept, no charges specified, there was no protection against self-incrimination, and counsel was not provided. Under those conditions, Gault was sentenced to a youth detention center until his twenty-first birthday, a sentence of six years for a crime that would have cost an adult two months imprisonment and a $50 fine. The case, formally known as *In re Gault* (1967) was ultimately appealed to the United States Supreme Court, which reversed the conviction and held children in juvenile court proceedings were constitutionally entitled to certain due process guarantees previously limited to adults in criminal prosecutions. The case tolled the death knell of the doctrine of *parens patraie*—the state's parentalistic authority to protect or promote the welfare of certain classes of person who are considered to lack the capacity to act in their own best interest—at least with regard to juvenile court proceedings (see Bersoff, 1976-77 and references therein). The Supreme Court concluded in *Gault* that the state was neither the sole nor proper representative even when the state sought to further what it judged to be children's interests. Perhaps more importantly, while earlier cases had held that children were entitled to constitutional protections, "*Gault* was the first case squarely to hold that children had constitutional rights" (Developments in the Law, 1980, p. 1228).

The broader impact of *Gault* was reinforced two years later when the Supreme Court explicitly declared in *Tinker v. Des Moines Independent Community School District* (1969) that children were *persons* under the Constitution and possessed fundamental rights the state was required to respect, even when those rights were exercised in the relatively controlled environment of the public schools. *Tinker*, thus, is important on at least three levels. First, it may be said to have ended educators' untrammelled immunity from judicial scrutiny. Second, by declaring children as persons it placed them directly within the protections of the fourteenth amendment's due process clause, which shields only those entities denominated as persons against arbitrary deprivations of life, liberty, or property by the state. Lastly, the Court intimated that at least some rights were evenly distributed among children and adults: "First Amendment rights are available to teachers and students. It can hardly be argued that either students or teachers shed their constitutional rights to freedom of speech or expression at the schoolhouse gate" (p. 506). However, the Supreme Court has also made it clear that children do not share equally in all provisions of the Constitution. In *In re Gault* (1967) the Court only afforded children in juvenile court proceedings some, but not the entire range, of the due process protections granted adult criminals. In *Ginsburg v. New York* (1968) the Supreme Court said that it was rational for the state legislature to prohibit the sale of sexually related material to minors even though it would not be allowed to do so with regard to the sale of the same material to adults. While it violates the eighth amendment's cruel and inhuman punishment clause to physically discipline adult prisoners, the Court ruled that corporal punishment of school children was constitutionally permissible *(Ingraham v. Wright,* 1977).

The Supreme Court's recent abortion-related decisions indicate that in some facets of personal life, certain children possess privacy rights that will be allowed expression even though to do so may conflict with parental wishes. In 1976 the Court declared unconstitutional a state statute requiring parental consent before a pregnant minor could obtain an abortion, saying "Constitutional rights do not mature and come into being magically only when one attains the state-defined age of majority. Minors, as well as adults are protected by the Constitution and possess constitutional rights" *(Planned Parenthood of Central Missouri v. Danforth,* 1976, p. 74). Thus it refused to uphold a blanket provision requiring the consent of a parent as a condition for all unmarried minors to obtain an abortion during the first trimester of pregnancy. A year later the Court was faced with a challenge to the constitutionality of a statute prohibiting the sale or distribution of contraceptives to children under sixteen. Given that it had previously concluded that minors could secure abortions without consent it felt that an absolute ban against access to contraceptives was even more violative of children's independent rights to privacy. "The State's interests in protection of the mental and physical health of the pregnant minor, and in protection of potential life are clearly more implicated by the abortion decision than by the decision to use a nonhazardous contraceptive" *(Carey v. Population Services International Inc.*, 1977, p. 694). Finally, the Court had the occasion in 1979 to once again rule on a minor's unencumbered right to abortion. In the light of the Supreme Court's decision in *Danforth*, Massachusetts amended its law so as to require parental consent for abortion but at the same time affording the child access to court if one or both parents refused to consent. Judges would have the discretion to prohibit the abortion if they found the youngster insufficiently mature to make a decision or if the abortion were not in her best interests. The Court ultimately found that even this new legislation unduly burdened minors' rights to an abortion *(Bellotti v. Baird*, 1979). Justice Powell, speaking for a four member plurality, said that the state could not require parental consent or even consultation if the pregnant minor could show an impartial adjudicator that she was able to make an intelligent decision concerning abortion on her own. If the adjudicator finds she does not meet this standard of competency, the young woman is still entitled to an abortion if it is determined that it would be in her best interests.

These decisions should not seduce the reader into thinking that children have been granted broad independent decision-making powers. Although the Court has extended to children the privacy rights previously granted to adults in earlier abortion cases, matters of procreation have received special treatment by the Court:

> The abortion decision differs in important ways from other decisions that may be made during minority. The need to preserve the constitutional right and unique nature of the abortion decision, especially when made by a minor, requires a State to act with particular sensitivity when it legislates to foster parental involvement in this matter (*Bellotti v. Baird*, 1979, p. 642).

Thus, there is no reason to believe that the independent rights of children will be honored in other domains where their interests may also be at stake (or even in abortion cases where the young woman is determined to be too immature to make decisions without parental consultation or court approval).[3]

That this hypothesis has validity has been borne out in *Parham v. J.L.* (1979), a most important Supreme Court decision rendered during the same 1979 term that it issued *Bellotti*. In *Parham*, the Court was called on to decide the constitutionality of a statute permitting parents to admit their children to mental institutions. When the state seeks to involuntarily commit adults they are afforded a number of procedural safeguards, including a hearing before an impartial decision maker and representation by an attorney. However, in almost all states, when parents seek to place their children in mental hospitals, it is considered a voluntary admission and children have no due process rights. In *Parham*, child advocates claimed that such admissions were voluntary in name only, that there were dangers of parents acting adversely to the interests of their children, and that, as a result, children should be given procedural protections similar to those of adults.

In considering these claims the Chief Justice, writing for a five-member majority, balanced the children's interest, the state's interest, and the parents' interest. Justice Burger acknowledged that children have a substantial liberty interest in not being confined unnecessarily for medical treatment and in not being labeled erroneously by institutional authorities. The state had an interest in restricting use of costly mental health facilities to cases of genuine need. On the other hand, it also had an interest in not imposing unnecessary procedural obstacles that would discourage mentally ill children and their families from seeking psychiatric assistance. What the Court disparagingly called "time-consuming minuets" (what others would call an impartial due process hearing) not only would interfere with the treatment activities of professionals but would prove too onerous, too embarrassing, or too contentious for parents. In the end, the Court found the interests of the parents paramount. It reiterated its traditional concern for the family unit and of the primacy of the family over the State. While noting the incidence of child neglect and abuse,

[3]*See H.L. v. Matheson* (1981) in which the Supreme Court upheld a parental notification statute for dependent minors.

it relied on what it called the "pages of human experience" to undergird its conclusion that "parents generally do act in the child's best interest" (pp. 602-603).

Most importantly for our purposes, the court renewed its belief that children are incompetent to make decisions. It said, "The law's concept of the family rests on the presumption that parents possess what a child lacks in maturity, experience, and capacity for judgment required to making life's difficult decisions" (p. 602) and concluded that "most children, even in adolescence, simply are not able to make sound judgments concerning many decisions, including their need for medical care or treatment" (p. 603). "Parents," it declared, "can and must make those judgments" (p. 603). The overall result of this tripartite interest analysis was to simply hold that a "neutral factfinder," i.e., a staff physician at the admitting hospital, should review all available sources of information to determine that parental requests for institutionalization were not in error.

These sentiments were echoed by the Court in *Bellotti* a few weeks after *Parham*. Justice Powell, announcing the judgment of the Court, made it clear that "States may validly limit the freedom of children to choose for themselves in the making of important, affirmative choices with potentially serious consequences" (p. 635). That power, he said, was "grounded in the recognition that, during the formative years of childhood and adolescence, minors often lack the experience, perspective, and judgment to recognize and avoid choices that could be detrimental to them" (p. 635). While acknowledging that children have constitutional rights that cannot be easily abridged, Justice Powell asserted that "the State is entitled to adjust its legal system to account for children's vulnerability and their needs for concern, . . . sympathy, and . . . paternal attention" (p. 635). In addition to its assumption that children are unable to "make critical decisions in an informed, mature manner" (p. 634), the Court felt justified in limiting children's rights to make independent decisions because of the "guiding role of parents in the upbringing of their children" (p. 637). "Legal restrictions on minors," Powell stated, "especially those supportive of the parental role, may be important to the child's chances for the full growth and maturity that make eventual participation in a free society meaningful and rewarding" (p. 638-39).

Parenthetically, it cannot go unnoticed that on the same day in June 1979 that the Court decided *Parham*, holding that the Constitution did not require hearings for children before they were involuntarily placed in mental hospitals, it decided *Fare v. Michael C.* (1979). In that case the Court held that a sixteen-year-old whose request for his probation officer was refused by the police who were questioning him and then made incriminating statements, waived his right under the fifth and fourteenth amendments to remain silent. Despite the fact that there was evidence that Michael was crying during the interrogation and that he had relatively little schooling, the Court asserted that he waived his constitutional rights knowingly and intelligently. Obviously, to a majority of the present Supreme Court, when children commit crimes they magically assume the decision-making ability of adults; when they are about to be placed in a mental hospital, they are but children who must rely on their parents' judgment of their best interests.

## Children's Right to Consent to Research Reconsidered

It is hoped that this lengthy litany of recent Supreme Court law gives readers some reference points to evaluate the current status and future possibilities for children's participation as independent decision makers in research. In the main, the law considers children generally incapable of knowing what is best for themselves. In their salutary goal to protect families from unreasonable state interference and in a more questionable desire to protect children from immature and potentially harmful autonomous decisions, the courts have presumed that parents, as preferred caregivers, are competent to represent their children's interests. Only when this presumption is rebutted by evidence of significant injury to the child do courts replace parents—either permanently or for limited purposes—with alternative decision makers. Although the right of parents to control the upbringing of their children has strong foundations in tradition and in the Constitution's preference for minimal state interference in family life, "that right is nevertheless unusual among constitutional rights in that it protects the ability to control another person. Ordinarily, constitutional rights do not protect an individual's power to control someone else" (Developments in the Law, 1980, p. 1353).

However, if parental prerogatives are also founded on the premise that children are incapable of making informed decisions, it may be possible to rebut that premise also, making it permissible not only to shift decisions from parent to state but also from parent to child. As we have seen, this has occurred in instances where a particular class of rights, e.g., child bearing and contraception, have been considered so fundamental that parental control and intervention have been ruled as unconstitutionally burdensome. Similarly, statutory and case law is presently affording adolescents greater freedom to seek medical and psychological help without parental permission, a change advocated by many writers and legal scholars in recent years (Bersoff, 1976-77; Foster & Freed, 1972; Holt, 1974; Kleinfeld, 1970, 1971; Wald, 1974). Many states now have statutes permitting minors to give valid consent to treatment for veneral disease and other sex-related problems (Note, 1975). One state permits those sixteen years of age or over to consent to treatment for emotional disorders from psychiatrists (Note, 1971). A joint commission of the Institute of Judicial Administration and the American Bar Association (IJA/ABA, 1977), while upholding the general principle of parental consent to medical care, has issued a set of recommendations that, if adopted, would significantly expand certain children's right to treatment without third party consent. For the treatment of chemical dependency, venereal disease, contraception, and pregnancy, the commission would only require the physician to obtain the minor's permission to notify (but not secure the consent of) parents to such treatment. Minor's objection to notification would be binding unless the physician judged that failure to inform would seriously jeopardize the health of the minor. Minors over fourteen who sought treatment for mental or emotional difficulties from psychotherapists or counselors would be permitted to do so for three sessions before notification would be required. However, for mature minors, i.e., those over sixteen, and for emancipated minors, i.e., those living separate and apart from parents and who are managing their own financial affairs, the commission would permit autonomous decision making without parental notification.

Despite these developments, the right of children to seek aid (or reject it) by giving valid consent is far from universal. In the light of the Supreme Court's overriding preference for parental control and its distrust of minor's ability to make mature judgments, it is unlikely that children will be granted the right to decide for themselves whether they wish to be enrolled as research subjects. More likely is that the courts will employ the analysis used in *Wisconsin v. Yoder* (1972), a case in which the Supreme Court upheld the right of Amish parents to violate state compulsory education laws and to keep their children at home once they completed eight grades. The exemption, the Court felt, was necessary to the free exercise of religion. In its positive light, the decision may be seen as allowing at least a limited class of parents the right to make decisions concerning family life even though it may interfere with a long acknowledged state interest, in this case compulsory education. On the other hand, it may be seen as another instance of adults generally failing to afford children the opportunity to articulate their own interests. Chief Justice Burger, who wrote the majority opinion, saw the case as involving only the "fundamental interests of the parents, as contrasted with that of the State . . ." (p. 232). Justice Douglas, dissenting in part, was the only member of the Court to recognize that the critical interests at stake were those of the children:

> On this important and vital matter of education, I think the children should be entitled to be heard. While the parents . . . normally speak for the entire family, the education of the child is a matter on which the child will often have decided views. . .
>
> It is the future of the student, not the future of the parents, that is imperiled in today's decision. . . .It is the student's judgment, not his parents, that is essential if we are to give full meaning to what we have said about the Bill of Rights and of the right of students to be masters of their own destiny (pp. 244-245).

Of course, the question arises in this and other cases we have described, do children have sufficient maturity and stability to make life-important decisions? Or, is the Court correct in concluding that they do not? Justice Douglas, to support his claim in *Yoder* that students not only had the right but the competency to be heard, cited the work of major developmental psychologists and sociologists as Piaget, Kohlberg, Gesell, Kay, and Ilg to the effect that cognitive capacity and moral judgment of young adolescents approximated that of adults. It must be said in the interest of intellectual honesty that while works cited by Justice Douglas lend substantial support to his assertion, many other scholars who have reviewed the research of those cited are not in total agreement with their colleagues. The failure to corroborate centers mainly around adolescents' failure to evidence the judgment and reasoning associated with the most mature states of intellectual and moral development theoretically possible in adults. There is little evidence that those stages are reached by adults themselves. One of the few studies to systematically investigate the issue of consent (Grisso & Vierling, 1978) with regard to treatment decisions concluded that minors below the age of eleven generally did not have the intellectual ability or sense of independence to give competent consent but that those over fifteen were not any less competent than their adult counterparts. The authors view the preadolescent's inability to give legally sufficient consent as developmentally related. An alternative hypothesis is that society in general and the law, through its reinforcement of parental authority, even as against a mature minor, particularly, have retarded children's ability to make appropriate choices. One does not want to create more responsibilities for an already overburdened school system but it may be possible to construct schools so that they will routinely and systematically include children in decisions that affect their lives. School people could model more equal relationships, mutual disclosure, and ordering of priorities. The role of the school could be expanded so that it would develop decision-making skills. In short, it could teach how to make choices and encourage children to do so.

## Conclusion

As this chapter has discussed, children, by and large, are not trusted with the right to make independent decisions because it is assumed that they are unable to give knowing, voluntary, and competent consent. Courts and legislatures have thus far ignored or are not (or have not been made) aware of the literature that does exist to the contrary. They can certainly be faulted for neglecting the data, but they may be right in doing so at this time. The available evidence is only tangentially relevant to the issue. In psychologists' terms, the data are not situation specific. Applied psychologists have an unparalleled opportunity to contribute to the judicial and legislative expansion of the right of children to be directly involved in decisions with regard to child custody (Bersoff, 1976-77), submission to psychological testing (Bersoff, 1973; Fischer, 1978), psychotherapy, or making contracts and voting (Holt, 1974). There have been some attempts by lawyers and psychologists to join forces to gather information in these and other areas (see especially Grisso & Vierling, 1978; Keasey & Sales, 1977; Tapp, 1976), but it is probably indisputable that, by and large—

> [M]ost developmental research has little to say about children and their daily lives . . . American developmental psychology . . . has tended to emphasize laboratory studies in which the child performs an unfamiliar task in a strange situation with a strange adult. It has tended to neglect the study of social settings in which children live and the persons who are central to them emotionally (Skolnick, 1975, pp. 5253).

It is in response to this criticism that psychologists who produce applied research have the greatest potential for contributing to judicial decision making. For those who want to engage in this process, it may be more helpful for psychologists to gather data directly relevant to legal issues than to devote themselves to "abstracted empiricism" (Skolnick, 1975). Psychologists who interact daily with children and their families in assessment or intervention settings, for example, have the capability of developing data of concern to the courts. It may be possible to rebut the judicial and statutory presumption that children are not able to give legally sufficient consent by gathering data in specific, appropriate situations. The successful accomplishment of this task is perhaps best performed by psychologists who possess research skills and familiarity with the relevant settings (e.g., homes, schools). Data gleaned in these settings and specifically related to a matter of judicial concern may be far more persuasive than statistics gathered in an isolated research setting and not readily applicable to the legal issue in question.

I personally believe that we should reverse our current presumptions. Rather than assume that children are too young emotionally, experientially, and cognitively to make "appropriate" decisions, we can alternatively presume that children are capable of making those decisions no less disastrously than adults. Only if there is a significant risk of irreversible damage or clear and convincing empirical evidence that at particular ages children do not have sufficiently developed skills to exercise discretion should parents and the state have the right to make unilateral decisions that meaningfully affect children. The burden would fall on those wishing to deny the right of children to choose; it would not fall to children and their advocates to show that children are capable. Such a proposal is in keeping with the legal doctrine that rights can be deprived only after a showing of incompetency, as is true when those called mentally ill are no longer allowed to control their finances or when parents are required to relinquish custody of their children.

Like others, my proposal is based on not much more than personal judgment. We need data, even at the risk of discovering that the Supreme Court's presumptions are correct. As a person, I think DHEW's proposal falls far short of recognizing the autonomy of children in those instances where their significant interests are at stake. As a psychologist, I believe that we need developmental, social, and educational psychologists to produce more situation-specific research to help the legal system make more reality-oriented decisions. From the perspective of a neutral observer and as a legal commentator, I must admit that the Commission's recommendations and DHEW's proposed rules comport with the current status of the legal rights of children. Insofar as these proposals recognize at least a limited right of direct participation in the decision-making process, they are an appropriate and positive advance.

## References

Annas, G., Glantz, L., & Katz, B. *The law of informed consent to human experimentation.* Cambridge, Mass: Ballinger, 1977.

Bellotti v. Baird, 443 U.S. 622 (1979).

Bersoff, D. The legal regulation of school psychology. In C. Reynolds & T. Gutkin (Eds.), *Handbook for school psychology*. New York: Wiley, 1982.

Bersoff, D. Legal and ethical concerns in research. In L. Goldman (Ed.), *Research for the counselor*. New York: Wiley, 1978.

Bersoff, D. Representation for children in custody proceedings: All that glitters is not *Gault*. *Journal of Family Law*, 1976, *15*, 27-49.

Bersoff, D. The ethical practice of school psychology: Rebuttal and suggested model. *Professional Psychology*, 1973, *4*, 305-312.

Carey v. Population Services International, Inc., 431 U.S. 678 (1977).

Comment, Evidence—Competency of child witness. *Rutgers-Camden Law Journal*, 1980, *11*, 339-347.

Cooke, R. Clinical research on children. In DHEW/NIH (Ed.), *Issues in research with humans subjects*. Bethesda, Md.: DHEW/NIH, 1980. (NIH Pub. No. 10-1858).

Department of Health, Education, and Welfare. Proposed regulations amending basic HEW policy for protection of human research subjects. *Federal Register*, 1979, *44*, 47688-47695.

Department of Health, Education, and Welfare. Proposed regulations on research involving children. *Federal Register*, 1978, *43*, 31786-31794.

Developments in the law, the Constitution and the family. *Harvard Law Review*, 1980, *93*, 1156-1383.

Ellis, J. Volunteering children: Parental commitment of minors to mental institutions. *California Law Review*, 1974, *62*, 840-916.

Fare v. Michael C., 442 U.S. 707 (1979).

Fischer, C. Collaborative psychological assessment. In C. Fischer & S. Brodsky (Eds.), *The Prometheus principle: Informed participation by clients in human services*. New Brunswick: Transaction, 1978.

Foster, H., & Freed, D. A bill of rights for children. *Family Law Quarterly*, 1972, *6*, 343-375.

Friedman, P. Legal regulation of applied behavior analysis in mental institutions and prisons. *Arizona Law Review*, 1975, *17*, 39-104.

Ginsburg v. New York, 390 U.S. 629 (1968).

Goldstein, J. On the right of the "institutionalized mentally infirm" to consent or refuse to participate as subjects in biomedical and behavioral research. In National Commission for the Protection of Human Subjects (Ed.), *Research involving those institutionalized as mentally infirm*, Appendix 2-1. Bethesda, Md.: National Commission, 1978. (DHEW Pub. No. (OS) 78-0006).

Grisso, T., & Vierling, L. Minors' consent to treatment: A developmental perspective. *Professional Psychology*, 1978, *9*, 412-427.

H.L. v. Matheson, 101 S. Ct. 1164 (1981).

Hauerwas, S. Ethical issues in the use of human subjects cited by Cooke, R. Clinical research on children. In DHEW/NIH (Ed.), *Issues in research with human subjects*. Bethesda, Md.: DHEW/NIH, 1980.

Holt, J. *Escape from childhood*. New York: Dutton, 1974.

*In re* Gault, 387 U.S. 1 (1967).

Ingraham v. Wright, 430 U.S. 651 (1977).

Institute of Judicial Adminsitration & American Bar Association. *Juvenile Justice Standards Project: Standards relating to rights of minors.* Cambridge, Mass.: Ballinger, 1977.

Katz, J. *Experimentation with human beings.* New York: Russell Sage Foundation, 1972.

Katz, S., Howe, R., & McGrath, M. Child neglect laws in America. *Family Law Quarterly,* 1975, *9,* 1-372.

Keasey, D., & Sales, B. An empirical investigation of young children's awareness and usage of intentionality in criminal situations. *Law and Human Behavior,* 1977, *1,* 45-62.

Kleinfeld, A. Balance of power among infants, their parents, and the state (I, II, III). *Family Law Quarterly,* 1970, 1971, *4, 5,* 320-349, 410-443, 64-107.

Macklin, R., & Sherwin, S. Experimenting on human subjects: Philosophical perspectives. *Case Western Reserve Law Review,* 1975, *25,* 434-471.

Milgram, S. Behavioral study of obedience. *Journal of Abnormal and Social Psychology,* 1963, *67,* 371-378.

Mnookin, R. *Child, family, and state.* Boston: Little, Brown, 1978.

Natanson v. Kline, 186 Kan. 393, 350 P.2d 1093 (1960).

National Commission for the Protection of Human Subjects of Biomedical and Behavioral Research. Report and recommendations: Institutional review boards. *Federal Register,* 1978, *43,* 56174-56198.

National Commission for the Protection of Human Subjects of Biomedical Behavioral Research. Reports and recommendations: Research involving children. *Federal Register,* 1978, *13,* 2084, 2114.

Note, Counseling the counselors: Legal implications of counseling minors without parental consent. *Maryland Law Review,* 1971, *31,* 332-354.

Note, Parental consent requirements and privacy rights of minors: The contraceptive controversy. *Harvard Law Review,* 1975, *88,* 1001-1020.

Parham v. J.L., 442 U.S. 584 (1979).

Pitkin, H. *The concept of representation.* Berkeley: Univ. of Calif. Press, 1967.

Planned Parenthood of Central Missouri v. Danforth, 428 U.S. 52 (1976).

Pratt v. Davis, 118 Ill. App. 161 (1905).

Prince v. Massachusetts, 321 U.S. 158 (1944).

Ramsey, P. *The patient as person.* New Haven: Yale Univ. Press, 1970.

Rule v. Geddes, 23 App. D.C. 31 (1904).

Schmerber v. California, 384 U.S. 757 (1966).

Skolnick, A. The limits of childhood: Conceptions of child developments and social context. *Law and Contemporary Problems,* 1975, *39,* 38-77.

State in the Interest of R.R., 79 N.J. 97, 398 A.2d (1979).

Tapp, J. Psychology and the law: An overture. In M. Rozenzweig & L. Porter (Eds.), *Annual review of psychology,* Vol. 27. Palo Alto: Annual Reviews, 1976.

Tinker v. Des Moines Independent Community School District, 393 U.S. 503 (1969).

Wald, M. Children's rights: A framework for analysis. *University of California-Davis Law Review,* 1979, *12,* 255-282.

Wald, P. Making sense out of the rights of youth. *Human Right,* 1974, *4,* 13-29.

Wisconsin v. Yoder, 406 U.S. 205 (1971).

Wyatt v. Aderholt, 368 F. Supp. 1383 (M.D. Ala. 1974).

Chapter 10

# LAWYERS AND CHILD CLIENTS: A CALL FOR RESEARCH

THOMAS GRISSO AND THOMAS LOVINGUTH

A FEW YEARS AGO, Michael Wald issued a lawyer's request for help from behavioral scientists in which he offered questions that might be addressed in their future research. One of his reflections was as follows: "I have often wondered, when I was representing a child in a delinquency or neglect proceeding, what it meant for me to go up to a nine- or ten-year-old and say, 'I'm your lawyer. Here I am; tell me what to do. What do you want me to do in representing you?'" (Wald, 1976, p. 5).

If the trend of the past decade continues in the 1980s, more and more children will be meeting with their lawyers. In many cases, neither the child nor the lawyer will have requested the conference; they will have come together at the request of a system or agency that has been compelled by law to protect the interests of the child. As the two sit facing each other, the child may have only vague notions of the purpose of the meeting or its implications for his or her future. The lawyer will understand the legal implications of the meeting but may reflect in vain upon any law school experience that prepared him or her for this moment.

How does a lawyer approach a child-client whose powers of self-determination and general knowledge of professional-client relationships might not be equal to those of adult clients? How different are children's perceptions of lawyers? What meaning does this have for the best way in which the lawyer can fulfill the duty to represent the child?

Very few behavioral scientists have come to the aid of Wald and his colleagues by addressing these questions empirically. It is not that we have been idle; recent years have produced significant research results concerning children's perceptions of law and rules (Tapp and Levine, 1974), their views on legal authorities (Stapleton and Teitelbaum, 1972; Torney, 1977), their grasp of the concept of a right (Melton, 1979; Torney and Brice, 1979), and their understanding of certain specific constitutional rights (Grisso, 1981). Studies focusing specifically on children's perceptions of lawyers and the lawyer-client relationship, however, have been few and less than definitive in addressing Wald's concerns.

The purpose in this chapter, then, is to acknowledge Wald's request for aid and to prepare behavioral scientists to accept his challenge. We will first examine the contexts in which questions of the lawyer and child-client relationship are raised, leading to a conceptualization of the questions in order to clarify them for purposes of future attention by behavioral scientists. Then we will review existing results of research on children's knowledge and perceptions of the lawyer's role. Finally, we will present two interpretations of the existing data, both of which offer potential for further research and for modifying those conditions that may now result in negative perceptions of lawyers by children.

## Where Children and Lawyers Meet

There are presently three circumstances that probably account for most of the lawyer and child-client relationships today: neglect and custody cases, the child in an institutional setting, and the child facing potential adjudication as delinquent.

It is becoming increasingly common for courts to take into consideration the expressed wishes and points of view of children who are the object of "placement" decisions due to neglect or custody battles between divorced parents (Fredericks, 1977). Some states require that the child be represented in court by counsel so that the child's interests and viewpoint can be weighed with those expressed by the attorneys for the two adult parties. This practice can be expected to become increasingly common as the result of supporting recommendations by the Juvenile Justice Standards

Project (Institute of Judicial Administration-American Bar Association, 1977).

· Children's rights in institutional settings—mental hospitals, child care centers, and schools—are undergoing active reform. While constitutional right to a child's self-determination concerning commitment to hospitals has been denied (*Parham v. J.L.*, 1979; *Secretary of Public Welfare of Pennsylvania v. Institutionalized Juveniles,* 1979), children's rights within institutional settings have gained wide recognition (Koocher, 1976). Along with these rights have come various procedures for their protection. These include the availability of counsel upon request and models for periodic consultation with children to monitor the provision of services and processes that children are legally due.

By far the most frequent setting for lawyer and child-client contacts, however, is in the context of delinquency proceedings in juvenile courts. One type of contact is in the context of police interrogation of juvenile suspects. Juveniles have a constitutional right to consult with a lawyer, if they choose to do so, prior to or during any interrogation regarding an offense that could result in a finding of delinquency.[1] Very few juveniles make this request (Grisso and Pomicter, 1977), and no state presently requires that juveniles be assigned legal counsel at pretrial interrogations unless they request it.[2] Nevertheless, some juvenile courts automatically assign public defenders to consult with juveniles before interrogations in order to assist them in deciding whether or not to waive their right to remain silent. Another context for lawyer and child-client contacts in delinquency proceedings is, of course, in preparation for and during adjudication hearings—that is, hearings on the question of the juvenile's

[1]In *In re Gault* (1967), the U.S. Supreme Court extended the rights to silence and to legal counsel to juveniles at critical stages of legal procedures in delinquency cases. Although the U.S. Supreme Court has never decided that pretrial interrogation is one of these "critical stages," almost all lower courts since *Gault* have assumed that it is.

[2]The automatic assignment of legal counsel to juveniles prior to pretrial interrogation, and at other critical stages of delinquency proceedings, has been recommended by the Presidents' Commission on Law Enforcement (1967), Paulsen and Whitebread (1974), Piersma et. al (1977), and the Juvenile Justice Standards Project (IJA-ABA, 1977).

alleged delinquency. Juveniles' representation by public defenders is more frequent at this stage of juvenile court process than at any other, and it is required in some states. Finally, where a separate hearing is held to determine disposition (incarceration, treatment) after a juvenile has been adjudicated, juveniles' interests may be represented at the hearing by a lawyer, usually the same one who has represented the juvenile prior to or during the adjudication hearing.

Somewhat more is known about the nature of lawyer and child-client relationships in delinquency cases than in custody/neglect cases or in institutional settings. This is probably because lawyer and child contacts in the two latter circumstances are a relatively new phenomenon and still infrequent; therefore, they have rarely been the focus of systematic study to date. In the remainder of this chapter, then, we will focus primarily upon juvenile court contacts between lawyers and potentially delinquent children. Let us examine more closely the nature of these contacts.

## The Lawyer-Client Relationship

At the heart of Wald's question, with which we began this chapter, is the fact that the lawyer-client relationship as traditionally construed was developed in the context of criminal and civil cases involving adult clients. A brief look at this relationship in adult cases will reveal why major conflicts may arise for lawyers when they enter lawyer and child-client relationships.

The lawyer's duty to the client, and to the legal system, is to zealously represent the interests of the client in legal proceedings. In order to do this, one of the lawyer's concerns in the earliest contact with a defendant client is to obtain truthful information from the client concerning the facts of the allegation so that the lawyer can begin to formulate meaningful legal advice. The great importance of honesty between lawyer and client is reflected in the protective veil of confidentiality, which assures the client that the lawyer may not inform anyone of information provided by the client in consultation except in order to zealously represent the client's interests. Most lawyers are aware that the promise of confidentiality alone may not be sufficient to ensure an honest and open dialogue with a new client. Some attention must be given as well to establishing a cooperative atmosphere by developing emotional rapport with the client.

The duty to represent the client's interest requires that the lawyer be especially aware of the client's desires at all times. The lawyer cannot take action that is contrary to the client's desires—for example, accepting the conditions of a plea bargaining session against a client's wishes. On the other hand, the lawyer's task is to educate the client as to the probable consequences of various possible decisions or strategies, and then to advise—and if necessary, to attempt to persuade—the client as to the course of action that in the lawyer's opinion (and in the lawyer's understanding of the needs and interests of the client) is the best of the available options. In the end, though, it is the client's decision that must prevail as the guide for the lawyer's subsequent activities in representing the client.

The lawyer-client interaction, then, involves far more than merely the giving of legal advice by a professional to a client. It is a dynamic relationship in which the adequate functioning of both parties is dependent upon mutual understanding and acceptance of the rules of client and lawyer in an advocacy relationship.

A client's ability to "play" the role of client to his or her own benefit would seem to depend on several factors. First, there must be a basic understanding of what an attorney is, and of the intended advocacy purposes of a defense attorney. Second, the client must expect or believe that the advocacy traditionally promised in lawyer and client relationships is not a fiction and that it can be realized in the client's relationship with his or her own lawyer. Third, the client should be capable of considering the advice given by the lawyer (whether or not the client accepts it), and the client should be able to weigh that advice rationally in the process of making a decision and formulating his or her own desires.

It is in this context that lawyers might wonder what it means to offer to provide legal counsel and representation to a child-client. Adult defendants are assumed generally to possess the aforementioned capabilities and comprehensions.[3] The assumption that children generally possess these requisite capabilities and understanding, however, is challenged by the fact of their varying degrees of immaturity and relative inexperience in comparison to most adults. That is, it is anticipated that in working with children the lawyer is more likely to encounter interference in traditional fulfillment of the lawyering role because of a child's lack of understanding of what a lawyer is, or because of attitudes that are in conflict with the desired cooperative relationship between client and counsel. Further, because of the question of the child's intellectual or social maturity, it is not clear whether an attorney should be bound (as is assumed in adult cases) by the preferences of the child-client in his or her representation of the child (Bersoff, 1976-77). On the one hand are juvenile advocates who claim that a lawyer should never act contrary to the expressed wishes of a child-client; on the other hand are those who argue that the attorney must sometimes make decisions for the child—or even contrary to the child's expressed desires—when the child is unlikely to possess the maturity to make a reasoned choice (Landsman and Minow, 1978).

How the attorney deals with these problems in his/her relationships with child-clients may have broader implications—beyond the goal of providing adequate legal advice and protection for children. For example, it is through observing the actions of their attorneys that many juveniles might develop faith in, or a distrust of, our society's legal system in general. Further, the attorney is frequently the only potential source of emotional support for juveniles who are faced with court proceedings. The attorney's relationship with a child-client, then, is important for reasons that go beyond the matter of legal advocacy. Yet, the ambiguities in the relationship, as noted earlier, can interfere with the attorney's ability to provide these emotional and legal benefits.

Neither the law nor the Code of Professional Responsibility for

---

[3]When there is doubt about an adult defendant's capacities in this regard, an attorney or a judge can instigate proceedings to declare the defendant incompetent to stand trial, meaning that the defendant is incapable of assisting the attorney in a defense or cannot comprehend the nature or consequences of the court proceedings (McGarry, 1973).

the legal profession provides guidelines to structure or to reduce the ambiguity in attorney and child-client relationships. In order to make the judgments necessary in their relationships with children, lawyers are in need of basic empirical information of several types: (1) children's understanding of what an attorney is and of what the attorney-client relationship is supposed to be; (2) children's expectancies about the consequences of consulting with an attorney; and (3) children's capacities to weigh information and to make a rational choice between options explained to them by an attorney. With this information lawyers would be better prepared to adjust their own behaviors to meet the needs and levels of understanding of their child-clients.

Exploration of the third type of information noted above (children's rationality) would require an extensive review of developmental psychological literature concerning the cognitive and emotional capacities of juveniles at various ages and stages of development. This is beyond the scope of the present chapter, but others have provided such reviews in relation to children's decision making in other legal contexts (Bersoff, 1976-77; Grisso and Vierling, 1978). In the remainder of this chapter, then, we will focus only on children's understanding and perceptions of the lawyer-client relationship itself.

## Children's Understanding of a Lawyer's Function

### *What a Lawyer Is*

The most basic question is whether children understand what a lawyer is and the general type of expertise that lawyers claim. In a project investigating juveniles' understanding of *Miranda* warnings, Grisso (1981) asked 431 juveniles (ages 10-16) in a detention center to define various words in standard *Miranda* warnings, one of which was the word "attorney." Responses were scored with objective criteria developed especially for this study. All but 6% of the juveniles recognized the term as synonymous with the word "lawyer" and were able to identify a lawyer either as a person who "knows the law" or as a person who helps someone else in legal proceedings. About two-thirds of the juveniles mentioned all of these elements; the percentage doing so was significantly greater at ages twelve through sixteen than in younger age groups. The results were not related to the number of prior arrests or police/court contacts of the juveniles. On the basis of this study, then, it would appear that most juveniles with whom juvenile courts deal in relation to delinquency and "status offense" referrals have some general sense of what a lawyer is.

### *What a Lawyer Does*

What do children believe that a lawyer is supposed to do in delinquency proceedings? Do they have a sense of what the attorney-client relationship is supposed to be? Only two studies have examined this question to date.

In a study in a Canadian juvenile court, Catton and Erickson (1975) interviewed twenty-two juveniles soon after their court hearings at which defense attorneys were present. "Several" of the juveniles, the authors reported, believed that thc defense lawyer "worked for the court" or "thought (the lawyer) was getting the facts for the judge."

In relation to the study reported earlier, Grisso (1981) examined juveniles' understanding of the intended function and significance of legal counsel. The assessment consisted of five standardized questions concerning the attorney-client relationship asked of juveniles in the context of hypothetical cases rather than in reference to their own cases. The same questions were administered to a large sample of adult ex-offenders and another sample of adult nonoffenders, all being of similar racial and socioeconomic status to the juvenile sample. About 85-90% of the juveniles and the adults said that: (1) the main job of the defense lawyer was to help the client or to protect the client's rights; (2) the client was supposed to trust the lawyer, to cooperate with his/her lawyer, or to answer the lawyer's questions truthfully; (3) the main thing that the lawyer and client would discuss would be the client's view of the alleged offense, how the lawyer could help, or what the client should do in relation to the allegations or impending court processes; and (4) a lawyer should provide an effective argument for the client's side in court.

The fifth question, however, asked why the lawyer would urge the client to tell him/her the truth about the client's behaviors that might relate to the allegations in the case. Two-thirds of the juveniles (compared to 90% of the adults) understood that the truth was necessary in order for the lawyer to build an effective defense. The remaining one-third of the juveniles believed that the lawyer must know the truth about the client's guilt or innocence in order to determine whether he/she should take an advocacy or an accusatory role. Specifically, they believed that if the client admitted guilt to the lawyer, then the lawyer would not represent the client or would be required to report the client's culpability or confession to the court. This belief was especially prevalent among juveniles with no more than one prior felony referral to the court, but was very rare among juveniles with two or more prior felony referrals.

These results suggest that while most ten to sixteen year olds with court contact perceive attorneys as having an advocacy function, less experienced juveniles (at all of the aforementioned ages) believe that the lawyer is required to change this stance and to become an agent of the court when a juvenile admits guilt. These results are consistent with the exploratory data of Catton and Erickson noted earlier. Yet both studies leave many questions unanswered. Further research could examine more specifically what powers juveniles believe are at the disposal of the defense attorney who takes an advocacy position—that is, specifically *how* they believe the attorney can be of help. Further, we need to know whether juveniles who do perceive attorneys as advocates believe that a client's wishes must always guide the lawyer's actions, or whether on the other hand they believe that the client is expected to have no decision-making power and must merely hope for the best at the hands of a benevolent lawyer. The existing studies, then, only touch upon the broadest questions concerning juveniles' understanding of the intended roles of attorney and client.

One's understanding of a lawyer's *intended* functions may not reflect what one believes about the actual behaviors or values of legal counsel. Let us look now at studies that have examined how children feel about lawyers, in contrast to their recognition of what lawyers are supposed to do.

## Children's Attitudes and Expectancies About Lawyers

### *Self-Reported Attitudes Toward Lawyers*

Rafkey and Sealey (1975) administered questionnaires to delinquent and nondelinquent youths to seek their attitudes toward legal authorities of various types. They found that one-half of their nondelinquent sample claimed to perceive lawyers as dishonest. The perception of lawyers as untrustworthy was even more prevalent in the delinquent sample, with 80% of black adolescents with arrest records reporting this belief. One should note, however, that this study involved juveniles' stereotypes about lawyers in general and not necessarily their beliefs about defense attorneys specifically.

Among girls who had been represented by counsel in delinquency proceedings, Connor (1972) found that two-thirds were disappointed in their lawyers' courtroom performances. Similarly, Catton and Erickson's (1975) post-hearing interviews with juveniles produced results indicating that few of the juveniles perceived legal counsel as adequate. Only one-third named their attorney as a person who was "on my side" or was there to help them; only about one-fifth of them believed that an attorney would have been the best person to tell "my side of the story" in court.

In contrast to these results, Grisso (1981) found that two-thirds of juveniles in a detention center recommended obtaining legal counsel, in response to hypothetical stories about juveniles' arrests. The difference between this finding and those in the aforementioned studies might be a function of methodologies or circumstances of the juvenile subjects involved. In the studies by Connor and by Catton and Erickson, juveniles were reporting on their own experiences following hearings in which they had been found delinquent or in need of court supervision. Attitudes toward defense lawyers at those times might well be different than when (as in the Grisso study) juveniles respond to hypothetical situations without direct reference to their own immediate experiences.

### *Juveniles' Behaviors in Relation to Lawyers*

Several studies have reported behaviors of juveniles in legal contexts, which suggested that they did not trust their defense lawyers or did not believe in their advocacy value. Among juveniles with court experience in a study by Walker (1971), 30% admitted to researchers that they had not told their lawyers "the whole story" about their illegal activities. Catton and Erickson (1975) observed initial lawyer-client consultations for twenty-two juveniles; in only three cases did the juveniles ask questions of the lawyer. In a sample of over 700 felony arrests of juveniles, Grisso and Pomicter (1977) found that juveniles chose to assert their rights to silence and to obtain legal counsel in less than 10% of the cases in which police attempted to interrogate the juveniles. Assertion of the rights was nearly nonexistent at ages fourteen and below.

These results might suggest that juveniles have little faith in the advocacy potential of defense attorneys. Yet the outcome of a project reported by Clendenen, Cullen, and Goldberg (1977) produced contradictory conclusions. Clendenen et al. provided free legal assistance to juveniles in a number of correctional institutions and treatment programs for delinquent youths in Minnesota. The lawyers made themselves available to juveniles on call, providing services ranging from ombudsman regarding institutional rights and privileges to helping juveniles resolve legal issues related to domestic and financial problems. They reported that the program evoked a very positive response from many youths, and their results indicated that juveniles did seek the legal services that had been made available. Under these circumstances, then, juveniles' attitudes toward the value of legal counsel appear to have been far more positive than in the studies mentioned earlier involving juveniles in the context of legal proceedings against them.

### Theoretical Explanations

There are at least two general ways to conceptualize the results of the research we have reviewed on juvenile's attitudes toward lawyers. First, one can conceptualize many of the results as being consistent with developmental theoretical perspectives of adolescents. Alternatively, one can view the results as manifesting juveniles' direct responses to the messages conveyed by lawyers themselves to juveniles. Let us briefly examine both of these viewpoints, since they may have implications for conceptualizing further research in this area.

### *Developmental Perspective*

Many of the aforementioned studies demonstrated attitudes toward legal counsel that could be characterized as rejecting, mistrustful, or pessimistic. The limited data available on juveniles' understanding of the *intended* function of legal counsel in delinquency proceedings suggests that most juveniles (ages 10-16) had a grasp of the advocacy *potential* of defense attorneys. Yet a significant proportion of them doubted the value of legal counsel. Can this be explained on the basis of developmental psychological principles?

The Piagetian notion of cognitive development suggests that the ages in question (but especially ages 10-14) are particularly important as a period characterized by the development of capacities for "formal operations." That is, in many children of these ages, cognitive capacities approach a level that is more characteristic of adult thinking in terms of logical thought processes. Corresponding to this stage is a period of heightened social awareness (Strommen, McKinney, and Fitzgerald, 1977). Indeed, there is some evidence that children in early adolescence are more concerned about meeting social expectations than are either younger children or older adolescents (Costanza and Shaw, 1966). Matza (1964) has built a convincing argument that this is no less so for the "delinquent" youth than for the obedient youth. Most delinquents, Matza has said, have not rejected society; they continue to accept its basic values and to desire conventional rewards, even though their behavior and words may superficially deny it.

One might hypothesize, therefore, that most juveniles who are arrested during the early adolescent years would be acutely aware of the social condemnation associated with the arrest. Attempts to deal with condemnation by society at this age could take several forms, among them reciprocal rejection of society on the one hand, or feelings of unworthiness and undeservingness on the other. In either case, the idea of a lawyer taking one's side could seem implausible. If one feels rejected by society and in turn has claimed to reject it, then it would seem inconsistent to hope that an attorney provided *by* "society" would take one's side against the adult society in which the attorney him/herself lives and interacts. If one feels unworthy in response to social rejection, then pessimism or feelings of being undeserving of the potential advocacy of legal defense would seem to be a likely outcome. The result in either case might be the unresponsive attitudes toward lawyers that characterize much of the research with juveniles we have examined. The point here is not that juveniles alone experience such feelings in the course of legal proceedings against them. It is that the characteristics of their stage of social development, combined with their relatively powerless and submissive status as children, might produce this dynamic and its consequent negative effect on the attorney-client relationship more frequently among juveniles than among adults.

The exceptions in certain studies reviewed earlier can also be accounted for by this theoretical explanation. In the project by Clendenen et al. (1978), for example, no social condemnation was present; under these circumstances, juveniles responded hopefully to the prospect of legal assistance.

This dynamic, which couples developmental theory with the concept of deservingness, can be tested by examining the self-reports and behaviors (both in experimental and real situations) of children of various ages toward lawyers in situational contexts that afford greater or lesser feelings of social condemnation. Yet there is a competing explanation with equal plausibility to which we now turn.

### *Effect of the Lawyer*

It may be that children's attitudes toward lawyers are not directly related to their level of developmental maturity or their reaction to social condemnation but merely reflect the behaviors of lawyers in their interactions with juveniles. That is, whether a juvenile doubts the advocacy potential of defense attorneys or perceives defense attorneys as a source of hope and support, these attitudes might simply reflect the ways in which defense attorneys have presented themselves to juveniles or their actions in representing juveniles.

There are several reasons why the results of studies in our earlier review, especially those which suggest that juveniles doubt the advocacy intentions of defense attorneys, could be a consequence of lawyering in the juvenile justice system.

First, there is disagreement within the juvenile justice system concerning the appropriate role of defense counsel to juveniles. On the one hand are lawyers and judges who believe that juveniles are entitled to a strong legal defense not unlike that which is appropriate in adult criminal courts (McMillian and McMurtry, 1969; IJA-ABA, 1977; Piersma et al., 1977). Proponents of this view argue that juvenile defendants are in jeopardy of penalties that are no less punitive than those received by adults in criminal cases. The U.S. Supreme Court in *In re Gault* (1967) pointed out that, although the juvenile justice system had been developed to provide treatment, in fact it has generally not met that promise. Therefore, the Court reasoned, juvenile defendants deserve some of the same general procedural protections as adults, including vigorous representation by legal counsel.

On the other hand are those who view the defense attorney more or less as an agent of the court and as one who shares the court's traditional duty as *parens patriae*. This view holds to the philosophy that the juvenile court provides treatment, which is in the child's best interest; therefore, it is the duty of defense counsel to work with the juvenile court in meeting the child's needs, not to take an adversarial stance against the court's interest in intervening in the child's life. One consequence of this view was the finding that many defense attorneys claimed that they would report to the court any admission of guilt by their juvenile clients, even if the admission were made in the context of confidential communications (Ferster, Courtless, and Snethen, 1970). This view of defense counsel as assistant to the court prevails in many juvenile courts (Stapleton and Teitelbaum, 1972; Kay and Segal, 1972-73; Landsman and Minow, 1978). Juveniles who have experienced this type of lawyering might be expected to develop a dim view of the advocacy potential in the attorney-client relationship.

Second, even attorneys who adopt a strong advocacy stance may sometimes find it necessary to take a position that is contrary to the expressed desires of the juvenile. This can occur when a juvenile's immaturity or short-sightedness is responsible for his or her desires, and when those desires are so clearly unrealistic or potentially damaging to the juvenile that the lawyer cannot work toward those ends. Some juveniles might therefore perceive the lawyer's well-meaning actions as a betrayal.

Third, many observers of legal counsel in juvenile courts (Catton and Erickson, 1975; Genden, 1976; Landsman and Minow, 1978) have commented on lawyers' frequent lack of skill in developing good rapport with juvenile clients, in explaining their own function to juveniles, in perceiving situations through the juvenile's eyes, and in being sensitive to juveniles' needs and concerns. For example, Catton and Erickson (1975) reported that in only two out of the twenty-two sessions they observed between lawyers and juveniles did the lawyers explain who they were and what was their purpose. At the end of one session with a public defender, the juvenile was heard to ask when his lawyer was going to talk to him! Clearly, juveniles cannot be expected to hold positive or hopeful views of the advocacy potential of defense lawyers who are unprepared to explain their function and to extend themselves interpersonally to juveniles.

In light of the argument that attorneys themselves may be responsible for juveniles' frequent skepticism about lawyers, it is interesting to consider the process used in the project by Clendenen et al. (1977), which we described earlier. Lawyers in this project initially met several times with juveniles in the participating institutions to describe to them examples of the advocacy roles they were prepared to take. They placed themselves at the disposal of the juveniles and proceeded to provide them client-centered legal advice, as well as to pursue legal remedies when possible, much as they would in adult matters of civil dispute. Under these conditions, the lawyers experienced general acceptance by juveniles, whose many requests for legal counsel over a period of eighteen months clearly demonstrated their belief in the advocacy potential of lawyers.

## Conclusions

The two theoretical explanations for juveniles' attitudes

toward legal counsel need not, of course, be in competition. Both may be true, and they suggest two types of research that are needed. The developmental explanation suggests the need for research not only on greater detail concerning juveniles' perceptions of legal counsel at various ages or developmental stages but also for research on what it means to a juvenile to be arrested and thereby to be faced with social condemnation. The explanation focusing on the quality of lawyering in juvenile justice requires research on lawyers' approaches to juveniles, and on the degree to which the system is committed to various philosophies of lawyering in juvenile courts.

In the review, we found that a better understanding of juveniles' attitudes toward lawyers was obtained by comparing results derived from studies in a diversity of situations. Future research should be done in a variety of circumstances, ranging from hypothetical to *in vivo* and with self-report and behavioral measures. Further, while at least a few studies have focused on legal counsel in delinquency cases, researchers have yet to examine attorney and child-client encounters in other circumstances such as mental health settings. It is important to do so, because we cannot assume that juveniles' attitudes toward lawyers in the context of juvenile courts are representative of their attitudes in other settings wherein lawyers and children are beginning to meet with increased frequency.

Finally, we must obtain information on the knowledge and expectations about lawyers among a much wider age range of children than is presently represented in the literature. Most of the studies we reviewed included only juveniles in the thirteen to sixteen year old range. Further, almost none of them included data on adults' understanding and perceptions. This will ultimately be necessary if we are ever to be able to make meaningful evaluative statements about juveniles' attitudes and perceptions, since evaluation requires some standard with which to compare juveniles.

If our society continues to take seriously the many questions of children's rights that have emerged in the past decade, lawyers and children will be meeting each other with increased frequency in a variety of contexts in the future. Sometime during the next decade, one hopes, behavioral scientists will be better informed by their empirical research to assist lawyers in resolving the critical ambiguities in lawyer and child-client relationships.

## References


Bersoff, D. Representation for children in custody decisions: all that glitters is not *Gault. Journal of Family Law,* 1976-77, *15,* 27.

Catton, K., & Erickson, P. *The juvenile's perception of the role of defense counsel in juvenile court.* Center for Criminology, University of Toronto, Canada. Unpublished manuscript, 1975.

Clendenen, R., Cullen, J., & Goldberg, M. Legal assistance to delinquents. *Federal Probation,* 1977, *41,* 8-15.

Connor, W. *The juvenile court: its impact on children adjudged to be delinquent.* Center for Criminology, University of Toronto, Canada. Unpublished Master's Thesis, 1972.

Costanza, P., & Shaw, M. Conformity as a function of age level. *Child Development,* 1966, *37,* 967-975.

Ferster, E., Snethen, E., & Cortless, T. The juvenile justice system: in search of the role of counsel. *Fordham Law Review,* 1970, *39,* 375-412.

Fredericks, M. Custody battles: mental health professionals in the courtroom. In G. Koocher (Ed.), *Children's rights and the mental health professions.* New York: Wiley, 1976, pp. 41-52.

Genden, J. Separate legal representation for children: protecting the rights and interests of minors in juvenile proceedings. *Harvard Civil Rights-Civil Liberties Law Review,* 1976, *11,* 565-595.

Grisso, T. *Juveniles' waiver of rights: legal and psychological competence.* New York: Plenum, 1981.

Grisso, T., & Pomicter, C. Interrogation of juveniles: an empirical study of procedures, safeguards, and rights waiver. *Law and Human Behavior,* 1977, *1,* 321-342.

Grisso, T., & Vierling, L. Minors' consent to treatment: a developmental perspective. *Professional Psychology,* 1978, *9,* 412-427.

*In re* Gault, 387 U.S. 1 (1967).

Institute of Judicial Administration and American Bar Association. *Juvenile justice standards project: standards relating to the rights of minors.* Cambridge, Mass.: Ballinger, 1977.

Kay, R., & Segal, D. The role of the attorney in juvenile court proceedings: a non-polar approach. *Georgetown Law Journal,* 1972, *61,* 1401-1424.

Koocher, G. (Ed.). *Children's rights and the mental health professions.* New York: Wiley, 1976.

Landsman, K., & Minow, W. Lawyering for the child: principles of representation in custody and visitation disputes arising from divorce. *Yale Law Journal,* 1978, *87,* 1125-1190.

Matza, D. *Delinquency and drift.* New York: Wiley, 1964.

McGarry, A. *Competency to stand trial and mental illness.* Washington, D.C.: U.S. Government Printing Office, 1973.

McMillian, T., & McMurtry, D. The role of the defense lawyer in the juvenile court—advocate or social worker? *St. Louis University Law Review,* 1969, *14,* 561-603.

Melton, G. Children's rights: children's own concepts and attitudes. Paper presented at meeting of the American Psychological Association, New York City, September, 1979.

Parham v. J.L., 47 U.S.L.W. 4740 (1979).

Paulsen, M., & Whitebread, C. *Juvenile law and procedure.* Reno, Nevada: National Council of Juvenile Court Judges, 1974.

Piersma, P., Ganousis, J., Volenik, A., Swanger, H., & Connell, P. *Law and tactics in juvenile cases.* Philadelphia: American Law Institute-American Bar Association, 1977.

President's Commission on Law Enforcement and Administration of Justice. *Task force report: Juvenile delinquency and youth crime.* Washington, D.C.: U.S. Government Printing Office, 1967.

Rafkey, D., & Sealey, R. The adolescent and the law: a survey. *Crime and Delinquency,* 1975, *21,* 131-138.

Secretary of Public Welfare of Pennsylvania v. Institutionalized Juveniles, 47 U.S.L.W. 4754 (1979).

Stapleton, W., & Teitelbaum, L. *In defense of youth.* New York: Russell Sage, 1972.

Strommen, E., McKinney, J., & Fitzgerald, H. *Developmental psychology: the school-aged child.* Homewood, Ill.: Dorsey Press, 1977.

Tapp, J., & Levine, F. Legal socialization: strategies for an ethical legality. *Stanford Law Review,* 1974, *27,* 1-72.

Torney, J. Socialization of attitudes toward the legal system. In J. Tapp & F. Levine (Eds.), *Law, justice, and the individual in society.* New York: Holt, Rinehart, and Winston, 1977, pp. 134-144.

Torney, J., & Brice, P. Children's concepts of human rights and social cognition. Paper presented at meeting of American Psychological Association, New York, September, 1979.

Wald, M. Legal policies affecting children: a lawyer's request for aid. *Child Development,* 1976, *47,* 1-5.

Walker, S. The lawyer-child relationship: a statistical analysis. *Duquesne Law Review,* 1971, *9,* 627-650.

*Chapter 11*

# NEEDS OF THE EDUCATIONALLY HANDICAPPED

T. KERBY NEILL AND KAY BLANTON STEVENS

THERE IS NO WAY to address a handicapped child's unique educational needs without creating an individualized, locally tailored educational program. Therefore, the way to get a free and appropriate public education for a handicapped child is to build it.

Because the main consumer of what we build, the child, does not know what to build, considerable responsibility falls on the child's parents. Because the parents are usually not sure of what they should seek or expect, they need to enlist skilled allies and a range of supports. This chapter will focus on key issues for both families and professionals who are concerned about an appropriate education for the handicapped.

The raw materials for building a good educational experience include the child, the family, the teacher, the school, professional resources, community resources, and advocacy groups. With the coming of Public Law 94-142 in 1975 and the provisions of Section 504 of the Rehabilitation Act of 1973, the educationally handicapped child and his family have an impressive array of tools at their disposal. We will begin by considering these tools. Next we will consider how to evaluate and work with the materials. Finally, we will consider what to build—what is an appropriate education.

## Legal tools

Although most parents, educators, or other professionals in

related services will never read P.L. 94-142, excellent summaries are available (in order of comprehensiveness) by Vergason and McAffe (1979), Ballard and Zettel (1977), Children's Defense Fund (1978), and Turnbull and Turnbull (1978). In addition, each state is required to promulgate information regarding the law and can provide concise and usually readable materials:

In capsule, P.L. 94-142 has several provisions:

1. States must provide an appropriate public education to all handicapped children. The handicapped include the mentally retarded, hearing and speech impaired, visually handicapped, learning disabled, seriously emotionally disturbed, orthopedically handicapped, and multiply handicapped. Details of the definitions are in State and Federal regulations (Department of Health, Education, and Welfare, 1977). The schools must provide for transportation and diagnostic services. A free appropriate education must be provided not only to those handicapped children who can attend public school but also for those who are homebound or in private schools, hospitals, and institutions. This applies to all individuals aged three to twenty-one (unless the State is not serving other children 3-5 or 18-21 in their regular educational programs).
2. Handicapped children must be educated in classes or programs with children who are not handicapped to the maximum extent appropriate (generally referred to as "mainstreaming" or the "least restrictive alternative").
3. More than one criterion must be used in the evaluation of a child. Evaluation materials and their administration must not be racially or culturally discriminatory.
4. An Individual Educational Program (I.E.P.) must be developed for each child. This should be a collaborative effort of the child's parents and appropriate educational experts.
5. A number of procedural safeguards exist. Parents must be given notice of any meeting or contemplated change affecting their child. This notice must explain all procedural safeguards, proposed plans, and their rationale. The information must be in a language understood by the parents. Parental consent must be obtained prior to an evaluation for placement. Parents have the right to seek and obtain an independent

evaluation, examine their children's educational records, amend records they feel are in error, utilize their own educational experts and have these experts or counsel present at meetings, and appeal decisions with which they disagree. Parents may also petition to obtain a hearing and, if necessary, may initiate civil action in order to obtain an appropriate program for their child.

The listing above is too sketchy for use in pursuing an actual case, but it provides a basic orientation for discussing our building project. A critical factor to understand is that the law provides a sequence of steps and safeguards for providing a free, appropriate education but says nothing about what the educational program should contain. The content issues regarding the planning of the child's educational program are thrown back into the laps of parents, teachers, and school personnel. The parents who must exercise the procedural safeguards are asked to make judgments about issues where they usually have little knowledge or experience. Often they may attend a meeting to develop (or rubber stamp) their child's I.E.P. This meeting is run by school personnel, whose jargon, familiarity with the system, educational level, and sheer numbers may easily overwhelm the parents. *The entire procedure cannot work without an assertive, questioning advocate for the child.* The law is written with the presumption that this advocate will be a parent. It is the contention of the authors that such parents are in the minority and that a significant number of parents will have an impact under this law only if the parents are organized and make appropriate use of educational expertise, probably from outside the system.

Pugach (1979) has discussed the potential conflicts between the bureaucratic mechanics of implementing the law and its spirit (i.e., providing a free appropriate education). She emphasizes that the I.E.P. is a process and not a document. Thus, if the I.E.P. is to become meaningful, teachers, parents, and interested parties should meet at regular intervals to assess progress, to modify goals, and to try new approaches. In the same way it is important to consider the diagnostic evaluation, which leads to the child's educational identification, as a continuing process. However, both of these processes can be easily lost in the paper shuffle, and the evaluations, because of limited diagnostic resources, are usually a one-shot process that offers only an approximate definition of the problem. Thus, often we end up with a program based on an incomplete and static evaluation that is being maintained because of legal mandates. When this is true, the very law that assures an education to all handicapped children can become a stumbling block. Actually the failure to make an I.E.P. truly effective is one of the more subtle forms of failure to comply with the law. Morsink (1979) lists four "Catch 22s" of the law that can result in ineffective compliance. For example, a child needing highly specialized attention may labor in a normal class, which is defined as the "least restrictive alternative." There are still many areas where families do not even confront the appearances of compliance. Five years after the passage of P.L. 94-142, a coalition of thirteen child advocacy groups found numerous examples of gross non-compliance with the law such as thousands of children on waiting lists for placement or the illegal expulsion of handicapped children from school (Children's Defense Fund, 1980a).

At times hearings or court action will be necessary, but one also needs to be realistic about what they can achieve. Court orders can mandate the provision of services, establish time tables, require evidence of compliance and *supposedly* monitor quality, but mandates are slow, cumbersome, and expensive to develop. Parents will remain the key monitors, and school personnel the key implementors. It is well to keep in mind the limited success the courts have had in mandating a better racial atmosphere in the schools in spite of regularly reaffirmed desegregation rulings.

All of this does not mean that parents cannot be fortunate in having a good system and a concerned and competent teacher with whom they work well. When good collaboration is present, it is not likely that parents will have recourse to hearings and civil suits. Assertive parents are still a key to collaboration (Rudberg, 1979). Pushing can be done politely, firmly, and collectively. Assertive behavior to enhance open communication does not have to imply confrontation. Positive as well as negative reinforcers can be forms of assertiveness. This is an issue we often remember when dealing with children but forget when dealing with school personnel.

## Building Materials

### *The Child*

The whole concept of individualization is child focused, but this is a difficult focus to maintain in practice. As soon as the child is labelled, which is an essential step in obtaining services, there is a tendency to focus on the "condition" rather than the child. It would be better to focus on a range of strengths and needs of the child as a full and changing person (Hobbs, 1975). In theory, P.L. 94-142 provides such a focus through the I.E.P. In practice, this means that attention should be given to areas in which the child can experience reasonable success as well as those areas of prevention and remediation that require the child to struggle uphill against handicaps. It means considering the full scope and sequence of skills the child will need to function in our society. In addition, it means considering handicapped children's abilities to speak for themselves. It is apparent that this capacity varies with the age and limitation of the child; however, it is also apparent that the capabilities of others to judge what is best for the child vary according to their own orientation.

> Now PJ was really something else. I've watched that guy and I can see in his eyes that he is aware. He knows what's going on. He can only crawl and he doesn't talk, but you don't know what's inside. When I was with him and I touch him, I know that he knows (Bogdan & Taylor, 1976, p. 276).

The quotation above is not that of a sensitive educator, but of a resident in a state school for the retarded who is communicating his understanding of his fellow-resident and friend. He is able to see beyond labels and is blissfully unaware of the "ideological monopolies" that Bogdan and Taylor (1976) suggest control many of our perceptions of the retarded.

In the course of their years in the educational system, handicapped children develop a sense of who they are. This is a process that is intimately tied to the child's understanding of his or her handicap and brings them squarely before the label they may bear. The development of a favorable self-concept therefore becomes a major educational goal. Siegel (1975) raises a number of questions as to the most effective ways of enhancing the child's self-concept. His questions are critical (and controversial) in any child-focused educational effort: Should the child be told about their handicap? If so, how, what, and when? What are the consequences of being grouped with nonhandicapped children or with other handicapped children?

Where do the schools stand in addressing these questions? In most cases the issue of helping a child address his own handicap is avoided in the public schools. This is understandable. Not only is it a "heavy" issue but experts have no consensus on how to deal with the problem. There are researchers, such as Edgerton (1967), who decry labels as archvillains barring the individual's struggle for a positive self-concept. He suggests it will be helpful if labels are found that suggest that a person's affliction is partial and may be amenable to treatment or training. Yet, even with our current, somewhat global labels, there is evidence which suggests that children with labels may be viewed more empathically by other youth, or by themselves, than youth with the same handicap who do not bear a label (Budoff & Siperstein, 1978; Foley, 1979; Rosenthal, 1973).

The issue of how handicapped children should be grouped—with themselves or with nonhandicapped children—is addressed by P.L. 94-142. The law is oriented away from separate grouping of the handicapped. Aanes and Haagenson (1978) and Switzky and Miller (1978) take a look at some of the key concepts that underlie P.L. 94-142, namely "Normalization" and the "Least Restrictive Alternative." Both pairs of authors caution against the danger of losing sight of the individual child in applying these valued principles. Our state of knowledge with regard to most issues that impact the esteem of the handicapped child is so limited that it is essential to gauge our programming by the reactions of each child rather than taking shot gun approaches to building an appropriate education.

### *Parents*

Because active parents and their lobby gave P.L. 94-142 shape, it is not surprising that the law gives parents considerable clout vis-à-vis the school system. The law presumes that parents are ready to exercise that clout; however, parents are generally unprepared for this task. Although federal regulations provide for training or counseling of parents, this is generally seen as counseling related to the parents' role in remediating the child's handicap (and for the school to provide it, it must be specified in the child's I.E.P.). The advocacy training that is necessary for parents to help decide what is best for their child with regard to his/her educational program is not generally available.

Parents' roles as advocates also depend on the way in which they have come to grips with their child's handicap. Are they discouraged and too pessimistic to work for the child's progress? Are they denying the child's limitations and demanding an unrealistic, "curative" education? Kurtz (1978) provides a good discussion of family approaches to the mentally retarded child that have a wide range of application to other conditions. He emphasizes psychotherapeutic, counseling, and educational approaches to parents, all forms of intervention with the parents. On the other hand, Tjossem (1976) suggests that "support, *not* intervention" is what parents need most. Such practical supports as programs for the child, a helping network of friends, or financial assistance all seem more promising for producing developmental gains. It is clear that Tjossem has in mind continuing support systems that begin with early identification and continue through preschool years into the public education system. This presupposes a strong system of coordinated linkages leading up to the school years, and also suggests that the schools take a key role in helping the child obtain adjunctive community services.

A critical factor for the parents is that they have to carefully think through the goals of the educational process itself—something most of them would assume that the school has already done. They must decide the priorities and follow the project through from start to finish (while other key personnel, those with the architectural expertise, may change annually).

P.L. 94-142 also envisions the parent in a key role of supporting the efforts of the child and supplementing the efforts of the teacher. This means that the parent may tutor the child in particular skills. This is the same as the role of any parent who is concerned about their child's school progress, but with the handicapped child it is both more necessary and more demanding.

In a standard social psychology demonstration, a group is presented with a cluster of lines and asked which is the longest. The answer is fairly obvious but all group members except the subject of the experiment agree on a wrong answer. The lone person, whose judgment tends to the correct answer, yields to the decision of the group. This is a common dilemma of parents who face school personnel that are unified around certain classic myths. A sampler of such myths might include, "One learning disabilities class is as suitable as another," or "All our elementary schools are equally supportive of their special education programs," or "This teacher has special education certification, so if your child isn't learning, it must be your child's fault." Against such dubious assertions, parents need to have their own judgments supported by fellow parents and professional allies.

### *Teacher*

The teacher is the primary architect of the child's educational experience, yet he/she is probably the forgotten figure in P.L. 94-142. The law simply assumes that teachers are ready to tackle the task: "Developments in the training of teachers and in diagnostic and instructional procedures and methods have advanced to the point that, given appropriate funding, state and local education agencies can and will provide effective special education and related services to the needs of the handicapped child" (P.L. 94-142, Sec. 3 (b) (7)). It is not likely that teachers are truly trained to meet the challenge or that conventional in-service training can effect such change. Teachers find it difficult to effect the individualization required by the I.E.P. or to employ the range of teaching techniques it may require. Albert Shanker (1980) (president of the American Federation of Teachers) is a vocal critic of P.L. 94-142. He cites a number of areas where the law mandates services but does not provide schools or teachers with the funds to develop them. He cites lack of teacher training as one of the "most disastrous failings" in the law. On the other hand, Shanker asserts that the I.E.P. makes such a demand on the teachers' time that it leaves "no time to teach." The authors must dismiss this last assertion as a bit of overstated union crying. The I.E.P. is what a number of good teachers have done for years. The I.E.P. is a creative tool. When it fails we would challenge the worker, not the tool.

The mechanics of developing and implementing an I.E.P. for handicapped children is not the only requirement for teachers as a result of P.L. 94-142. The law expects teachers to be able to promote social development between handicapped and non-handicapped children and to create a more favorable perception of handicapped persons among all children. Research (Serafica & Harway, 1979) suggests that many teachers and administrators will have to modify their own views of the handicapped before imparting healthier, more accepting attitudes on their students.

Another factor affecting teachers' attitudes is the longstanding push of teachers' unions and similar groups toward smaller class size and the elimination of "problem" students in regular classes. As Pugach (1979) indicates, such emphasis has reinforced teachers for classifying children as handicapped. They have learned to exclude those children rather than learning how to teach them.

An understanding of the teacher's role in P.L. 94-142 must be based on a more general analysis of the teacher's place in the school. Sarason has written perceptively on this issue. In 1966 (Sarason, Levine, Goldenberg, Cherlin, & Bennett) he outlined the isolation of the teacher. Most teachers labor and have little regular contact with their principals or fellow teachers. There is almost no provision in the school day for teachers to share common frustrations or helpful solutions. Outsiders often view the school principal as a powerful supervisor of the educational process yet principals spend most of their time with matters that do not impact the teaching situation. The frequent presence of the principal in the classroom is more likely to be viewed as threatening than supportive. The infrequency of supportive, problem-solving meetings in schools is striking when compared to the ways most businesses operate.

The bottom line with regard to the effectiveness of P.L. 94-142 is the teacher-student interaction. There is no substitute for a creative teacher who produces enthusiasm and growth in a child. When this is happening it is probably not worth seeking a more specialized program for a child, even if the child's label warrants it. There are many students who have found their best advocate in a teacher rather than in their parents. Certainly advocacy for those you serve is an expected part of most professional codes. Our educational system would be far advanced if advocacy for those served was a more prominent part of its professional practice.

Adequate help for the handicapped child also implies a close working relationship between teachers and parents. The teacher should be able to communicate with parents and plan collaboratively. He/she should be responsible for setting up regular and frequent channels of communication via notes, meetings, calls, etc.

Whereas P.L. 94-142 offers major financial incentives (or penalties) on the level of state and local school systems, there are no direct incentives for the teacher. Rather than getting better pay or extra benefits, teachers who embrace the spirit of P.L. 94-142 (by accepting and working with handicapped children) just get more work. The handicapped child will benefit most when educators are prepared to deal with their educational and social development, receive reinforcement and support for effective teaching from administrators and fellow teachers, and realize financial incentives in the form of higher pay or extra benefits.

### *School*

Both programmatically and architecturally, the handicapped need to be integrated into the school program. The identity issues mentioned above imply an active preparation of the nonhandicapped students for dealing with the handicapped. This also means that the administrative and supportive staff of the school are prepared and oriented towards the role they play in creating a proper social and educational environment for the handicapped in the full range of extracurricular activities available within the school.

Many self-contained classes and resource rooms are still located in portable classrooms outside the main building, on the auditorium stage, or in other areas not originally designed for class use. The presence of special children in remote or makeshift facilities suggests that they are accorded a generally lower status both in the eyes of school personnel and possibly in the eyes of the parents who accept facilities they would not accept if their child were not handicapped.

Just as there are no special incentives for teachers to respond to the needs of the handicapped, the law mandates no special incentives for principals (although a few school systems have instituted them). The law also presumes that the schools can achieve rather significant institutional change in order to meet the needs of the handicapped. As Sarason (1971) has so deftly described, schools have their own culture that is often reflected in their structure and in their strong resistance to change.

There is much need for administrative leadership if P.L. 94-142 is to move from dry ritual to become a meaningful force in the lives of children.

### *Professional Resources*

Depending on the nature of their child's handicap, parents will encounter a variety of professionals over the years that their child attends school. Notable handicaps may first come to the attention of the pediatrician. Pediatricians often play a key role in families and are the most likely professional to follow a child from infancy into adulthood. As Accardo and Capute (1979) warn, even if the pediatrician "denies any special competence in, for example, deciding on an appropriate school placement, parents will invest his slightest bias with disproportionate significance" (p. 155). They go on to stress the need for pediatricians to be thoroughly familiar with the professional and educational resources of their community so that they might be able to direct families to the help they need. Granted, there are many families who lack regular or continuous medical supervision, but of all the professional resources used by a family, medical services are likely to have the greatest continuity.

The lack of continuity in the services of professionals who assist a family with a child's educational handicap is a matter for both parental and professional concern. Maybe families with educationally handicapped children need to think in terms of a family psychologist, a family educational consultant, or a family resource teacher—one who can follow the child through the full span of their education. For now, it is probably up to the parents to recruit the resources they need. As we become more sophisticated in this area, new patterns of service may emerge that will provide more than a year-to-year perspective on a handicapped child's education. There are some specialized centers that provide continuous programming for particular handicaps, but such centers are the exception and are generally located only in larger urban areas. The future may bring more programs of this scope both inside and outside our school system.

Section 4 (a) (17) of P.L. 94-142 requires the schools to provide or obtain for the child such "related services" as may be required to assist the child's educational progress. This may simply involve transportation but can also involve a wide range of developmental and corrective services, including speech services, audiology, psychological services, physical and occupational therapy, recreation, and counseling services. In fact, the only major exception is that medical services can be provided only for diagnostic and evaluation purposes and not for treatment. It is not only important that related services be provided, but the law envisions their coordination into a total program (I.E.P.) for the child. Hopefully this will reduce the fragmentation that traditionally characterizes the delivery of such disparate services. With a little push, isolated professionals will begin talking to each other and school personnel will gain expertise in the integration of their services.

In many parts of the country the "related services" just are not there. In such instances the law means little, but it may create some impetus to make better use of existing professionals and regional resources.

A special area of concern in the delivery of professional services under P.L. 94-142 is the requirement that the assessment of children may not be racially or culturally discriminatory. The large scale misplacement of children who are ethnically distinct from the white, middle-class norms has received growing attention in both the professional literature and the Courts (esp. *Diana v. California State Board of Education*, 1970; *Larry P. v. Riles*, 1972). Mercer (1973) has gone to particular length to distinguish those who are retarded in both intellectual skills and adaptive measures from those who are both economically and ethnically removed from the cultural mainstream and who are retarded in intellectual skills but not adaptive skills. She calls this latter group the "quasi-retarded" and sees them as the most frequently mislabelled group under traditional assessment procedures. Mercer and Lewis (1978) have provided a system for correcting such errors, which merits the attention of all psychologists providing evaluations for school placement. However, as Goodman (1977) has pointed out, there is still a great distance between correcting a diagnostic bias and producing a coherent educational plan.

In the same spirit in which the authors have advocated the integration of evaluative techniques into teaching, we wish to advocate the integration of teaching techniques into the evaluation process. The case for such an approach is most obvious in the area of learning disabilities. This diagnosis covers a range of conditions that no single discipline can encompass. Yet, most communities lack good interdisciplinary diagnostic centers, and strong research into most of these conditions is still lacking (Brown, 1979). This means that most local diagnoses are only an approximate (or inappropriate) definition of the problem. Although specialized testing techniques may identify important problem areas, there is probably no better overall system of assessment than one that establishes a baseline measure of skill, provides stepwise learning opportunities (including varied approaches), and then evaluates the learning. Lerner and Egan (1979) have described such clinical teaching methods. A measure that reflects a child's progress or lack of it, in a well-conducted learning situation is probably of much greater assessment value than a traditional psychological test, provided the child has been taught the skill and not simply trained in the responses needed for the assessment instrument.

### *Community Resources and Advocacy Groups*

Although the law mandates many resources be made available to the handicapped child in the educational environment, the educationally handicapped often need a wide range of other community resources. These resources may provide success experiences that are not available in school or, like the Special Olympics, provide sports experiences that would not be possible unless they were particularly designed for the child with handicaps. Community programs can provide camping, participation in the arts, involvement in agricultural projects, or vocational experiences that enable youth to achieve successes at the same time they acquire occupational experience.

The most important community supports are those that support the parents and the families of the handicapped child. The parents of handicapped children are often bewildered about what to do for their child. They may feel isolated, think they are unique in their mixed feelings, or experience awkwardness in asking for the help they need. They find that existing school organizations such as the P.T.A. do not relate to their problems. Larger communities usually have parent groups for specific handicapping conditions. In small or rural communities, there may be distinct advantages for parents to form a group for mutual support, information sharing, and advocacy for a cross-section of handicapping conditions. Clout with school system and community is rarely obtained in isolation. In Ohio, parents representing a wide range of handicapped children have formed a statewide network, which not only shares information about the law and resources available to parents or school but impacts the legislature and the State Department of Education as well as local schools (Children's Defense Fund, 1980).

Advocacy groups will have to pave the way for ancillary services needed by the educationally handicapped, such as tutoring services or respite care for parents whose children make unusual demands for care on the family system. Advocacy groups are also needed to address the needs of those youth who will require special support when they reach adulthood in the form of working and living arrangements or recreational and social opportunities.

The process of educating the handicapped also involves educating the community. Both advocacy groups and school systems can take an active role in increasing community awareness regarding the needs of the handicapped persons and ways in which persons in the community can respond to them most helpfully. The experience that the parents of children with serious handicaps will acquire dealing with the educational system may serve them well in dealing with other systems that must be responsive to their child.

Aside from parent advocacy, some states have advocacy mechanisms established within their state educational system. These offices of advocacy may be staffed with attorneys and educational specialists who can assist a parent who is not served by the local educational agency.

## Goals

No issue in the education of the handicapped looms as large as the problem of deciding what is an "appropriate education"—what are we going to build? Turnbull and Turnbull (1978) state that the "burden of proof is on the school system to document exactly what curriculum and educational environment constitutes an *appropriate* education" (p. 159). There are three major questions to be addressed when considering educational goals for the handicapped: first, to what degree can traditional educational goals be extended to the handicapped; second, what personal and psychological goals must be considered for the handicapped student; and third, what distinct goals must be established for the handicapped in order to provide them with the necessary skills to function in our society?

### *Traditional Goals*

The stated goals of traditional elementary and secondary education usually run something like this: to produce an adult with competence in basic academic subjects who is ready to find an occupation, to serve as an informed citizen in the community, and to enjoy a range of mature interests. Yet, it seems that the guiding principles in the development of most curriculum materials are to prepare the high school graduate for more education rather than for life as an independent adult. The classic example of this phenomena was the introduction of "new math." New math was oriented towards giving youth the basic theoretical underpinnings of advanced academic mathematics rather than a practical array of skills for everyday living. A strong academic orientation is particularly chararacteristic of elementary school curricula. It is here that youngsters either advance or fail and thereby sift themselves into the major separations that emerge in junior high and high school. However, even those children who cannot keep to the high academic track usually just get a watered-down version of the same academic curriculum. The more curricula deviate from a college-bound academic preparation, the more they are considered "special."

There seem to be two main forces contributing to the primacy of academic goals even for the handicapped (in contrast to vocational goals or social goals).These forces contribute to the shape of the curriculum when viewed as a totality as well as elements of the curriculum that affect each year's program. The first of these forces is the test book and curriculum establishment with its strong orientation towards the college-bound student.

The second of these factors is the equal opportunity myth. Weintraub and Abeson (1974) speak of the common belief that "America's public schools are the great equalizer of America's diversity," yet point out that this has not been true for the handicapped. The implication is that opening educational doors opens the doors to "equal opportunity." This is a pervasive myth that, when combined with inertia and a general lack of understanding of handicapping conditions, leads to the irrational extension of conventional approaches to the handicapped. There is no reason why youth without intellectual handicaps (though they may be blind, deaf, or physically disabled) should not pursue the regular academic curriculum to the greatest extent possible. Youth with clear intellectual handicaps will need different goals, goals that recognize the needs of their ultimate adult adjustment. The consequences of offering such youth a watered-down version of the regular curriculum are devastating. It invests great energy in preparing children for major skills they will never acquire. It reinforces their sense of frustration and failure. It wastes time that could be focused on adaptive skills they lack.

In discussing the trainably retarded, Hirshoren and Burton (1979) acknowledge that a wide range of academic performances can be drilled into children using operant conditioning methods, but they emphasize that such skills are useless unless the skills are both generalizable and contribute to the student's ultimate adjustment. A distressed aide recently reported a typical example of such teaching with a group of educably retarded third graders. The children (for the third time) were being taught about antonyms and synonyms. During the class period the children seemed to be making limited progress, but a few days later there were no signs of retention. Such inappropriate teaching is particularly likely in ill-prepared, mainstreamed classes.

Errors in teaching the educationally handicapped occur not only because of irrelevant content, but also because of poor sequencing of material. The justification for the inappropriate material is often that it is in the regular curriculum at the child's assigned grade level. The classic example of poor sequencing occurs when poor readers are moved into more advanced reading programs that are focused on increased comprehension and an expanded vocabulary while the children are still laboring with phonics and basic word recognition.

### *Personal and Psychological Goals*

In discussing the requirement for becoming an adequate adult in American society, a distinguished developmental psychologist, Jerome Kagan (1976), has said: "Competence in academic subjects is the *sine qua non* for the American child. It is difficult, if not impossible, to fail this requirement completely and retain a sense of dignity and worth in adulthood" (p. 89). The consequence of Kagan's premise is that children who will not make normal academic progress need to have the maintenance of their self-esteem considered as an integral part of their educational goals. Second, as discussed earlier in this chapter, a goal of education must be to help each child come to grips with the meaning of their own handicap. Finally, the educational goals for the handicapped must take account of the deficits in the child's socialization that are imposed by the child's own handicap. Social deficits may result from programs that do not allow for adequate socialization with children without handicaps, from limited mobility due to physical handicaps, or from social barriers imposed by communication disorders. For example, deafness can be a profound form of social isolation. Deaf children need adequate opportunity to communicate with other deaf or normal children who can communicate by signing. Without such opportunities, these children miss the whole range of experiences necessary for a successful adolescent passage.

### *Distinct Goals for the Handicapped*

For the child who is not capable of mastering the regular curriculum, the goals must be changed. Hopefully what we will build under P.L. 94-142 are educational programs that teach the skills needed for the educationally handicapped to live in the least restrictive environment. A critical question posed by a shift in educational goals away from academic tasks is whether the traditional classroom is the adequate locus of this new education for all handicapped students. Gunzburg (1974) asserts that "education for many handicapped youth" must extend far outside the classroom boundaries and must be directed even to those aspects of learning "which are usually left to the informal and haphazard teaching by life itself" (p. 630). If it is true that there is a limited capacity to transfer learning to the community among the retarded or the blind, for example, we must look for classrooms to reflect real-life social, commercial, and vocational environments or for the students to learn in real-life settings.

Each educationally handicapped child needs a structure for his or her own education. To build the structure we need appropriate goals, cooperative and competent teachers, community professionals who are both informed and ready to follow a child over a long period of time, a supportive and well-designed school environment, and parent advocates who are strongly supported by their community reference groups. When all of the above are available, P.L. 94-142 provides an ideal process for orchestration of the whole project.

## References

Aanes, D., & Haagenson, L. Normalization: attention to a conceptual disaster. *Mental Retardation*, 1978, *16*, 55-56.

Accardo, P.J., & Capute, A.J. *The pediatrician and the developmentally delayed child.* Baltimore: University Park Press, 1979.

Ballard, J., & Zettel,J. Public law 94-142 and Section 504: what they say about rights and protections. *The Exceptional Parent*, 1977, *7*, 177-184.

Bodgan, R., & Taylor, S. The judged, not the judges: an insider's view of mental retardation. *American Psychologist*, 1976, *31*, 47-52.

Brown, D. Learning disabilities: the need for cross disciplinary research. *Journal of Clinical Child Psychology*, 1979, *8*, 144-145.

Budoff, M., & Siperstein, G.N. Low-income children's attitudes toward mentally retarded children: effects of labeling and academic behavior. *American Journal of Mental Deficiency*, 1978, *82*, 474-479.

Children's Defense Fund, *94-142 and 504: numbers that add up to educational rights for handicapped children*. Washington: Children's Defense Fund, 1978.

Children's Defense Fund, Handicapped Denied Services. *CDF Reports*, 1980, *2*(3). 1; 7 (a).

Children's Defense Fund, Ohio parents network for handicapped students. *CDF Reports*, 1980, *2*(6), 2-3 (b).

Department of Health, Education & Welfare, Office of Education. Education of handicapped children: implementation of part B of the Education of the Handicapped Act (Rules and Regulations). *Federal Register*, 1977, *42*(163), 42473-42518 (Tues. Aug. 23).

Diana v. State Board of Education, Civil No. C-70, 37, RFP (N.D. Cal., January 7, 1970 & June 18, 1973).

Edgerton, R.B. *The cloak of competence: stigma in the lives of the mentally retarded*. Berkeley: University of California Press, 1967.

Foley, J.M. Effect of labeling and teacher behavior on children's attitudes. *American Journal of Mental Deficiency*, 1979, *83*, 380-384.

Goodman, J.F. The diagnostic fallacy: a critique of Jane Mercer's concept of mental retardation. *Journal of School Psychology*, 1977, *15*, 197-205.

Gunzburg, H.C. Educational planning for the mentally handicapped. In A.M. Clarke & A.D.B. Clarke (Eds.), *Mental deficiency: the changing outlook* (3rd ed.). New York: Free Press, 1974.

Hirshoren, A., & Burton, T.A. Teaching academic skills to trainable mentally retarded children: a study in tautology. *Mental Retardation*, 1979, *17*, 177-179.

Hobbs, N. *The futures of children*. San Francisco: Jossey Bass, 1975.

Kagan, J. The psychological requirements for human development. In N.B. Talbot (Ed.), *Raising children in modern America*. Boston: Little Brown, 1976.

Kurtz, P.D. Family approaches. In J.T. Neisworth & R.M. Smith (Eds.), *Retardation: Issues, assessment and intervention*. New York: McGraw Hill, 1978.

Larry, P. v. Riles, Civil No. C-71-2270, 343 F. Supp. 1306 (N.D. Cal. 1972).

Lerner, J.W., & Egan, R.W. Clinical teaching: updated. *Journal of Clinical Child Psycholgoy*, 1979, *8*, 219-222.

Mercer, J.R. *Labelling the mentally retarded*. Berkeley: University of California Press, 1973.

Mercer, J.R., & Lewis, J.F. *System of multicultural pluralistic assessment (SOMPA)*. New York: The Psychological Corporation, 1978.

Morsink, C. Implementing P.L. 94-142: the challenge of the 1980's. *Education Unlimited*, 1979, *1*, 20-22.

Pugach, M.C. Education for the handicapped: are we making any progress? *Education Unlimited*, 1979, *1*, 11-14.

Rosenthal, J.H. Self-esteem in dyslexic children. *Academic Therapy*, 1973, *9*, 27-39.

Rudberg, C.T. Working within the system. *The Exceptional Parent*, 1979, *9*, C26-C28.

Sarason, S.B. *The culture of the school and the problem of change*. Boston: Allyn And Bacon, 1971.

Sarason, S.B., Levine, M., Goldenberg, I.I., Cherlin, D.L., & Bennett, E. *Psychology in community settings*. New York: John Wiley & Sons, 1966.

Serafica, F.C., & Harway, N.I. Social relations and self esteem of children with learning disabilities. *Journal of Clinical Child Psychology*, 1979, *8*, 227-233.

Shanker, A. Public law 94-142: prospects and problems. *The Exceptional Parent*, 1980, *10*, 51-56.

Siegel, E. *The exceptional child grows up*. New York: E.P. Dutton, 1975.

Switzky, H.N., & Miller, T.L. The least restrictive alternative. *Mental Retardation*, 1978, *16*, 52-54.

Tjossem, T.D. Early intervention: issues and approaches. In T.D. Tjossem (Ed.), *Intervention strategies for high risk infants and young children*. Baltimore: University Park Press, 1976.

Turnbull, H.R., III, & Turnbull, A.P. *Free appropriate public education, law and implementation*. Denver: Love Publishing, 1978.

Vergason, G., & McAffe, J.K. A layman's guide to parents' rights under P.L. 94-142. *The Exceptional Parent*, 1979, *9*, R13-R15.

Weintraub, F.J., & Abeson, A. New education policies for the handicapped: the quiet revolution. *Phi Delta Kappan*, 1974, 526-529; 569.

Chapter 12

# THE CHRONICALLY ILL CHILD: A MATTER OF LIFE AND DEATH

JAMES S. HENNING

THE DIAGNOSIS OF chronic illness symbolizes "death" to many people. Their primary reaction is similar to that of having a loaded gun held by a killer pointed at their head (Gelder, 1978; Spinetta, Spinetta, Kung, & Schwartz, 1976). Fear, panic, and vulnerability enmesh the patient and the family. Then the gun does not go off. It remains directed at the victim and is held there for days, months, or years. Contemporary medicine has lengthened the life expectancy of many patients with chronic diseases (McCollum, 1974). The victim and the victim's family experience a myriad of emotions and inner conflicts. Anger, separation, fear of pain, dismemberment, loss of control—all these emotions kaleidoscope inside the victim (Easson, 1970; Travis, 1976). There is also a threat to bodily integrity and self-image. There is a fear of being dependent for survival, for care, for life itself. Adults conjure up these emotions and fears in their minds. Adults have had experiences that help them organize, rationalize, and systematize these concepts. What happens to children who developmentally are still not able to conceptualize? What happens to children who are just starting to formulate abstract thinking? What reaction does the teenager have who has just begun puberty? What happens to a child with cystic fibrosis, kidney failure, leukemia, or any other life-threatening disease? What rights do they have? What emotions do they experience?

Children with chronic illnesses have problems different from adults with the same illness (Anthony & Koupernik, 1973; Azarnoff, 1974). Working with children who have a chronic or terminal illness demands different skills, different treatment modalities, and different language (Kaplan, Smith, Grobstein, & Fishman, 1977; Koocher, 1977). Children are not small versions of adults. They do not have the experiential knowledge or the ability to abstract conclusions that adults have.

The diagnosis of a chronic illness or fatal disease in a child produces stress that pervades the child's environment. The child, the child's parents, brothers and sisters, relatives, friends, the physician, and health care staff are affected and enveloped in emotional tension (Kirkpatrick, Hoffman, & Futterman, 1974). Children, even very young children, who are repeatedly exposed to medical staff and clinics become aware that something is wrong and it is not going away. Children read adult expressions and reactions and learn that these people are not happy about what is happening. The parents frequently do not know how much or how little to say to a child, or what words to use. Traditionally, physicians have collaborated with the parents to say nothing until a child asks questions, and then answer with information that will not upset the child. This point of view ignores the fact that indirect communication frequently clues the child into what is happening. It has been suggested (Smith, 1968) that we get away from the idea that, with children, we need to soften blows in a special way. Facts cannot always be softened, but through exploration and sharing, the impact may be less concentrated and acute. The emotional and cognitive development of the child needs to be considered in these cases.

While contemporary medicine continues to forge progress in conquering malignancies, life expectancy has been prolonged in many diseases with remissions far longer than was possible in the past. Illnesses that were terminal fifteen years ago are now labeled chronic. The sequelae are legion. Children diagnosed early in their lives and formerly doomed to die early now live longer, go to school, and many grow to ages where they are capable of understanding their own illness and exactly what it means.

The family is also directly affected. What once was a short-term stress, crisis, or grief now is lengthened over months and years.

Parents of children with chronic illness whose initial response was grief for the expected death now are forced to drag that grief out, sometimes unable to complete the mourning process and arrive at closure since their child may live for an unpredictable period of time. Parents encouraged to treat their child "normally" find themselves faced with economic, emotional, and social stresses that increase in duration. The situation stretches for endless days and uncountable hours.

There are three primary forces to consider while working with the chronically ill child. The first is the diagnosed child, the second is the parenting group or family, and the third is the ancillary medical staff. Each of these three forces has three categories to evaluate: strengths, conflicts, and defenses. These forces contribute unique responses to the stress of the illness. In the ensuing chapter, the responses will be examined and the strengths, conflicts, and defenses reviewed.

## THE CHILD

### *Strengths*

When a child is diagnosed with a terminal or chronic illness, the course of that child's natural development begins its first detour. Brothers and sisters will continue on their own natural stage-appropriate development, gaining insights, garnering new skills, and accomplishing appropriate grade goals more or less within normal limits. They will continue on in regular classes, going to school each day, attending Blue Birds or soccer practice. The diagnosed child will be required to keep doctor's appointments, meet unfamiliar adults, and submit to "blood lettings" at regular intervals. There will be sick days and classes missed, parties disregarded, and friends ignored.

At this initial stage of diagnosis, it is paramount to emphasize the natural skills and talents the child does have. Despite, or in spite of, the disease, the child is not robbed of skills already achieved. If the child is good at art, then encourage the child to continue to express feelings and emotions with drawings and picture paintings. Focus on the natural existing talents to sustain a rhythm and semblance of progress/achievement.

> Lisa was a 4½ year old girl who was attacked by a neighborhood dog. The dog jumped her, forcing her to the ground and bit into her neck, ripping the larynx and neck muscles. After surgery, she was left with a tracheotomy and she frequently had to be suctioned. During play therapy sessions she liked to draw. First she drew pictures of herself and her sister. In the drawing of herself, there was no sign of the tracheotomy. When she drew her sister she put the trach tube in, suggesting both denial of her condition and anger at her sister for escaping the tracheotomy. Utilizing the drawings over sessions, she drew pictures of dogs, family friends and eventually a picture of the trach tube, her insides, and all "the muck" that had to be suctioned off. She became less afraid of the tube and the reaction of others to the tube.

Other natural talents like swimming and sports for competitive teenagers help them achieve and maintain some age-appropriate self-image. Discretion is advised to help the child achieve realistic goals and to not allow the talent to become an avenue of failure. Employing natural skills can help the child center on the part of his/her life that will stay the same and enrich life itself.

While the family and siblings begin to make adjustments—economic, daily, and medical—it is useful to establish as quickly as is reasonable a familiar routine. Maintaining the family's routine may become the most problematic part of the treatment plan. The purpose behind the routine is to help the child maintain a secure position within the family constellation. Children quickly learn that they can control the family through their asthma, dialysis, or leukemia. If discipline is not consistent for all children in the family, then the diagnosed child will learn how to manipulate the parents even when she/he is not sick. Parents frequently feel that because the sick child must come to the hospital, have blood drawn, receive shots and IV lines, they should not be disciplined any further. "After all, their life is painful enough." The consequences of this logic is the tail wagging the dog. Even young two-year-olds sense when there is favored treatment and they can use it maximally. The non-diagnosed children see the sick child as getting her/his own way and begin to imitate. Sometimes siblings of the sick child will come to the clinic asking for shots because they see their brother or sister receiving all the attention from adults and then being rewarded for the painful treatment by going to MacDonald's after the clinic visit. For all family members, the familiarity of routine brings both sanity and security.

Knowledge of Piagetian stage development theory is *de rigueur* for understanding what words to choose and what logic to select with children. All children have a sense for reasonableness. Not all children or adults choose to be reasonable, however. The diagnosed child has a right to know what is going to happen to him/her when in a clinic or hospital room. Choosing words and concepts to explain procedures is advised. Choose words that are age and stage appropriate. A review of child development helps to construct explanations that are best suited for a three- to five-year-old versus a nine- or ten-year-old. Teenagers are in a class by themselves and need to be treated in their own special way.

Chronic illness does not provide a time and space for surprises. Pediatric doctors and staff are acquainted with and have even been bruised by a child who has not been told that they are due for a spinal tap or bone marrow aspiration. It is not fair to expect a child to cooperate when she/he has not been informed of the pending procedure. The time taken to explain to a child, in appropriate words and sequence, what is going to be done to her/his body will be regained in cooperation during the procedure. Relaxation techniques and hypnosis are also available as auxiliary tools for helping the child. It is not appropriate to tell a child a shot "will not hurt." It hurts adults and some faint; why expect a child to be different? Laboratory technicians and nurses are learning to say that "this needle will be like a bee sting or a mosquito bite and then it will be over." Utilize a child's natural intelligence to interest him/her in a more active role in the management of the disease. It can be helpful to show them slides or x-rays. Time and interest invested in children is returned ten times over in cooperation and trust.

One of the consequences of coping with a chronic or terminal illness is that a child is faced with adult responsibilities. Diabetics start to manage their own insulin; leukemics look for bruises or mouth sores and inform parents; children with asthma, renal failure, or cystic fibrosis monitor their health. Frequent visits to clinics and hospitals place them in contact with adults more often than their peers. Hospital staff and parents place expectations on the children that are not placed on siblings. As a result, some children begin to emotionally mature faster and act more socially alert. This has both benefits and dangers. Adults are pleased that the child is responsive to treatment and cooperative and may expect more from a child. Socially, the child may have learned some cues necessary for survival but cognitively the child is still a child.

### *Conflicts*

Reflecting that children are cognitively at different stages, one conflict that the child faces at the time of diagnosis is that she/he is no longer omnipotent. The world and life do not hold out to this child limitless possibilities any longer. Limits are being set on the child—limits not fully chosen. All children experience this termination of omnipotence, but chronically ill children face the experience as if running into a brick wall, not through repeated mastery of self. Limits not wanted are limits that can become concrete walls separating the child from fun and peers. The child's fantasy life is intruded upon. Here limits are set also. In some ways, adult reality testing has been forced upon the child because of her/his chronic illnesses. "These things are now possible, those are not," they are told. "You must be here for this appointment, or you must take this medicine." The world, adults, and strangers force upon children's minds the reality that their time is limited, their potential is reduced.

The next phase is that life is also limited. Days are numbered and the numbering of those days does not belong to the child. Again, the outside world, i.e., the disease and its cure, force the child to face a reality other children are not faced with until later years. The child sees and learns of other children in the clinic who died with the same disease. Depression is often not far behind. Rarely, however, will the child be able to identify the cause of the depression. It is important to remember that children under seven years of age have little cognition of the meaning of death. A pet dies and is gone; a bug is smashed by a roller skate. The child feels that this is "not real;" it is like play. At the age of seven, the Piagetian stage of concrete operations and Erickson's stage of industry versus inferiority, the child begins to recognize that death is inevitable. It is not until the age of approximately ten that most theorists believe that children understand that death is irreversible.

The disease process can create an artificial or premature splitting off from family or friends. Then "why me and not my sister" questions arouse desires for rational explorations that cannot be given. The child senses that this process separates him/her from school mates or family, he/she is different, this child is unique and will never blend back into the commonweal again. There is among children, especially, a desire to think, act, look, walk, and talk like everyone else. A disease curtails this process of acceptance and oneness.

Psychodynamic conflicts also emerge when the child's natural impulses to be and do the things of children are stopped by the reality of constraints. This conflict is compounded by disease limitations. The ego's conflicts are passivity or quiet acceptance of all that is being done to her/him as a consequence of something they have merited or deserved by bad deeds versus an active interest in the process of getting better because they wish to participate actively in the mastery of their body, self, and world. Withdrawal versus acting out, object closeness versus distance are also basic conflicts that a developing ego struggles with to express external versus internal polarities. Psychosexual dynamics include: separation versus merging, needing to be nurtured versus resourcefulness, basic trust versus mistrust, independence versus autonomy, and Oedipal resolution. Super-ego dynamics are an expression of aggression versus fear of retaliation, good self-esteem versus poor self-esteem, and control versus external authority.

### *Defenses*

The personality profile exhibited by children with chronic diseases or handicaps fall along a continuum ranging from overdependence, overanxious, and pervasive withdrawn patterns to overindependent, aggressive modalities with strong denial of the illness. The reappearance of thumbsucking in infants and younger children or return to the bottle can be a regression in the service of the ego. Bedwetting and encopresis, more demanding and clinging, aggressive behavior, as well as the temporary lapse of learned speech or walking, are also regression behaviors. In latency and older children, more aggressive behaviors appear with the same frequency, such as inability to share with siblings, difficulties in learning and concentration.

Children under the age of four can be vulnerable to separation from the mother, which may be interpreted by the child as punishment or desertion. Such fears evoke childhood anxiety and regression. Older children may express anxiety about the functioning of certain organs: genital inadequacy, muscular weakness, hair loss, feelings of inferiority. These feelings can cause struggles for identity and independence and may interfere with a teenager's cooperation with treatment.

Eating and sleeping disturbances, mood swings, and changes in motoric levels sometimes accompany chronic illness. Pain may be interpreted as a punishment for real or imagined transgressions. Fear of body mutilation is frequent in young children.

In summary, the child is a complex individual who deserves the attention of all who help him/her cope with the illness. Each child is unique, each has reached a particular stage of development when diagnosed. It is the responsibility of the adults who work with them to address their stage development appropriately, listen to their needs, and help their understanding of the illness. It is *their* illness. It is *their* treatment. It is *their* life that is being developed as well as assaulted.

## THE PARENTS AND FAMILY

The mental health professional needs to address the feelings and thoughts of the parents and extended family as well as the child's feelings.

Families who have a child with a chronic or terminal illness experience a crisis and can be "at risk" (Caroff & Debrof, 1975; Moos & Tsu, 1977). The diagnosis creates a disequilibrium following the course of events to which previous coping efforts are now maladaptive. This diagnostive event is perceived as a threat to instinctual needs or integrity, or as a loss, or even as a challenge. The emotional response to threat is anxiety (Rapoport, 1965), the response to loss is depression, and the response to challenge can mobilize problem-solving efforts. Families with a chronically ill child can perceive the diagnosis as a loss, either present or potential. The present loss is of a healthy, developing child who played an active role in the family construction. The diagnosis of chronic disease requires a shift in the ecology of the family system resulting in juggling roles and adopting new ones. The family's ability to respond to each member's new needs may be more difficult (Hill, 1965). The manner in which the family carries out their new role affects the structure of the family and alters their perception of how "at risk" they will be (Koos & Folcomer, 1948).

The stress of the chronic illness can be perceived by the family as completely external: as an enemy from outside or as foreign to the family constellation. Such a perception enhances the unification of the family as they ban together for mutual comfort and solidarity against the attacking outsiders. One danger is that this can create an isolationist family policy and they see themselves as the solitary support for one another and reject all attempts to involve the outsiders in the healing process. When the family system redefines its roles it can also shatter the solidarity of the family ecology. Then the stress is no longer outside the family but within as well. This causes more difficulty in resolving the crisis of new role identities (Futterman & Hoffman, 1973; Hill, 1965). These dilemmas of withdrawal, introspection, self-recrimination, and new role identities need family intervention. Family members are rarely able to work out stress independently. The family unit can learn to sustain the stress, and individual members can learn new roles.

At the initial diagnosis, family members appear to be most receptive to outside help. At this point even minor therapeutic interventions produce magnified results because coping mechanisms are the most pliable (Rapoport, 1965). The family unit may not, however, be an open system. Some family systems permit outside intervention only through a liaison family member. The parents and extended adult family members exercise strong control over other members. The exercise of such strong control will either facilitate or obstruct the therapeutic intervention with the diagnosed child. Kaplan, Smith, Grobstein, and Fishman (1977) suggest a family approach to this crisis intervention. Ultimately, it is the family system that will determine how the collective family will reestablish harmony. A careful look at the strengths, conflicts, and defenses of the family's functioning will aid the intervention into the family system (Parad & Caplan, 1960).

### *Strengths*

The advantage that parents/adults have over children is experience: experience of life, experience of life cycles, and experience of suffering and recovery. Even on the most rudimentary level, this experience is not to be minimized. Parents of the chronically ill child sometimes report, "I don't have the strength or the courage to face this disease." In reality, the parent fears the unknown, the unpredictable. The health professional can review with the parent his/her past experiences of coping with exasperating events, meeting the challenge of those events, and surviving intact. For those parents who have already mastered months of chemotherapy, a review with them of what changes they have already met and what challenges they have overcome helps them to focus on achievements, not on future unknowns. No one can live in the future; the future does not exist yet. Helping the parents and siblings look at each day's goals and achievements keeps them reality-oriented. Open, honest communication between staff and family are essential to trust and cooperation.

The relationship between parent and child is created on trust; trust that no harm will be inflicted, shelter and food will be provided, and love will nurture. When a chronically ill child begins to see that the parents can no longer protect him from harm or guarantee housing/diet that the child will encounter in the hospital, only love remains as the thread of trust. It is advised that parents guard carefully that thread. Telling a child "This shot won't hurt" or "This IV needle doesn't hurt" is *not true.* It does hurt but it does not last forever! It is more like a bee sting or mosquito bite than an enduring pain. Teaching parents to be accurate in communication will protect the thread of trust. Being present, physically as well as mentally, provides the child with the emotional environment necessary to feel wanted, loved, and helped. This may mean, for the parents, an explanation of their roles as "providers" and how that role might change during the course of the disease. The love they give can and does more for a child than many parents think. Again, honest communication with their child provides the atmosphere where trust encourages love. Children know quickly adult moods; they intuit. They also have a good sense of how sick they are and can read from adult reactions the rest of the story.

> Philip was a thirteen-year-old who came to the hospital with what appeared to be an inflamed appendix. In the operating room it was discovered that he had a large tumor in his lower bowel and a major part of the intestinal tract was removed and a colostomy performed. When Eric woke up in the recovery room he still believed he had his appendix removed. However, he began to sense that something else was wrong when his mother did not talk about the operation, and the doctors talked outside of his room door and outside of his hearing. He didn't know why he had a colostomy bag. He began to ask the nursing staff what had happened in surgery.

Trying to hide a diagnosis from a child only fools the people perpetrating the charade. The pretense does not usually fool the child. The parent may feel more comfortable but then the child must find someone else to talk to about feelings. It is a shame and a pity when that person is not a parent. The parent loses the opportunity to share with the child critical parts of a life cycle. However, for some adults, death is too threatening an event to investigate their own feelings let alone share them with a child.

The instincts in parents to protect and provide for their children are strong. The maternal instincts have been acclaimed the strongest of all drives. When a child with a chronic illness is suffering and needs to undergo treatments, it is frequently the mother who is required to bring the child. The father's working hours sometimes prevent him from being present. The role typically devolves on the mother. Her instinct to protect this child from future disease allows her to stand by the child's side and watch treatments, answering the child that this procedure is for his/her own good. Such a process can build a conflict in the mother: looking for and creating long-term goals leave the present moment vulnerable. Stress builds as the mother continues to tell her child that all these treatments will help. Sometimes they do and sometimes they do not. The medical staff needs to be aware that mothers enduring this stress also need words of comfort and communication about what is happening. They have placed themselves on the line backing the doctors against the child's feelings. The staff need to inform her of the facts so she can continue to nurture the child. In addition, the mother is also the communicating link between the staff and her husband. Support and communication to the mother spell compliance and cooperation from the family and the child.

In brief, parents' realization of their own internal endurance, trust, and an open line of information flowing from parents to staff to parents can enhance the quality of life for the parents of the diagnosed child and the child as well.

### *Conflicts*

Parents of children with chronic illness begin to see their children as no longer perfect. These children will not grow up to be replicas of themselves. Guilt follows quickly upon these realizations. "Did my baby get this from me, from my side of the family?" "If I had taken better care during my pregnancy this wouldn't have happened." "What did I do to deserve this for my child?" These are questions that have no answers but leave a residue of guilt in the person asking the questions.

Parents also question what kind of future this child will have. What will the quality of life be for their child? What kind of life would the child have if the parents died, who would take care of the child? Is life worthwhile hooked up to machines? These types of questions avoid the main issue: What is happening today? Can I face it? And what am I going to do right now? The guilt feelings and excessive ruminations about an imperfect child do not change reality; they simply refocus attention away from the problem onto a suffering parent. Support, realistic counseling, and direct conversation can help these parents refocus the attention back to the child. Both parents need to be addressed. Parent groups, where the parents can meet one another, can facilitate an alleviation of guilt and anger.

When working with the fathers, medical staff should be aware that despite macho external appearances, it is difficult for fathers to tolerate the invasive, violent treatment procedures most chronic illnesses require. Preparation and open communication with a father can facilitate more cooperation from the child. Without explanations of the procedures you are less likely to surmise a father's reaction, e.g., fainting, revulsion, anger at the staff, aversion. With preparation you can achieve a strong and persevering ally.

Similar to the child's reaction to a long-term illness, parents also experience the desire to escape from the problems. This is a common, typical reaction that is also typically reacted to with guilt, self-recriminations, or shame. Talking with the parents about these inner feelings allows them to realize that they are not abnormal parents, that they can feel angry at the process, and at the same time still feel love for their children.

### *Defenses*

Some defenses used by the parents of chronically ill children are enumerated below. It should be noted that not all defense systems are malappropriate or maladaptive. Defenses become maladaptive when they prohibit the person from an accurate perception of reality. The major question is whether the defense is productive, recognizing the dynamic maturational and developmental continiuum. Stress can produce some productive defenses to allow the individual to incorporate data from the outside. In reviewing defenses that appear during a long-term illness, it is appropriate to look at both the appropriate and maladaptive sides.

ISOLATION: Intrapsychic separating of affect from content, resulting in repression of either idea of affect or the displacement of the affect to a substitute.

DENIAL: Seeing but refusing to acknowl-dge what one sees or

hears. Unlike repression, it affects the perception of outside data more than internal feelings.

INTELLECTUALIZATION: Control of feelings and impulses by thinking about them instead of experiencing them. It is a systematic excess of thinking, deprived of feeling in order to defend against anxiety due to unacceptable feelings.

CONTROLLING: Excessive attempts to regulate events in the environment in the interest of minimizing anxiety and solving internal conflict.

REPRESSION: Expelling from awareness an idea or feeling before it becomes conscious.

Rapoport (1965) states that there are three stages to crisis: impact, recoil, and post-traumatic period. In families diagnosed with a chronically ill child, this cycle is repetitive as the child goes through diagnosis, remission, relapse, remission, and terminal phase. The sequence may repeat itself over and over again. The family unit experiences the crisis in layers over a long period of time. This is a different kind of experience than those individuals who dealt with one single catastrophic event, such as the Coconut Grove fire (Lindemann, 1965). The family unit will experience the stress repeatedly for days and months and even years. They will need to rely on appropriate defenses, call up their inner strengths, and come face-to-face with conflicts they thought they could never endure.

## THE MEDICAL STAFF

Similar to the parents of the ill child and the child as well, the medical staff experiences strengths, conflict, and defenses. It is a recent concept in the field of psychology that health care givers are at times profoundly affected by the health care they give. Names like "burnout" and "wellness" are terms that are premiering in the field as professionals analyze their own personal dynamics.

The families of chronically ill children have, they occasionally believe, only the worst to anticipate. Freud (1965) pointed out that we are homeostatic-seeking human beings. We look at or anticipate the long-term illness of a child with great difficulty. Mental health professionals, nursing staff, and physicians that make themselves available to families can become the embodiment of the crisis. They become the symbolic crisis. The parents realize that the professional has come to discuss a painful event. The parents counter with conversations of food, weather, or school needs for the child. The health care professional approaches the family unit with the tools of support and the knowledge of experience. At the same time the health care professional needs to monitor his/her own skills, conflicts, and defenses to present a viable package of care giving.

### *Strengths*

The field of health care is a *chosen* profession. People select it for a variety of personal reasons but the common denominator is a wish to help other people who are afflicted. That wish to help has some extremes such as playing God, acting out a messianic complex, or fear of dying. Overall, most health care professionals care about the quality of human life and wish to help others enjoy their inalienable right to life, liberty, and the pursuit of happiness in a healthy way. They care and will take time to enhance the lives they are caring for given their individual personality disposition.

This dynamic provides the sick child and family a natural selection process in which they can find a friend or confidant to help them progress through the illness. The disposition of the staff also naturally inclines them to be more attracted to one patient than another. What is required of the staff, professionally, is an openness to an enriching experience of working with a seriously ill child day after day, allowing a recognition of the feelings that emerge, and a sharing of what is appropriate to enhance the life of the child.

Primarily, the staff supplies the means by which the child gets better: diagnosis and treatment. This is their job. This is their training. This is what establishes confidence and trust in a child patient. At times, it is not easy to be the person that brings medical pain to a child, e.g., IVs, spinal taps, or bone marrow aspirations. Yet, at the same time, the confidence that a child invests in the staff-patient relationship allows pain because the child believes that the staff person wants the child to have a healthier life. The relationship is important and not to be denied.

This is well evidenced on pediatric wards by the ability of some staff to give injections or IVs to some patients and not to others.

Experience is the mother of solace. The medical staff have the historical perspective to help parents and children understand the disease process. It is similar to a teacher who watches thirty children a day in the classroom being a better diagnostician about social adjustment than the parent who sees only one or two children. The medical staff tends to see more of the same kinds of cases per week or year and can conceptualize for the family an outcome or the sequence of the process and how other children have compared or responded to the experience. This is an invaluable service and when accurately used can benefit the family enormously.

### *Conflicts*

The conflicts for the medical staff center around two major areas: (1) the unpredictability of the body and its reaction to drugs, surgery, or treatment, and (2) the recognition and acceptance of the value of life and the inevitability of death in one's own life and the life of another.

The ancient philosophers used to debate the mind/body duality. The nineteenth century scientists considered that debate is futile and dealt only in the observable phenomenon. Today, again, medicine is facing the results of what the mind can do for and to the body. Anecdotal information abounds about the manner in which patients have recovered. New methods are being developed to facilitate the mind in aiding the body's struggle for health, e.g., biofeedback, stress management, guided imagery, hypnosis, even humor as suggested by Dr. Norman Cousins. The body is still an unpredictable phenomenon—the personality even more so. Helping the patient gain mastery over the body and disease through an understanding of the emotions and "willfulness" is not an easy task. Neither is it a task that is to be denigrated.

The second major conflict in working with terminal or chronically ill patients is directly looking into the meaning of death; death in the abstract and one's own death. It is a troublesome problem for medical and mental health professionals.

It means a sincere or honest look at belief systems and life values. Avoidance of those issues makes the staff impotent to help anyone else who is dying. It is not a matter of projecting onto the patient your belief system but of a willingness to listen to someone else's, allowing room for tolerance of foreign beliefs and practices, and finally acceptance of the reality of the finality of death. This is not simple, and certainly not easy, but the rewards from the open relationship with patient can be hundredfold.

### *Defenses*

Some basic defense systems utilized by professionals in the care of the chronically ill child are listed below. Not all defense systems are inappropriate to the circumstances.

DISTANCE: Physical removal from proximity to the person or event causing emotional conflict.

INCORPORATION: A primitive wish for union with another person, who loses all distinction and function as an individual. The other individual is completely assumed into the world of the subject.

IDENTIFICATION (with parental role): An unconscious adoption of the role or mental picture of the parenting role and the patterning after that role; seeing oneself like the person used as the pattern.

RATIONALIZATION: Justification of attitudes or behavior that might not be acceptable by applying just reasons or the invention of a convincing fallacy.

In chronic illness the cliche "which is worse, the treatment or the disease?" is frequently asked, sometimes rhetorically, sometimes in desperation. There are few people who would wish to return to the medical practices of fifty years ago and allow chronic illnesses to take their natural course, unabetted by modern medicine. Increased interest as well as more sophisticated intervention designed to support the emotional needs of chronically ill children and their families have emerged. The quest for solutions to the social consequences of modern technology has been less than vigorous. Mental health care of the seriously ill patient has only been acknowledged recently.

All staff engaged in helping the family of the chronically ill child cope with the disease can enhance the process. Each discipline brings to the intervention a historical tradition of skills and development. More open, interdisciplinary communication as well as treatment plans are needed. Children are many faceted. Treatment plans also need to be many faceted.

## Summary

Children and their families deserve every opportunity to cope with the loss or theoretical loss of life itself. They need every resource the psychosocial sciences can make available. This includes emotional support as well as professional services. The most important and major ingredient of support services for families is communication focused on educating the family about the child's illness or on educating the family to deal with the prospect of a child's death or death itself (Lansky, 1974; Lascari & Stehbens, 1973). Those are the major ingredients of communication. The other ingredients include regular and systematic communication of other issues, i.e., personal, familial, financial. Repeating to the family that communication of any concern whether or not it directly relates to the child's illness is important will help bear the stress. Decision making then is not done in haste and regretted later. Help can be provided about community resources, financial aid, or child developmental processes. If no direct assistance can be afforded, then the family still understands they have someone with whom they can unburden feelings and that some people are trying to understand their problems. Communication, care, and comfort are the important contributions professionals can give to children and their families, and receive them as well in return.

## References

Anthony, H.J., & Koupernik, C. (Eds.). The child in his family: The impact of disease and death. *Yearbook of the International Association for Child Psychiatry and Allied Professions*, Vol. 2. New York: John Wiley & Sons, 1973.

Azarnoff, P. Mediating the trauma of serious illness and hospitalization in children. *Children Today*, 3, 1974.

Caroff, Phyllis, & Debrof, Rose. The helping process with bereaved families. In B. Schoenberg, I. Gerber, A. Wiener, A.H. Kutscher, D. Peretz, & A.C. Carr,

(Eds.), *Bereavement: Its psychological aspects.* New York: Columbia University Press, 1975.

Easson, W.M. *The dying child.* Springfield: Charles C Thomas, 1970.

Freud, Anna. *The writings of Anna Freud: The ego and the mechanisms of defense.* New York: International Universities Press, Inc., 1966.

Futterman, E.H., & Hoffman, I. Crisis and adaptation in the families of fatally ill children. In J.E. Anthony, & C. Koupernik (Eds.), *The child in his family: The impact of disease and death* Vol. 2. New York: Wiley and Sons, 1973.

Gilder, R. Group therapy with parents of children with leukemia. *American Journal of Psychotherapy,* 1978, 32 (2).

Hill, Reuben. Generic features of families under stress. In H.J. Parad (Ed.), *Crisis intervention: Selected readings.* New York: Family Service Association of America, 1965.

Kaplan, David M., Smith, A., Grobstein, R., & Fishman, S.E. Family mediation of stress. In Rudolf H. Moos (Ed.), *Coping with physical illness.* New York: Plenum Medical Book Company, 1977.

Kirk, Patrick, K., Hoffman, I., & Futterman, E.H. Dilemma of trust: Relationship between medical care givers and parents of fatally ill children. *Pediatrics,* August, 1974, *54*(2), 169-175.

Koocher, G.P. (Ed.). Special issue on death and the child. *Journal of Pediatric Psychology,* 1977, *2*(2).

Koos, Earl., & Folcomer, D. Families in crisis. In E.M. Duval, & R. Hill (Eds.), *Dynamics of family interaction.* New York: Women's Foundation, 1948.

Lansky, S.B. Childhood leukemia: The child psychiatrist as a member of the oncology team. *Journal of the American Academy of Child Psychiatry,* Summer, 1974, *13*(3), 499-508.

Lascarl, A.D., & Stehbens, J.A. The reactions of families to childhood leukemia: An evaluation of a program of emotional management. *Clinical Pediatrics,* April, 1973, *12,* 210-214.

Lindemann, Erich. Symptomatology and management of acute grief. In H.J. Parad (Ed.) *Crisis intervention: Selected readings.* New York: Family Service Association of America, 1965.

McCollum, A.T. Counselling the grieving parent. In L. Burton, (Ed.), *Care of the child facing death.* London & Boston: Routledger & Kegan Paul, 1974.

Moos, Rudolf H., & Tsu, Vivien. The crisis of physical illness: An overview. In Rudolf H. Moos (Ed.), *Coping with physical illness.* New York: Plenum Medical Book Company, 1977.

Parad, Howard J., & Caplan, Gerald. A framework for studying families in crisis. *Social Work,* July, 1960, *5,* 3-15.

Rapoport, Lydia. The state of crisis: Some theoretical considerations. In H.J. Parad (Ed.), *Crisis intervention: Selected readings.* New York: Family Service Association of America, 1965.

Smith, Clement. Help for the helpless. *Rhode Island Medical Journal,* 1956, *39,* 491-9.

Spinetta, J.J., Spinetta, P.D., Kung, F., & Schwartz, D.B. *A Handbook for parents*. Leukemia Society of America, 1976.

Travis, G. *Chronic illness in children*. Stanford, California: Stanford University Press, 1976.

Chapter 13

# PAIN CONTROL IN CHILDREN

MARGO McCAFFERY

THE RIGHT TO BE relieved of physical pain and suffering, if possible, seems reasonable and humane. In writing and many times in lecturing to health team members I have stated that the patient has a right to pain relief (McCaffery, 1979). However, for some of the reasons discussed in this chapter, health team members and laymen may disagree with this statement.

## The Emerging Science of Pain

In spite of pain being universal and plaguing mankind since the beginning of time, the science of pain and its relief is very new. Professional interest in pain has surged in the last ten to twenty years. Progress has been made, but controversy remains. Much of what has been learned about pain has not been widely disseminated. Nevertheless, agencies have been established to assist with pain relief, notably hospices, which provide care for terminally ill patients and their families and pain clinics.

Unfortunately, children with pain have not yet benefitted very much from this growing interest in pain. To date, Johns Hopkins has the only pain clinic in the United States for children with prolonged pain (Epstein and Harris, 1978). Many hospice programs will not accept children. Although publications about pain have risen dramatically, very few papers are published about children with pain. For example, between 1970 and 1975, 1,380 articles on pain were published in the medical literature but only thirty-three dealt with pediatric pain (Eland and Anderson, 1977).

In spite of these problems, some information has become available that makes the relief of pain in children more feasible. Some of what has been discovered about relieving pain in adults can be applied to children. Reported clinical experiences with children have also increased knowledge of what may be effective.

However, misconceptions and myths about children in pain make it difficult to utilize what is presently known. Health team members and parents often harbor incorrect ideas about how the presence and intensity of pain can be determined in the child. The health team, parents, and also the child may have erroneous information about the need for and safety of certain methods of pain relief.

In the reality of clinical practice, helping the child with pain must usually begin with an attempt to identify what misconceptions are operating to hamper assessment and relief of pain and who believes these. It is obvious that if health team members or parents do not believe the child has pain, it is unlikely they will do anything to relieve the pain. If they do believe the child has pain but feel that the pain is in some way serviceable or that pain relief would be dangerous, it is again unlikely that much will be done to relieve the pain. Before significant progress can be made toward relieving a child's pain, misconceptions must be identified and confronted.

The misconceptions are divided into (1) those that hamper assessment of pain and (2) those that hamper relief of pain. These misconceptions are ones I have most frequently encountered in almost twenty years of reading about and being involved with the care of children with pain. Without conclusive research, it is difficult to state that the following misconceptions are absolutely false. Rather, it is possible to say that based upon current information they are certainly open to question.

## Misconceptions That Hamper Assessment Of Pain

The experience of a localized sensation of bodily pain is entirely subjective. Its existence and characteristics are truly and fully known only to the person who has the pain. However, relief of that pain may at times be largely dependent upon actions taken by others. When a child is in pain, those responsible for his care, usually parents and health professionals, may possess erroneous information and mistaken beliefs that cause them to overlook that the child has pain or that the pain is intense enough to warrant relief.

***Misconception***: Infants and young children do not perceive as much pain as adults.

*CORRECTION:* The precise age at which the child perceives a sensation of pain in the same way as an adult is simply unknown. However, it is no longer felt that infants lack the neurophysiological equipment with which to perceive pain. It was once thought that the infant's incomplete cortical development and myelinization of nerve fibers meant lack of pain perception. It is now known that complete myelinization is not necessary for the perception of pain and that myelinization occurs rapidly during the first weeks of life (Swafford and Allan, 1968). Further, while the undeveloped cortex in the infant may limit memory or localization of pain, it is fairly certain that the infant feels pain (Gross and Gardner, 1980). For example, the newborn usually reacts to needle punctures with bodily withdrawal and crying.

Some surgeons and anesthesiologists erroneously believe that infants less than three months old are insensitive to pain, and they allow surgical procedures to be performed without benefit of anesthesia in this age infant (Peiper, 1963). Such practices are clearly deplorable and unjustified.

There is some evidence that children are actually more sensitive to pain than adults. Haslam's (1969) study of children five to eighteen years of age showed that the younger child had a lower pain perception threshold than the older child. In other words, the younger the child, the more susceptible he was to feeling pain. Thus, if comparable stimuli are applied to children and adults, it is quite possible that children will experience more, not less, pain than adults.

***Misconception***: Children who do not act like they are in pain are not in pain.

*CORRECTION*: A child in pain will not always respond with visible physiological and/or behavioral manifestations of pain. While responses such as crying or a rapid heart rate may be useful clues that pain may be present, their absence does not mean that pain is absent.

For many reasons, behavioral and physiological responses to pain become minimal or nonexistent for periods of time. This adaptation may result because pain and illness are fatiguing. Thus, the child may be too exhausted to cry about his pain. The child may try to please others by minimizing his responses to pain, trying not to be a "sissy." Or, the child may value self-control and expend considerable energy being "brave." Other times the child's remarkable ability to be distracted leads to periods of minimal or no response to pain because he is attending to other stimuli, yet the pain is still there (McCaffery, 1977).

The child's high level of physical activity may be especially misleading. Under similar painful circumstances, children tend to be more active than adults. Physical activity is one of the child's coping mechanisms (Eland and Anderson, 1977). Being physically active not only distracts the child from pain but performing recently acquired developmental skills, such as standing or walking, probably also helps him retain a sense of mastery over himself and his environment.

Failure to believe a child has pain simply because he "doesn't act like he's in pain" may have dangerous consequences. If affection or pain relief are given only when the child cries, remains inactive, or otherwise "acts like he's in pain," then these behaviors are reinforced. Always ask yourself, "How would the child have to act for me to believe he hurts?" Then ask yourself, "Do I want to encourage the behaviors that convince me?" Probably not. Such behaviors are likely to be physically and emotionally detrimental to the child (McCaffery, 1979).

***Misconception***: Health team members can rate the intensity of pain in children more accurately than children.

*CORRECTION:* There is no way that a sensation of pain can be felt by anyone except the experiencing person. This is unlike most other symptoms with which the health team deals. If the child reports a sensation of warmth, he may feel warm to the touch of others and this can be checked with a thermometer. Pain cannot be felt by an outsider, and there are no "pain thermometers." As difficult as it may be to obtain information from a child, especially infants and young children, parents and health professionals must live with the sometimes exasperating fact that only the child can tell us about the existence and characteristics of his pain. Therefore, we must endeavor to observe as closely as possible for any indications of pain, realizing that they will sometimes be inadequate and misleading. The uncertainty of the situation is inescapable.

***Misconception:*** If the child denies pain or cannot localize pain, he does not have pain.

*CORRECTION:* Young children do not necessarily have the language ability or body image concepts that enable them to effectively communicate the existence and location of pain.

If a child is questioned about pain, the language used is extremely important. Children younger than six years rarely know the meaning of the word *pain* (Eland and Anderson, 1977). Naturally, they will deny its existence unless other words, such as sting or hurt, are used. Older children may also better understand words other than pain, since pain tends to be reserved for those sensations that are intolerable.

A child may deliberately deny pain. Reasons for this include fear of receiving injections or "bad tasting" medicine, fear of being kept in the hospital longer, or fear of treatment such as surgery or dressing changes. In this culture, school age children are becoming increasingly aware of drug abuse. Fear of becoming addicted is one reason some children will refuse narcotic analgesics, implicitly denying pain.

Sometimes the child will admit that he hurts or will appear to be in pain, but upon questioning he will not be able to localize the discomfort. This may be especially true when the pain sensation is internal and/or without external cause or when the pain has persisted at the same intensity for a long time. By contrast, the child usually easily communicates the existence and location of pain when it suddenly occurs or increases in intensity, when evidence of pain is visible to the child (e.g. an external lesion), or when an external event causes the pain (e.g. application of pressure to an internal injury).

Sometimes the child does not know the name of the body part. Asking the child to point to the area of his body that hurts or asking him to mark his discomfort on a predrawn human figure may be very helpful. Research has shown that children can probably communicate better by marking their pain on graphic human figures than they can by communicating verbally (Eland and Anderson, 1977). Another helpful approach is to begin at the top or the bottom of the child's body, touching each major body part and asking him if that hurts. In using this approach, it is wise to go slowly and give the child plenty of time to consider his response.

### Misconceptions That Hamper Relief Of Pain

Once caretakers recognize that the child experiences pain, other misconceptions may discourage efforts to relieve the pain. Following is a discussion of some common problems concerning whether or not the child's pain should be relieved and, if so, whether or not certain pain relief methods should be employed.

***Misconception***: Infants and young children probably do not remember pain.

*CORRECTION:* Remembrance of pain most likely requires more complete cortical development than is present at birth. Thus, the newborn probably does not remember pain, but the age at which the child is capable of remembering pain is unknown (Gross and Gardner, 1980). Nevertheless, "As long as the onset of remembrance of pain is unknown, the neonatal infant has the same right to analgesia and anesthesia as older patients" (Swafford and Allan, 1968, p. 132).

In addition, denial is a common defense mechanism of the child who is faced with an overwhelming situation. Thus, children who are perfectly capable of memory will sometimes fail to remember a protracted episode of pain such as occurs with burns and their treatment (Nover, 1973). This does not mean the event has no emotional impact upon the child. It is fairly well recognized that forgotten life experiences may exert an influence upon a person's life for many years.

***Misconception***: Children tolerate pain better than adults.

*CORRECTION:* Children usually do not report or respond to pain in the same way as adults. The child's problems with acknowledging the existence and location of pain have already been discussed as well as the fact that a child may have pain but may not "act like" he has pain.

A further problem is lack of persistence in reporting pain. The child usually communicates the onset of pain by various verbal and nonverbal behaviors such as crying, holding the affected part, or naming the painful area. However, when pain persists, the child does not necessarily persist in reporting pain. An adult, on the other hand, may recognize that repeated or regular reference to pain is necessary. Otherwise, others may think the pain has disappeared or is not bothering him.

***Misconception:*** The child needs to experience some pain.

*CORRECTION:* There is no evidence that experiencing pain will hasten recovery from illness or benefit the child in any other way. Some people feel that pain "develops character," but as discussed below, it more likely produces undesirable qualities in the child. Others feel that experiencing some pain will keep the child alert and motivated to recover from illness; that is, pain will instill the "will to life." To the contrary, almost all evidence suggests that prolonged, uncontrolled pain leads to depression, sleep disturbances, and other physical disruptions that interfere with recovery (Marks and Sachar, 1973; McCaffery, 1979).

***Misconception***: Children learn to cope with prolonged pain.

*CORRECTION:* Part of this misconception may be based upon the child's tendency to distract himself from pain and to be more physically active than an adult. Thus, the lack of pain expression is misunderstood as meaning lack of significant or distressing pain.

Even in relation to adults there is the general belief that the longer pain lasts the better able the person will be to cope with it. There is no evidence to support this. In the majority of instances it appears that adults suffer more as pain lasts longer or as the frequency of pain increases (Bonica, 1966; Collins, 1965; Kotarba, 1977; Merskey, 1975). It has been noted that children with recurrent pain tend to be more hostile, dependent, anxious, excitable, and generally negative than do children without pain (Gross and Gardner, 1980).

It is possible that lack of pain relief may even have long-term psychological consequences (Poznanski, 1976). Indeed, lack of pain relief probably decreases the child's trust in others. One wonders how well the child will be able to master developmental tasks if he must regularly expend his energy to deal with pain. Beales (1979) feels that relief of pain in chronic childhood diseases is an important way of avoiding interference with normal psychological development.

***Misconception:*** Children with pain are less upset when their parents are absent.

*CORRECTION:* When the child experiences pain, the presence of his parents can be the most potent and safest of pain relief measures. Of course, this is not always true since a very anxious or angry parent can increase the child's fear and interfere with the child's ability to cope with pain. However, if someone takes the time to talk with the parent, providing information and allowing the parent to express his feelings, the parent can usually become an effective means of supporting the child.

Sometimes the child is more expressive about his pain in the presence of his parent, and this can be easily misunderstood. It is quite possible that the child expresses his suffering with pain more to the parent in an effort to mobilize the parent to help relieve the pain. The young child often thinks the parent has an unrealistic degree of control over events. Also, the child may fear being expressive in front of health professionals whom he does not know well, but may feel that his parent is more understanding and accepting of his behavior.

Along with being more expressive in the presence of his parents, the child may exhibit some regressive behaviors. Regression is another defense mechanism used by children in especially difficult situations. A certain amount of regression is a very constructive way for the child to deal with the situation. Regression may include baby talk or greater demands to be held. Parents sometimes fear that responding to these behaviors with attention and affection will only spoil the child. They need to understand that regressive behaviors may benefit the child by reducing his anxiety and providing him with a means of asking for help (Gross and Gardner, 1980).

In recent years there has been increasing emphasis in the health care literature about the parents' right to be with their hospitalized child (Hilt, 1976), the child's right to his parents' presence (Medenwald, 1980), and ways this can be accomplished in spite of lack of accommodations (Hardgrove & Rutledge, 1975). Parents may be encouraged to bring cots or sleeping bags to stay overnight with hospitalized children. Parents who meet opposition may ask the physician to write an order that they are to be allowed to stay with the child. A U.S. government publication advises parents "to be prepared to insist quietly but firmly" (p. 18) if they wish to stay with their child and participate in his care in the hospital and to explore their rights with a lawyer if they cannot overcome opposition (Pizzo, 1977).

***Misconception:*** Do not tell the child something will hurt because this will only frighten him and make him hurt worse.

*CORRECTION:* As Beales (1979) points out there is some truth to this. Expecting pain and focusing attention on the sensation may indeed increase the perceived intensity of pain, and knowing that pain may occur will probably increase anxiety. However, Beales and many others (Eland & Anderson, 1977; Gross & Gardner, 1980; McCaffery, 1979; Mennie, 1974) stress the importance of being honest with the child about impending pain. If the child is not warned of pain or is misled into believing that something will not hurt, the child's trust and confidence in others may be severely damaged. Thus, the possibility of feeling more discomfort because of being forewarned appears to be a small price to pay for maintaining the child's trust.

The possibility of increased pain due to expectation can probably be offset to a great extent by giving the child some choices. Regarding the pain, he can be given some control by making decisions such as whether or not he wishes to cleanse the area for injection. Ways of relieving the discomfort can be suggested such as wriggling his toes or singing a song while the injection is given, and he can choose among the possibilities.

***Misconception:*** Analgesics are far more risky than simply letting the child suffer.

*CORRECTION:* If the dosage and frequency are carefully calculated and the effects monitored, analgesics can be used safely. Although narcotic analgesics may cause sedation and respiratory depression, the dosages can be adjusted to prevent this, or naloxone, a narcotic antagonist, can almost immediately reverse these effects. Like other drugs, narcotic and nonnarcotic (e.g. aspirin) analgesics have potentially harmful side effects. Like other drugs, they must be used with care. When knowledge and observation accompany the use of analgesics, they usually pose no more danger to the child than do other drugs.

There are dangers associated with inadequate use of analgesics. A child whose pain is inadequately relieved may suffer lack of trust and confidence, sleep disturbances, and decreased appetite. The child may not cooperate with procedures necessary for diagnosis or recovery. He may be extremely fatigued. Further, as pointed out by Gross and Gardner (1980), the long-term psychological effects of overwhelming acute pain may be much more serious than the adequate use of properly monitored narcotics.

Inadequate utilization of narcotics for relief of pain poses a sizable problem. It has been well documented that over the last twenty years there has been a trend toward the undertreatment of acute pain with narcotics in adults (Marks and Sachar, 1973). This problem may occur in children to an even greater extent. One study of twenty-five children between five and eight years who were hospitalized for surgery showed that thirteen were never given any medication for pain relief throughout hospitalization. The remaining twelve received only one to three doses. The frequency and potency of these doses appeared to be entirely inadequate for the degree of pain that was probably present. For example, for one child with second and third degree burns over 65% of his body received only one dose of acetaminophen (Tylenol®). Investigation showed not only that physicians probably underprescribed but that nurses usually underused the analgesics, e.g. they did not give the analgesics as frequently as the physician allowed (Eland and Anderson, 1977).

Many reasons have been cited for the inadequate use of narcotics. These include fear of respiratory depression and sedation, fear of creating addiction, failure to believe the child has pain, and guilt or reluctance associated with administering a narcotic injection to a child who responds with excessive crying or striking out. Some of these have already been discussed, and space does not permit a thorough discussion of all the possible reasons. However, since fear of creating addiction is one of the most common reasons for withholding narcotics from someone in pain, a simple and brief clarification of this issue follows.

***Misconception:*** Giving narcotics to the child for pain relief will create addiction.

*CORRECTION:* The literature shows that the probability of addiction occurring from the use of narcotics to relieve acute pain or prolonged cancer pain is between 0 and 3% (McCaffery, 1979). This percentage of risk is rarely considered sufficient for withholding any treatment that is indicated. Thus, it simply does not appear that addiction is sufficient cause to withhold narcotics from a child who needs them for relief of pain.

No universally accepted definition of addiction exists, and this creates some confusion. Addiction is now generally regarded as psychological dependence consisting of compulsive use of a drug for nonmedical reasons. This behavioral response is considered separately from the possible physiological effects of regular use of a narcotic for pain relief. Physiologically, drug tolerance may occur after a period of time, necessitating a larger dose to relieve the same amount of pain (the larger dose is generally safe because tolerance to respiratory depression and sedation also occurs). Physical dependence may occur eventually, that is, withdrawal symptoms occur when the narcotic is abruptly discontinued. It is no longer felt that drug tolerance and physical dependency automatically lead to addiction (Jaffe, 1975). In fact, they occur far more frequently than addiction and need not pose significant problems. Drug dosage can usually be safely adjusted upward to cope with drug tolerance in prolonged pain, such as may occur in the terminally ill. Withdrawal symptoms will subside on their own. If they are severe, they can be treated with decreasing doses of narcotics (Jaffe, 1975; McCaffery, 1979).

***Misconception***: The combination of meperidine, promethazine, and chlorpromazine is an effective way to relieve pain in children. (This is often referred to as DPT after the proprietary names of Demerol®, Phenergan®, and Thorazine®.)

*CORRECTION:* Chlorpromazine and promethazine are often added to meperidine, a known narcotic analgesic, to potentiate meperidine's analgesia. There is no evidence that either drug is a potentiator of narcotic analgesia. In fact, there is some evidence that promethazine will actually increase the intensity of pain. Primarily, these so-called potentiators simply sedate (Dundee, Love, & Morre, 1963; Keats, Telford, & Kurosu, 1961; McCaffery, 1979). Sedation cannot be equated with pain relief; a person can be both sedated and in pain. A child who receives DPT may obtain very poor pain relief but he may be too sedated to communicate this verbally or nonverbally. While sedation may be desirable, it can be obtained with many drugs. Promethazine is highly sedating but, based upon available information, it is a poor choice for someone in pain because of its potential antianalgesic effect.

## Summary

Many erroneous beliefs must be reexamined if the child is to receive adequate pain relief. There is little doubt that the persistence of so many misconceptions has resulted in an appalling lack of pain relief for children. Not only can it be argued that the child has a right to be relieved of pain but also that unrelieved pain may result in physical and psychological damage.

## References

Beales, J.G. Pain in children with cancer. In J.J. Bonica & V. Ventafridda (Eds.), *Advances in pain research and therapy* Vol. 2. New York: Raven Press, 1979.

Bonica, J.J. Management of intractable pain in general practice. *General Practice,* 1966, *33,* 107-123.

Collins, L.G. Pain sensitivity and ratings of childhood experience. *Perceptual and Motor Skills,* 1965, *21,* 349-350.

Dundee, J.W., Love, W.J., & Moore, J. Alterations in response to somatic pain associated with anaesthesia. XV: Further studies with phenothiazine derivatives and similar drugs. *British Journal of Anaesthesia,* 1963, *35,* 597-609.

Eland, J.M., & Anderson, J.E. The experience of pain in children. In A.K. Jacox (Ed.), *Pain: A source book for nurses and other health professionals.* Boston: Little, Brown, 1977.

Epstein, M.H., & Harris, J., Jr. Children with chronic pain: Can they be helped? *Pediatric Nursing,* 1978, *4,* 42-44.

Gross, S.C., & Gardner, G.G. Child pain: Treatment approaches. In W.L. Smith, H. Merskey, & S.C. Gross (Eds.), *Pain: Meaning and management.* Jamaica, N.Y.: Spectrum Publications, 1980.

Hardgrove, C., & Rutledge, A. Parenting during hospitalization. *American Journal of Nursing,* 1975, *75,* 836-838.

Haslam, E.R. Age and the perception of pain. *Psychonomic Science,* 1969, *15,* 86-87.

Hilt, N.E. Pride, prejudice, and parents! *Pediatric Nursing,* 1976, *2,* 32-25.

Jaffe, J.H. Drug addiction and drug abuse. In L.S. Goodman & A. Gilman (Eds.), *The pharmacological basis of therapeutics* (5th ed.). New York: Macmillan, 1975.

Keats, A.S., Telford, J., & Kurosu, Y. "Potentiation" of meperidine by promethazine. *Anesthesia*, 1961, *22*, 34-41.

Kotarba, J.A. The chronic pain experience. In J.D. Douglas & J.M. Johnson (Eds.), *Existential sociology*. New York: Cambridge University Press, 1977.

Marks, R.M., & Sachar, E.J. Undertreatment of medical inpatients with narcotic analgesics. *Annals of Internal Medicine*, 1973, *78*, 173-181.

McCaffery, M. Pain relief for the child: Problem areas and selected nonpharmacological methods. *Pediatric Nursing*, 1977, *3*, 11-16.

McCaffery, M. *Nursing management of the patient with pain*. Philadelphia: J.B. Lippincott, 1979.

Medenwald, N.A. Children's liberation—in a hospital! *American Journal of Maternal Child Nursing*, 1980, *5*, 231-234.

Mennie, A.T. The child in pain. In L. Burton (Ed.), *Care of the child facing death*. Boston: Routledge and Kegan Paul, 1974.

Merskey, H. Pain, learning and memory. *Journal of Psychosomatic Research*, 1975, *19*, 319-324.

Nover, R.A. Pain and the burned child. *Journal of the American Academy of Child Psychiatry*, 1973, *12* 499-505.

Peiper, A. *Cerebral function in infancy and childhood* (3rd ed.). New York: Consultants' Bureau, 1963.

Pizzo, P.D. *When your child goes to the hospital*. Washington, D.C.: U.S. Government Printing Office, DHEW Pub. No., (OHD) 76-30092, 1977.

Pozanski, E.O. Children's reactions to pain: A psychiatrist's perspective. *Clinical Pediatrics*, 1976, *15*, 1114-1119.

Swafford, L.I., & Allan, D. Pain relief in the pediatric patient. *Medical Clinics of North America*, 1968, *52*, 31-36.